AN INSIDE JOB

From Life in a Maze, to an Amazing Life

A Memoir by

Dejuan DJ Verrett

From life in a maze, to an amazing life best describes *De'Juan "DJ"* *Verrett*. On February 6, 1990 DJ Verrett was arrested on drug charges at the age of 19, and was sentenced to 19 1/2 years of imprisonment. After serving 16 years 10 months and three day in some of America's most notorious federal prisons DJ Verrett was released on November 1, 2006.

The day he was released DJ Verrett made the decision to change everything about him. He immediately began to give back to the community by volunteering his time with an organization called "GETTING OUT BY GOING IN" (G.O.G.I) and through this program; he began to work with "At-Risk Youth and Adults" to encourage and influence them not to make the same poor life choices he had made.

During his time of association with (G.O.G.I.), he has spoken at numerous events that focus on Youth Awareness/ Empowerment, Drug / Alcohol Prevention and Gang Prevention. DJ Verrett also spearheaded a unique after school program that taught students how to crochet while slipping in Cognitive Behavioral Therapy (CBT). The crocheting exercise taught the students about focus and concentration, thereby applying these same principles to their normal classes.

For his outstanding volunteer work DJ Verrett was acknowledged and given an Award of Appreciation by the Inglewood Unified School District and Inglewood's Former Mayor Roosevelt Dorn.

DJ was also a major contributor to the book, *"Prison, Getting Out by Going In, Freedom before Release"* by Mara Leigh Taylor, published by Lightning Source Inc. You can also find DJ's story in the New York Times Bestseller *"Moments of Clarity"* by Christopher Kennedy Lawford published by Harper Collins Inc.

Since coming back to America as DJ likes to call it, his life has been nothing short of amazing, having just finished recording his first CD Titled *"Make It Hot"* and completing his memoir called *"An Inside Job, From Life in a Maze, To an Amazing Life*, DJ Verrett's journey has been truly inspiring to all, barring witness to the power of self revolution.

On December 24, 2008 DJ Verrett received an early Christmas gift via the United States District Court by the request of his probation officer. The same judge that sentenced DJ to 19 1⁄2 years of imprisonment witnessed the power of this transformation and terminated his probation four years early.

On April 19, 2010 DJ received an Award of Appreciation from Lee Baca of the Los Angeles County Sheriff Department for his outstanding volunteer work in working with male and female inmates as well as juvenile wards of the state.

"Come as you are, but don't leave as you came" is DJ's message, whether it's in the many schools where he speaks, or jails. His message of self discovery and positive change is not only thought provoking, it is powerful and compelling.

"OUTTA MYSELF"

Now once upon a time,
when I was on the grind,
out committing crimes,
I thought the world was mine.
When I was in my prime,
I was just trying to shine,
but I was truly blind.
I couldn't see the signs.
I'm getting outta myself
by going into myself,
and if I don't,
that's the end of myself.
Now I got those clear eyes,
with a clear mind.
I'm in a clear space.
Now I'm about to shine."

Mista DJ

To my Mother, Catherine, and my sisters, Tomeka and Shonie, my nieces, Niara, Tiara, and Nyla, and to my nephews, Terry Jr. Londen and Little Solomon.
I love you all.

FOREWORD

By Christopher Kennedy Lawford

I had been working on my second book, *Moments of Clarity: Voices from the Front Lines of Addiction and Recovery*, for a year and a half, wrangling celebrities and some normal people to get them to tell me about a part of their lives that many had no interest in putting into the public consciousness. It was not an easy process and I was glad it was over. No way was I interested in chasing anybody else. I was done. However, I have learned in twenty-five years of my recovery, that *my* plan is not necessarily *the* plan.

A call came in one morning from a publicist friend of mine who is also in recovery with a client who she said just had to be in the book. She went on to tell me about a guy she was representing who had just gotten out of a federal prison after being incarcerated for eighteen years for selling drugs.

I told her that the book was finished, but she persisted, so I told her she could have her client call me hoping that he would not and knowing that if he did I would probably dodge the call. The next thing I remember is making a plan to meet someone named DJ at a Starbucks near my house, despite my conviction to blow him off. I thought, "I'll buy him a latte, listen to him for fifteen minutes and then go on my way," figuring it was the least I could do for someone just out of maximum security prison. I showed up in a Starbucks on Lincoln Boulevard near my house that I had never been in before. I looked around for someone who looked like they had been in prison, didn't see him and figured 'another flaky alcoholic.' I was almost out of the parking lot when I got a call it was DJ.

"Where are you, man?" he asked, with just enough irritation to piss me off.

"I'm at Starbucks, man. Where the hell are you?" I asked.

"At Starbucks," he said.

"Well, so am I, but now I'm in my car. I've been waiting for fifteen minutes."

"Well, I'm standing by the door."

"What do you look like, man?" I questioned, having figured it was his job to recognize me.

"I'm a light skinned African American man with a ponytail, and I'm 5'8", DJ said matter-of-factly.

"There is no one like that at this Starbucks," I said, hoping we were done.

"Which Starbucks you at, Dawg?"

"Lincoln & Maxella."

"Oh, shit. I'm at the one on Lincoln and Manitoba," he said.

"Figures!" I thought. Well, I had tried. I could finally blow him off.

"I'll be right there, man," DJ said and hung up.

"Fuck." I waited in spite of myself because that's what I'd learned how to do imperfectly in recovery. Show up. And more often than not, keep my word.

Twenty minutes later, DJ walked into Starbucks and I was delivered to that magical place I had come to recognize in the work I do, where in spite of my absolute certainty about what is happening, and how things are going to play out, I am delivered to a place where my expectation is obliterated in the wonder of human experience. We sat in that Starbucks for an hour and a half and he told me his story. It was like many of the other stories in my book in that it was powerful, transformative and beyond inspiration. His circumstances, though, were different from any I had come across. Eighteen years in a prison for selling drugs and he was a kid! There is something wrong in a society where that can happen. Everything in this man's life would justify a boatload of anger, resentment and retribution, but that's not who was sitting in front of me. DJ Verrett had been touched. Like many of us in recovery, he had been delivered to a different path, and the darkness that should have infected his soul and the rest of his life was gone, but this isn't what really surprised me, for I had seen many transformations. What touched me was his humanity. After eighteen years of hell, there was gentleness and an enthusiasm. The guy who was sitting before me, who after all he had been through, was telling me he was grateful for the experience and I believed him.

DJ's story is the last story in my book, *Moments of Clarity*. It's there in spite of me because it needed to be there. The book wouldn't be the book it is without it, but more importantly, I made a friend that day who reminds me not to take myself too seriously, to be grateful for the time and the freedom I have on this planet, and to continue my advocacy to change the policy that robs young people of their freedom because they have a disease and because they were born in circumstances where very often the only opportunity for economic gain is illegal.

It's an honor for me to write this foreword to a book that delivers a message of hope with the conviction that the human spirit can survive in spite of the limitations of our society.

ACKNOWLEDGEMENTS

First and foremost, I want to thank my Higher Power, who I like to call God, for giving me the strength to make it through some very difficult times. And from those difficult times I was given the inspiration to write this book, but it could not have been possible without the very supportive people that God put in my life. They gave me the courage to trudge forward with their unwavering and unconditional love, loving me until I could love myself.

I want to thank **Liz Tucker** for always being there for me, and **Russell Solomon** for his wise *Jedi Mind Trick* advice; you have been extremely instrumental in my new way of life.

Jaia Lee, I'm blessed to have you in my life. You have taught me so much.

Mara Leigh Taylor, big ups to you and G.O.G.I (*Getting Out by Going In*), for keeping me so busy during my re-entry process that I didn't have time to come up with anything slick. I'm like that airplane quote: "Climb young plane, climb."

William B.T. Taylor, thank you brother for keeping it one hundred percent with me at all times.

Deborah Cameron, words can't express my gratitude. You have the biggest heart on the planet! Your patience, love and understanding are boundless and cannot be measured with words. Because of you, I now believe in angels. You have taught me valuable life lessons and exposed me to the world and all its possibilities. I cannot thank you enough. I humbly thank you. Oh yeah, I can only drink tea with creamer now!

CONTENTS

CHAPTER 1

—

The Decision

"Mr. Verrett, I am only going to say this once, you can plead guilty and accept the government's offer of twenty years of imprisonment, or if not, I will push for the maximum sentence allowable by law, twenty-seven years of imprisonment, this offer is only valid for sixty seconds, the decision is yours.

The judge's countdown began. "Fifty-nine, fifty-eight, fifty-seven…"

There was a deadly silence as I sat in the judge's chambers, Everyone was waiting on me, I looked to my attorney for guidance but his eyes revealed how I felt inside, powerless. Frantic thoughts raced through out my mind. I was desperately trying to figure out what to do, I had to make a decision and fast.

"Forty-two, forty-one, forty..."

The room was cool but I was sweating profusely, the noise in my head was deafening and I was sure everyone could hear it.

"Thirty-three, thirty-two, thirty-one..."

My ego began to crumble as the seconds ticked away. "You could still win," the voice in my head, said shouting to be heard above all the other voices. I was involuntarily holding my breath as my body became rigid with tension. It felt like I was free falling to earth without a parachute and nothing could save me.

"Nineteen, eighteen, seventeen…"

My toes curled in my snakeskin shoes as my fists formed tight little balls revealing only white knuckles as a calming voice was trying to cut through the panic I was feeling. "Do the math, De'Juan, do the math," I said to myself. I was only nineteen years old and if I lost, I would be almost fifty when I would be released. I saw a vivid picture of the fifty something year-old me standing outside of the prison walls. He looked old and worn, defeated and lost. The world had passed him by; his life had passed him by.

I felt powerless as reality set in, I knew I couldn't beat the United States government, I couldn't win, not with three co-defendants willing to point the finger at me. The government's case was strong, but if I took the deal just offered, I would be only thirty-six or thirty-seven when I would be released; at least I would have some chance at a normal life.

"How did I get in this situation?" I asked myself, this was not normal for a nineteen year old to have to make these types of decisions and choices. I should be in college playing baseball or something, not heading for prison.

"Eleven, ten, nine…"

I felt the vibration in my stomach at first; my heart was summoning the courage to accept the twenty-year prison sentence offer as my body began relaxing. My toes uncurled as I raised my head while my hands began to unlock from the tight little fists. My heart rate was beating even faster if that was possible, bump-bump, bump-bump, bump-bump, and then the low tone vibration began travelling up through my chest.

"Seven, six, five…"

My mouth opened as the words struggled to escape.

"Three, two…"

"Okay, okay, I'll take the twenty years," I stammered, gasping for breath after the words escaped my mouth.

Breathing heavily now, I listened to the Chief Prosecutor, "You made the right decision, Mr. Verrett," he said.

I will never forget the smirk on his face.

The U.S. Marshals immediately cuffed me and led me away. I thought about how I had ended up here. My big homie's had never talked about this side of the game, the ugly side. All I had ever wanted was to be like Bosco.

CHAPTER 2

Leader of the Pack

One of the guys I looked up to when I was a kid was Bosco. He was loved and respected by everybody in the neighborhood. Well, almost everybody, Bosco is what we called hood famous.

When I would see him, he would acknowledge me like a big brother would do. If I could've had a big brother, I would've picked Bosco no doubt.

I lived with my mother and two sisters. My mother was a good woman, and she did the best she could to provide for us. I never even knew that we were poor because we always had food, clothes and toys. I never had a memory of ever being hungry.

My mom was a great cook she could cook anything. I really loved her desserts; my two favorites were banana pudding and her famous peach cobbler even to this day.

When the streetlights came on that meant it was time for dinner, and no matter where I was in the projects she would stand on the porch and shout my name.

Whatever I was doing and wherever I was, when I heard her call my name I would bolt home ready to eat. My sisters would always help my mom set the table and I would come in and sit down ready to eat. My mom would say, "Boy, you better go and wash those dirty hands."

My mother had just gotten a permanent job as a dockworker and she seemed really excited about it.

Holding the letter in her hand, she shouted, "No more welfare!" while singing the theme song to the Jefferson's.

Most of my family is from the harbor area, which consists of San Pedro, Harbor City and Long Beach, and in that area, everybody knows everybody. I never really knew that the world was any bigger than what I had seen because people in my area really didn't go too far from home.

My Grandmother moved to San Pedro in the 1940s from Louisiana. Then she met my Grandfather, they married and she gave birth to fifteen kids, 8 boys and 7 girls. And just like all my uncles and aunts, my sisters and I were born at the same hospital, San Pedro Peninsula Hospital, and we all lived in San Pedro, just like the rest of the family.

I was born at 5:20 a.m. on May 31, 1971, that was the day I came into America! I would be the next generation to live and run the streets, have kids and die in the harbor area.

As kids, we 'patrolled' our neighborhood it was a real learning experience for us because we would see a lot and get to know who's who! When it came to Bosco, I watched him closely and noticed how everybody loved to be around him. When my friends and I would ride our bikes to where Bosco would hang out, he would always smile and give us the "What's up" head nod, it felt good to be recognized by him.

We knew everyone that was with Bosco, we even knew who their mothers were and those whose fathers were around we knew them too. That's what we did as kids in the hood, patrolling, watching and learning how stuff was done in our world.

Most of my friends had their own fathers, or the next best thing, an older brother, but me I didn't have a father or an older brother so I studied my uncles and the older guys in the neighborhood.

One of my uncles was missing in action for a while and I asked my mom where he'd gone, she would only say that he'd gone out of town and he'd be back soon. It seemed like a hundred years had passed when my uncle finally returned, but he looked different, his eyes seemed cold and angry, and his muscles were all buffed out like a super hero action figure but with tattoos.

My family had a big party for him, but he really didn't seem too happy at the party. I asked him where he gone, and if he'd fun while he was there because I wanted to go there when I got older so I could have

4

a big party when I returned, but he never talked about his trip to us kids. A few months later another uncle disappeared for a while and he came back looking the same way. Then a lot of the guys in the neighborhood began disappearing too, but nobody ever really talked about it.

That was how life was for us, everybody had a place to maintain, so you found your space and stayed there. Now for me it was a different story because I realized that I was different, I looked different from my little crew. I was black, but my skin wasn't, and my light skin color and my wavy hair had caused me a lot of unwanted problems, I was always being teased for being light skinned and having wavy hair.

I was once told a story about the Willie Lynch Syndrome. During the time of slavery, a slave owner named Willie Lynch had written a declaration and sent it out to all slave owners, telling them that he'd figured out a way to keep the slaves separated and in bondage for at least four hundred years. Divide and conquer was his motto.

He told the slave owners, "I've figured out a way to keep the Negro slaves divided, by separating the light-skinned slaves from the dark skinned slaves, pitting the young against the old, separating the males from the females, pitting the fathers against the sons and mothers against the daughters and the slaves in the house against the slaves in the field, they will fight amongst themselves and we can control them for hundreds of years."

Now I realized that I'd become a victim of the Willie Lynch Syndrome, I had to fight for my place amongst my peers, I hated my light skin.

I was called Yella Boy, High Yella, White Boy, White Bread and Half-Breed, and those were not choice names for a kid just wanting to fit in. I had to be faster, stronger, tougher and braver than all my friends in the hood, and even the ones that were almost as light as I was would tease me just to keep the heat off them. Consequently, I started doing foolish things to take the attention off my appearance just to show that I was one of them.

When school was out for the summer, we would all meet and ride all day in the neighborhood staying in the safe zone. We would always raid Mr. Gomez's trees for fruit, and just like clockwork he would always come out the back door yelling at us as we hopped over the back yard fence and ran down the alley with our loot of oranges. We'd find a place to rest in the shade and prepare for our weekly bicycle race.

Now bicycle racing was a big deal to us because the winner was the leader of the pack for the week and the title was challenged every week. This week I was determined to be the leader because the pack followed the leader without question.

As we prepared for the weekly challenge, every one of us took the ritual very seriously. We all made sure that our bicycle chains had the correct amount of tension. Before the race began we all stuffed our pant leg into our sock and then we all lined up.

I was extra focused on being the leader of the pack, I imagined myself guiding my little crew to wherever I wanted to go without being called names or teased, but being called they're leader.

On the starting line, I prayed that my legs would pump me to victory.

P.J. called it, "On your mark, get set, go!" I had a perfect take off. I felt the adrenaline shoot through my body and I peddled like a madman. Focusing on the finish line, I blazed past the finish line like a runaway train as P.J. declared me the winner, but I kept riding feeling the wind on my face. It seemed as if I was going two hundred miles per hour, but in reality it was about ten miles per hour. I returned back to the other guys and every one was still breathing hard.

P.J. said, "Damn, man! You rode like Mr. Gomez was chasing your ass!"

I just smiled and thought; "Now I'm the leader."

CHAPTER 3

—

Acceptance

One hot afternoon when we all met up for our ride, I announced the plan for the day. We started out with things like jumping curbs and riding wheelies just to get warmed up. We left the projects and headed for the park taking our normal shortcuts through the alleys. I felt special in a funny way and nobody teased me in any way. I had finally earned the respect of my peers, but there was more to come that day. It was going to be a really special day for me.

I was wearing my favorite Casper the Ghost t-shirt with my tough skin pants and a pair of old tennis shoes. The night before, I had fever-ously detailed my bicycle making sure there was not a speck of dirt on it. I polished my chrome rims with some dried turtle wax I had found. We took care of our bikes like the older guys took care of their cars. As we hit the entrance to the park I saw Bosco sitting on the hood of his car, and just like me he was the leader of his pack. The only difference was, they he had girls in his pack. I recognized Tammy, Pattie and Anna and some other girls, but I didn't know their names.

They weren't doing anything, but they seemed to be having fun doing it. Bosco had a navy blue 1964 Chevy Impala convertible with hydraulics. Rob-Dog had a sparkling gold Nissan truck with gigantic speakers; his truck had the loudest music I had ever heard. Gangsta had a silver Coup de Ville Cadillac and Chuck T had a mint green Regal with a sparkling paint job. Bosco, Gangsta, and Chuck T all had the same rims; they were called Dayton's.

When Rob-Dog would start his truck it roared like an awakening lion, so I decided to tape old playing cards to the forks of my bike so that when the wheels turned the spokes would strike the cards making a roaring sound. The faster I peddled, the loader the roar.

Seeing all those shiny and sparkling cars reminded me of a small personal car show, and we were lucky enough to be up close to the action. I could see myself being in Bosco's position the center of attention. I wished I could be just like that! Everybody loved him. I believed Bosco is what every man should be, and I wanted my life to be like his.

As we coasted by the small car show, I noticed that everyone had a drink in his or her hand and they were smoking. None of them were really any paying attention to us, Well, no one except for Bosco.

I guess Bosco was saying something funny because everybody was laughing, I never really saw Bosco get angry, and he always had a smile on his face. As we got closer Bosco stopped sipping his drink and shouted from a distance,

"What are you young nigga's doing riding around like a pack of dogs?"

"We just riding," we all said.

As far as I was concerned, Bosco was our American Idol. He was the man and our hero, he is what we call "Hood Famous". He motioned for us to come over to him, at first we weren't sure that he was talking to us.

"Bring your young ass's over here." he said in a loud voice.

I immediately wanted to bolt out of there, but I couldn't because I was the newly appointed leader of the pack, and my subjects looked to me for guidance. My heart began beating fast as I took a deep breath and slowly headed towards Bosco.

He looked down at me and started laughing I nervously smiled back. "That's the perfect name for you," he said.

I remained silent because I was clueless as to what he was talking about and so was my crew.

"What do you mean?" I asked.

"Your t-shirt, you will now be called *Casper the Ghost*," he said, pointing at me.

8

Gangsta said, "That name fits him," and the girls all agreed.

I didn't know what to say I looked down at my t-shirt, and then looking back at Bosco, he smiled and said.

"Casper, take your road dogs out of here and don't get into any trouble."

Obeying his command, riding away I felt something happen inside of me I didn't know what it was but it felt good. Bosco had just handed me the power I had been looking for. I instantly embraced what I looked like and I was no longer ashamed of having light skin. The Willie Lynch curse had been lifted and it had taken Bosco to do it.

The day seemed even brighter than it was. "I'm now Casper the Ghost," I said silently to myself, leading my pack to a nearby hill to rest my heart was still beating fast, not from riding, but from the excitement.

We all turned our bikes upside down instead of laying them on their sides because kickstands weren't cool as we talked; I began spinning the rear wheel looking at Bosco and his crew.

Tony asked Shawn, "What do you want to be when you grow up Shawn?"

Shawn said, "A basketball player."

When we were in the sixth grade Shawn was dunking the ball on an eight-foot rim at the elementary school, and he loved the game. He also loved the Harlem Globe Trotters and Dr. J, but when we started the seventh grade he stopped taking his Harlem Globe Trotter lunch pail to school I didn't understand why, but I continued to carry mine.

Tony wanted to be a sheriff because the deputies would drive through the projects and hand out baseball and basketball cards to us kids and that's why Tony wanted to be a sheriff. It seemed like every time the sheriffs would leave, Bosco and his crew would show up, just missing them. I thought maybe they had just outgrown baseball cards.

Then somebody asked Vincent what he wanted to be.

He said, "I want to be a professional skateboarder."

Jose Gonzalez said, "I really don't know yet."

"I don't know either," P.J. said.

"How about you, Casper the Ghost?"

I was lost in a trance and wasn't used to my new name yet, I was focused on the people in the parking lot.

P.J. tapped me on the shoulder and said, "Casper the Ghost, what do you want to be?"

I was still looking into the parking lot imagining myself standing there next to my car with a forty ounce in my hand with everybody around me.

"De'Juan!" Tony yelled.

"Oh, what's up?" I said.

"Man, we were calling you," Shawn said. "What do you want to be when you grow up?"

I was still spinning the back wheel, looking through the spokes, and that's when it came to me.

I stood up and said, "I want to be like them," and pointing towards Bosco and his crew.

"That's what I want to be, like them."

CHAPTER 4

—

Road Dogs for Life

I was close to my friends, Tony and Vince, and the others from the pack, but Shawn and I were close like brothers. We would ride our bicycles to school together, and then ride home together after school.

My mother loved Shawn; she had known him before she knew me because he was born almost two months earlier. His mother and my mother had grown up together and were good friends.

I really didn't see his mother that much because she went on vacations a lot, so Shawn would live with his aunt. On the weekends Shawn would take me to the Rolling Hills Golf Club to collect golf balls and turn them in for money.

"Shawn, why ain't Tony and Vince coming?" I would ask.

"So we don't have to split the money four ways," he answered.

"How much do you think we can make?"

Shawn said, "About eight dollars apiece."

Eight dollars was a lot of money to me, I could shop for months at the candy lady's store. Sometimes, when Bosco would see us in the projects he would ask if we had some money and we would say as if on cue, "No", then Bosco would take us on a shopping spree to the candy lady's house to buy sweets.

The candy lady was a short overweight Mexican lady with flaming red hair who lived in the projects. The inside of her apartment resembled a shrine with candles and incense burning around the statues of

Jesus hanging on the cross, the entire house was decorated with pictures of Jesus.

The living room was dark except for the flickering candles around the mini statues and all the furniture was covered in plastic, which looked very uncomfortable to sit on if you were wearing shorts, but we were there to get some sweets, not sit down. The candy lady had almost everything a regular store had, but with affordable prices. You couldn't buy anything from a real store with three cents, but with the candy lady you could buy three pieces of licorice. I guess she was making a lot of money because the inside of her apartment sure didn't look like the other apartments in the projects.

Shawn was a hustler, a young businessman in the making and I became his protégé. We started out by renting gas lawn mowers with rakes; we'd also post flyers around the projects about our landscaping business. Yeah, even people who lived in the projects took pride in the small patch of grass that was allotted to them. Sometimes we would mow five lawns in one day.

Don't get it wrong, Shawn and I would still raid the fruit trees in the neighborhood. From being the former leader of the pack, I still had the speed so if I got too far in front of him I would slow down to let him catch up, I would never leave him behind and he would never leave me, we were brothers.

We did a lot of things together, but there were some things that we didn't do together, like play baseball. I was good at it and Shawn was okay, but when it came to playing basketball, Shawn was a young Dr. J.

I really enjoyed everything about playing baseball running, sliding, diving for balls and getting dirty. I took the game seriously. We then started to see less and less of each other. We were still close we just found different things to do and enjoy. It was agreed that we would still collect cans and golf balls together.

CHAPTER 5

—

Crushed

Mark Holt is the only man that I ever called Daddy the day I found out that he was not my father I was crushed!

It was 1979 or 1980 I was at Mark's father's house, the man I called Grandpa. In the living room there was a big wooden coffee table and I would drape a blanket over it to make a fort and I'd lay there with my green army men positioning them to protect the fort.

From my vantage point under the table I could see people coming in and out of the front door, I could watch TV and even take a nap in the safety of my little fortress. I could also lay still and listen to what the adults were saying without them seeing me.

One day, Gloria, Grandpa's girlfriend, came into the house and I peeked from under the blanket and smiled at her. Then my little sister came into the living room, and Gloria asked, "Who is this little girl?"

Grandpa answered, "She's Mark's daughter."

Then Gloria asked, "Is he Mark's son too?"

"No, he's not Mark's son."

When Grandpa said that, I couldn't believe it, why would he'd tell a fib like that. It felt like I'd been kicked in the stomach I was too shocked and embarrassed to leave the safety of my fort. My throat hurt as I lay there and silently cried, making sure that no one heard me. I had thought that I was a good Grandson and that Grandpa would be proud to be my Grandpa.

Everything became dark and I drifted off to sleep. When I woke up it was very quiet as I peeked out from under the table. I saw no one, so I slipped from under the table and sat on the couch. There was a pen and piece of paper on the table and I wrote on it, "I hate myself." I signed it DLV and left the house.

I rode my bike through the projects, I wanted to ride as fast and as far away as I could get, those words 'No, that's not Mark's son' echoed in my head and fucked me up! I had just lost a family. Mark was not my father, Grandpa wasn't my Grandpa, Granny wasn't my Granny, and Uncle Spencer wasn't my uncle anymore!

Then I started wondering about everyone in my family, were my sisters really my sisters? Was my mother really my mother? Where did I come from? Why was I here? I started to question everything, my world had crumbled and I felt different inside.

The streetlights came on with an orange glow, which was my cue to head home. My mother was on the porch as I arrived home, and she said, "I was just about to call you boy, is everything all right?" she asked. "What's wrong, De'Juan?"

"Nothing," I said. "Just hungry."

I went upstairs to wash my hands for dinner and looked into the mirror, I had no one to talk too; I was all by myself now.

I have never called another man daddy since I found out that I was not Mark's son. The word daddy had lost its magic, it became just another word to me, the feeling and the meaning were lost forever.

I wondered if everybody knew the truth, why did Mom lie to me? Everyone had lied to me, where was my real father, and why didn't he want me?

Now I understood why my sisters and I all had different last names.

CHAPTER 6

—

Stepped Up

My mother had two children from two previous failed relationships when she met Mark Holt. They met in 1975 or 1976 when I was five or six years old. My youngest sister, Shonie, was my mother's last child, and Mark's first. I had no other memory of any other man who lived with us, except for Mark.

He had accepted me, and my sister Tomeka as his own, and he had always done the father things like teaching us kids how to ride a bike. I had a white Evel Knievel bicycle with a red white and blue banana seat, I remember the day the training wheels came off. We were in the parking lot of the projects where we practiced. This was the first time that I rode my bike without the assistance of training wheels.

Mark said, "D, today we're going to ride without the training wheels, okay?"

I responded with an unsure, "Okay, Daddy."

He would guide me up and down the parking lot with encouraging words, saying, "You're doing it, you're doing it!" giving me all the confidence in the world.

As we made another run up the parking lot, the ride felt smooth as I pedaled. I thought he was still holding the seat then I looked back and saw that he wasn't holding the seat and I panicked. I could hear him in the distance yelling, "Keep pedaling, De'Juan! Keep pedaling!" and I did, but I couldn't stop and I crashed.

He ran up to me and said, "You did it you did it! I'm so proud of you" That was all the validation and encouragement I needed to continue, the scraps and bleeding elbows didn't even hurt.

A few years later, when Mark and my mother split up, I would be taught and encouraged to do negative acts by men that I looked up to as role models.

When baseball season came, Mark took me to the local park to sign me up for little league. He and my mother would be there at every game supporting me. It felt good to see my family in the stands cheering me on.

A few seasons passed and I became pretty good at the game, and then Mom wanted me to play at a different park. I didn't want to go because all of my friends were in Harbor City, but she signed me up at this place called Navy Field. Yeah, the fields were better looking and they had real uniforms, but I wanted to stay with my friends.

Navy Field was in another city where mostly white people lived. As my mother was in the office signing a bunch of papers, I walked around to check out the place. All the equipment looked brand new nothing was old or taped up and they even had new bats. The grass was cut just like I'd seen on the professional fields on TV.

The first day I was introduced to the team and the coach, Coach Stevens was a white guy with a beard who drank beer and smelled like cigarette smoke. He asked me what position I played.

I said, "I'm a pitcher."

Coach Stevens shook his head like something was wrong and said, "No, you look more like an outfielder."

When I played in Harbor City I was a star pitcher and starter, but at Navy Field I was labeled an outfielder. I didn't want to be a problem from the beginning, so I did what I was told.

It felt lonely in the dugout I was the only black kid on the team. After three or four games had passed, I was still riding the pine, wondering why my mother had sent me here in the first place. I was not happy!

In Harbor City I was a star here at Navy Field with these white people I was a nobody if Coach Stevens would only let me play, he would see that I would be one of his best players.

Game after game I went home with a clean uniform I missed coming home dirty and sweaty with grass stains on my uniform and having something to talk about at school.

My uncle would see me in my uniform and ask, "Did you have a game today, or did you take team pictures?"

"Yeah, I had a game today, no pictures," I answered.

And his friends would say. "Then how come you ain't dirty?"

"They're saving me for the playoffs," was my reply.

One day, as I walked into the house, I heard my uncle say to his friends, "Why did Cathy sign that boy up to play with those crackers? Those crackers ain't gonna let no niggas play there." They didn't know I was in the kitchen and had heard every word.

Coach Stevens probably thought because I was smaller than the rest of the team I would be liability, thereby causing the team to lose. He never really tried me out to see if I had a good arm or anything, so inning after inning, and game after game I sat in the dugout watching the game in my clean uniform.

Finally, I got the chance to play in one game because it was almost a mercy rule which means that the other team was losing by ten runs or more in the fifth inning, so Coach Stevens put me in. I was so excited I was finally getting to play and my family was cheering. I started to walk toward the pitcher's mound when Coach Stevens stopped me and told me to go to right field. In Little league nobody hits the ball to right field it's called no man's land.

Disappointed but happy to finally be on the field, I jogged to my position got into my stance and waited for something to come my way.

The umpire called, "Batter up!"

The first batter was a lefty I said a little prayer, "God, let the batter hit it my way." The first batter struck out and then the next. The last batter hit a pop fly and the game was over, I walked back to the dugout grabbed my jacket and met my family.

Mom had a strange look on her face and so did mark. We piled into the family car a Volkswagen bug, and drove home. In Harbor City I was somebody amongst my friends, I had earned my place as the leader of the pack, my size and skin color didn't matter. It was my ability and determination that made me a leader, and I was determined to show Coach Stevens that I was good baseball player.

The weekend had arrived and Shawn came over to hang out to do what we usually did on weekends. Shawn already had our day planned. "Come on, Casper we've got a lot of golf balls to collect," he said.

"I can't go I need to practice," I said.

"You have all summer to practice."

But I was determined to stay close to home and practice my pitching.

Shawn said, "The guys are waiting for you."

"I ain't going."

Shawn said, "Okay then I gotta jam."

As Shawn rode away I grabbed my glove, a few tennis balls and a stick of chalk. I drew a box on the side of the building and started practicing my pitching.

As I was throwing the ball against the wall, this new white kid from Tennessee rode by on this bike and watched me. His family lived in our building.

Every day he would watch me practice my pitching from a distance. Watching him from the corner of my eye, I figured it was time for an introduction, I took a break and walked over to him and said, "What's up? I'm Casper the Ghost," and extended my hand in friendship.

He stood up to his full height and replied, "I'm Kyle."

Kyle was tall for his age and skinny! "Is that your real name?" he asked.

"No, but my friends call me that," I replied.

Kyle asked if he could practice with me.

I said, "Sure." I was bored practicing by myself and it would be good to have someone to practice with.

He laid his General Lee bicycle next to my Huffy and grabbed his glove. As we started playing catch, Kyle asked if I was on a team.

I said, "Yeah, but I don't get playing time."

At the Rolling Hills Country Club, I had not only collected golf balls, I had also collected a lot of tennis balls. Sometimes the tennis players would hit the balls into the dirt field and I would be there to collect them. I accumulated about a hundred tennis balls and stored them in my closet. My mother would get upset because I had so many of them,

18

but I was waiting for the perfect time to use them, and now was the time. I couldn't practice throwing with a hard ball against a brick wall because it would make too much noise, so the tennis balls were perfect.

Kyle and I would practice chasing high flies until the streetlights came on. Then, like clockwork when the streetlights came on, all the mothers in the projects would stand on the porch and call their children home and even his Nana started doing it.

I loved to ride my bike with my friends I had worked hard to become the leader of the pack proving that I was just as good as anyone. Now I had a new challenge to face at night as I lay in my bed I would imagine myself as the starting pitcher with my family cheering me on as the announcer called my name.

"And the starting pitcher number thirty one, De'Juan Verrett."

After school and after homework, Kyle and I would meet to start my training. While we warmed up, he would tell me stories about Tennessee and his friends there and how they played baseball.

"Today he said, "We're going to work on your pitching I see that you can already track down pop flies now I want to see how much control you have on the mound."

I was confident that I had control; I did well at Harbor City Park. I didn't hit that many batters, but I was open to learning something new. I had to be better than everybody else on the team and work twice as hard I had to be like two people.

Kyle drew the box on the wall and then measured out forty-two feet and two inches. That was the distance from the pitcher's mound to home plate on a little league field.

"Now," Kyle said, "let me see your wind-up."

I got into my stance, imagining myself on the Navy Field mound I went into my wind-up and let it rip, the tennis ball hit just outside of the box on the wall.

"Good," Kyle said, "All lefties have a natural curve, but you ain't following through lefties are hard to hit against."

I never knew there was a difference I did what was necessary to get the ball across the plate. Kyle walked over to the makeshift mound like a coach would do and corrected me.

"Show me your fast ball," he said.

19

I grabbed the tennis ball and showed him.

"Now show me your curve ball," he said and I did.

He looked confused and said, "You're throwing palm balls."

I didn't understand what he meant, so he grabbed a couple of tennis balls and held a ball in front of me. He showed me how to hold the ball and how to flick my wrist upon release. I noticed the ball did something different before it hit the target square center.

Kyle said, "It's all in the wrist and the follow through." I grabbed a dozen tennis balls and practiced my curve ball. Kyle said, "Man, you're a natural!"

I said, "You're a good coach," that day he taught me how to throw a drop ball, a slider and a knuckle ball. Knuckle balls were the hardest ones because I had small hands. Kyle would tell me to calm down and relax; the game waits on the pitcher. He was so wise to be only fourteen years old.

Next Kyle said that we were going to work on my batting, so I stood in the makeshift batter's box and he pitched to me. As I stood in the box Kyle said, "That's weird. You throw with your left hand, but you bat on the right side."

I never thought it was weird because that's what seemed natural to me. "This is how I learned," I said.

Standing in the batter's box, Kyle went into his wind-up and he released the ball. I tightened up my grip and swung as hard as I could, and missed.

Kyle said, "Good cut." It may have seemed like nothing to him, but it meant everything to me.

He was throwing little speeding green comets at me I swung and missed. Kyle didn't take it easy on me and struck me out every time. If you could have seen his wind-up it was perfect, it was like he'd been doing it his whole life. It was really something to see, I wanted to pitch like that, and I was determined to do so.

Kyle saw that I was getting upset and called for a break. I threw down the bat and walked to the mound, which faced the side of the apartment building.

He said, "Don't get upset it's just a game."

I replied, "It's a game I love and my coach won't let me play! and you struck me out every time!"

"I'm bigger and stronger than you that's why I throw harder than you, I've played longer than you, I used to be in your position before that's why we're here. You'll get used to playing with me, and your timing will be better than your teammates. They only play against kids their own age, but we're training you to play two leagues ahead of them."

After the break Kyle said, "We're going to work on you bat speed. I'll be right back." While he was gone I grabbed a tennis ball and practiced holding the ball split finger and thinking.

Kyle returned with a broomstick, "What's that for?" I asked curiously.

Kyle replied, "Back in Tennessee we used to play stick ball, and it helped our bat speed and it'll help you to keep your eye on the ball."

"You can't hit a tennis ball with a broom stick," I said.

"Pitch me a few then," he said, smiling.

I grabbed a couple of tennis balls and stood on the mound. I went into my wind-up and threw a perfect curve ball and Kyle sent the tennis ball rocketing over the building. Every ball I pitched Kyle sent sailing over the building.

When he saw that I was getting frustrated once again he walked over to me and said, "All I'm doing is showing you something that somebody showed me."

What I liked about most about Kyle was that he never made fun of what I looked like he liked me for me I didn't have to prove anything to him I could just be myself. We spent many days practicing, and when he wasn't around I would take my mother's broomstick outside and pretend I was at bat.

Kyle had taught me how to throw a variety of pitches he liked to call junk balls. I remember the day we went to the side of the house to practice. I warmed up my arm, and stood at the mound while Kyle stood in the batter's box. The first ball I threw was a curve ball and he swung and missed. I expected the ball to sail over the building as usual, but it didn't. Taking my time to focus on my pitching I threw a few more and to my amazement, I finally struck Kyle out.

Now it was my turn to bat, I took a few swings and a deep breath. Kyle went into his wind-up and released it, the ball hit the wall with a hard thud, I didn't want to take the first pitch. Then he threw the next ball it felt right, I swung and made contact with the ball we both watched the ball sail over his head! Everything seemed as if it was in slow motion, we both smiled. The feeling I had was unexplainable.

When all my training was over, Kyle had taught me how to bat on both sides of the plate and how to throw with both arms. He said, "Now you're like two people; ambidextrous."

"What does that mean?" I asked.

"You can use both arms to do the same thing with the same skill no one on your team can do what you can do."

CHAPTER 7

—

I'm Ready

We arrived at Navy Field a little early just as they were dragging and lining the field with white chalk. My sisters eagerly led my mother straight to the snack bar while Mark and Kyle went to the bleachers, but me I trudged my way to the dugout dreading every step. Coach Stevens was filling out the team's roster I knew my name wasn't on it. As I walked into the dugout he gave me one of those "Oh not you again" looks which made me sink deeper into my own self-doubt. I found a space on the bench and removed my Members Only jacket my aunt had bought for me. Only one of my teammates spoke to me to the rest of the team I was invisible.

I grabbed my glove and joined my teammates on the field to warm up, I thought to myself, "Why am I warming up when I never play?" I had no idea that today was going to be very different. The umpire called the game, as my team took to the field first and all the parents started cheering; as usual I was left in the dugout with the coaches and equipment.

I looked into the stands; my family members were the only ones not cheering. My uncle had just arrived and my mother said something to him then he looked at me and clapped. Kyle and Mark joined in, and then my sisters followed it felt really good to have at least five fans.

It was the top of the third inning I then looked into the stands, I actually could see steam coming out of my mother's ears. She had watched

Coach Stevens make substitution after substitution, and I was the only one he hadn't put in and she was about to blow. I had never seen my mother that angry before. When a black woman has had enough, get out the way. Now Mark and my uncle had the same identical pissed off look on their faces.

Coach Stevens had no clue as to what was about to happen because he was focused on the game.

Then it happened as I watched in horror, Mark and my uncle could not contain my mother any longer. The look on my sisters looked faces was, "Oh, shit. Someone's in trouble now."

There was nothing anyone can do stop her now! She leaped out of the stands like a lioness focused on her prey. All the white parents in the stands looked on in horror as this wild-eyed angry black woman made her way to the dugout. I pretended that it had nothing to do with me but I was the only black kid on the team.

The only one that stayed calm was Kyle; his attention seemed to be on something else.

As my mom entered the dugout with Mark and my uncle right behind her, I wanted to crawl into the ball bag and hide. My stomach was in knots and I felt like I had to use the bathroom. If I'd had one wish it would've been to be invisible. Well, in Coach Steven's eyes I already was invisible.

"Coach Stevens!" my mom yelled angrily.

I looked at her in complete shock.

Coach Stevens turned to see who was calling him in that manner and saw my mother coming at him.

My mother said, "I didn't pay all that damn money to have my boy sitting on the bench in a clean uniform!" Now everyone's attention was focused on this angry black woman who had two black men standing behind her. "You put my boy in right now!" she demanded.

This was a new side of my mother that I had never seen before. In a way it felt good that she was standing up for me because I hadn't had the guts say anything to Coach Stevens myself. I was glad my mother did because I was really tired of sitting in the dugout.

Coach Stevens said something to her that I couldn't hear, and my mom's face relaxed, and Mark and my uncle backed away from the dugout.

Coach Stevens grabbed his clipboard and called a time out for a substitution. I looked into the stands and saw that my mother was still talking, but she seemed a little more relaxed. Kyle was still focused on the field, while Mark and my uncle stood next to the bleachers, talking.

Coach Stevens walked up to me and said, "You're going in to pitch the next inning, De'Juan."

"All right," I responded, trying to keep my voice from cracking. Then Coach Stevens ordered a teammate to go warm me up to get my arm ready for the next inning.

As I stepped onto the field, there was an announcement, "Now pitching for the Angels, number thirty one, D. J. Verrett," just as I had imagined.

My family began cheering and then both sides of the bleachers began cheering me onto the field. Everyone then took his or her seats except Kyle. He was the only one still standing as our eyes locked, he pulled out a tennis ball from his pocket and held it up for me to see, and I became instantly relaxed and ready to have some fun.

I had trained hard for this very moment, yeah it was only little league, but I felt like I was on the mound at Dodger Stadium with fifty thousand people watching me. I was going to make my coach really proud of me. Stepping onto the mound, I surveyed the field to make sure all my team-mates were in position. The umpire gave me five practice pitches, which all hit their target. I was cool and relaxed, not scared anymore. I had my family and Kyle all there supporting me.

The umpire called, "Batter up!"

I glanced at Kyle one last time for reassurance, then went into my wind-up as I had practiced thousands of times, and let it rip!

Almost immediately, the umpire called, "Stee-riike!" which seemed to become the umpire's favorite word. I struck out most of the batters, and the ones that did get hits only grounded out, while the infielders did their job.

I felt like a big leaguer. Each time I entered the dugout Coach Stevens would tap the front of my hat and say "Good job."

Coach Stevens had me in the line-up in all the games that followed, and Kyle was always there to support me. When the season ended, Coach Stevens told me I had a place on his team next season. I still have the hardball that was signed by my team naming me the MVP of the season. I had proved to myself and to Coach Stevens that my size and skin color didn't matter. It was my determination and support that mattered, and oh yeah, Kyle!

When the season was over, a lot had happened. I had grown not only in height, but also in confidence in myself, and I learned never to judge anyone by his or her appearance. I had a better understanding of Martin Luther King's 'I have a dream speech', and now I was dreaming awake.

CHAPTER 8

—

The Apprentice

1984 was the year when my life changed, a year prior to that, Shawn and I were at his Aunt Wanda's house watching an old western movie. We were into them at the time. The movie was about a cowboy and an Indian who formed a bond like brothers. I remember this particular scene in the movie where they wanted to become blood brothers. The Indian went on to say that when two men from different tribes form a strong bond as if they were birth brothers, they must also share the same blood thereby completing the bond and becoming blood brothers.

The Indian pulled out a knife and sliced the palm of his hand, then the cowboy did the same, then they locked hands and squeezed mixing their blood completing the ritual. They were now blood brothers. After the movie ended, Shawn and I sat on the sofa and talked. We didn't have a brother and we both were from different tribes and had known each other our entire lives, so it seemed only right that we become blood brothers. Shawn suggested that we do what the cowboy and Indian had done.

"Shawn, does your Aunt have a needle?" I asked.

Shawn replied, "Yes, I think so."

I didn't think using a big knife to cut us mattered blood was blood plus, neither of us had the guts to use a sharp knife. Shawn came back with his Aunt's sewing box and found two needles.

I asked him where we should prick ourselves, Shawn suggested our fingertip and I agreed. We both counted to three, and then pricked ourselves and both winced in pain.

Shawn said we should squeeze our fingers which we did and a small bead of blood appeared. Before we touched our fingers together we both said, "Nothing will ever come between us." We both waited for a minute.

I said, "Can you feel my blood in you?"

Shawn responded, "Yeah, can you feel mines?"

I replied, "Yeah, I can." We became brothers on that day.

I continued to collect golf balls and mow lawns, but Shawn couldn't make it most of the time. He said he had another job. For his fourteenth birthday, I had saved enough to buy him a brand new lock for his bike he really didn't seem too excited about the lock but he said, "Thank you I needed a new one."

Shawn was almost two months older than me he had shown me a lot especially how to hustle golf balls to keep money in my pocket. One day I was at the local park waiting for Shawn so we could sign up for the basketball league, but he never showed up. Later that day I was at home in my room when Shawn came over to see if I could spend the night. I asked my mom if that was okay, and she didn't object. I put some clothes in my backpack and headed out the door.

When we got outside, I hopped on my bike and said to Shawn, "Where's your bike?

"I don't need it anymore," he said.

I was confused. Shawn said, "Leave your bike here I have something to show you."

My mind raced with thoughts as we walked into the night.

"I have a car now," he finally said.

"Yeah, right!"

Shawn pulled some keys from his pocket and dangled them for me to see. We stopped in front of an old brown Grand Toreno.

"Get in," Shawn said.

I sat in the car in amazement he was only fourteen years old and had his own car! He was still too young to even get a driving permit, but that didn't mean anything; he had a car. My mom didn't even have her own car yet. He told me he'd paid five hundred dollars for it, and I quickly tried to add up the amount of golf balls I would have to collect to earn five hundred dollars.

It was a great car, except it didn't have a passenger window or a stereo, but other than that it was a great car. I felt like an adult sitting in my brother's car. We were like two grown men I had twenty-seven dollars in my pocket from collecting golf balls, cans and mowing lawns. It felt good just to know it was there if I needed it, and just in case we were going to the arcade.

We arrived safely at his Aunt's house in Long Beach and went to the back of the house to chill. I followed Shawn to the back room where we found Donte cutting something on a plate with a razor blade. He had a big gold chain around his neck and something that looked like a garage door opener on his belt.

Donte looked up and said, "What's up, Shawn?" "Nothing. Ready to clock some dollars," Shawn said.

Now I understood how Shawn had bought his car, and why he'd stopped collecting golf balls.

Shawn pulled out a plastic bag with a golf ball in it. Well, at least I thought it was a golf ball. He held it up and said, "This is going to make me eight hundred dollars tonight," and he proceeded to cut the golf ball-sized rock into smaller pebbles. Shawn said each one was worth twenty dollars.

I had heard about cocaine, but had never seen it, I wanted to tell Shawn to take me home, but I didn't want to look like a punk.

Then he asked me, "Do you want to make some money?"

I hesitated at first, then answered with a shaky, "Hell, yeah."

That's when Donte's older brother, Lamont, walked in and said to me, "Boy, what are you doing here?"

"I'm spending the night."

Lamont was like family he knew Shawn and I were tight.

Then Donte blurted out, "He wants to start slanging now."

I shot Donte a look that said, "Shut up!" but now I was on the spot.

That's when Shawn came to my rescue and said, "He wants a double up twenty-five dollars."

Lamont looked at me and said, "Is that right?"

I replied with a sheepish, "Yeah."

He smiled and said, "Your momma will kill you if she finds out you selling rocks."

"She isn't going to find out," I said.

Lamont just laughed, and then asked, "What if you get caught by the police?"

I hadn't thought about that part that's when Shawn interrupted and said, "Don't trip. I'll teach him."

Lamont walked up to Shawn, putting his face right in Shawn's face and said, "He's your responsibility."

I wanted to bolt out the door and go home, but I was compelled to stay. I gave Lamont my hard earned twenty-five dollars and he gave me the three and a half grams of rock cocaine.

Lamont said, "Usually those cost a hundred dollars," then left the room.

I had only two dollars cash left on me, but if things worked out tonight like Shawn predicted, I'd make close to three hundred dollars. That was like three summers of mowing lawns, collecting golf balls and cans!

I sat in my chair like a good student while Shawn schooled me on how to cut the marble sized rock into smaller rocks that were worth twenty dollars apiece. We even rehearsed what I was to say to the customers.

That night I watched Shawn at work, he made it look easy just like at LAX the summer before quick easy exchanges. Then it was my turn to be up and I was nervous.

Shawn called my name, "Casper, you up!"

I approached the car, and the customer said, "I want a hundred worth."

I quickly counted out five rocks and said, "Show me the money," the customer flashed five twenty dollar bills, and we made the exchange. I was so nervous I didn't see Shawn standing behind me as I turned and I bumped into him. Still clutching the money, I couldn't believe I'd made a hundred dollars that fast.

Shawn instructed me to check it to make sure it wasn't marked. I quickly looked at it, then stuffed it into my pocket and took my position back in the shadows.

That night I made my quota. Donte supplied me with more and I sold that too. We all sold out, then headed back to his Aunt Wanda's house to sleep, but I couldn't sleep. I lay in bed counting my money. I had six hundred eighty-two dollars in only two hours; I'd made six hundred and eighty dollars in drug money only the two dollars was golf ball money.

The next day we went to the neighborhood park to hang with some friends. Shawn told me to wait in the car, so I did. I wondered why he wanted me to wait, but to pass the time I counted my money once again. I had kept only the two dollars in my Velcro wallet. Then Shawn summoned me to come over where everybody was drinking forty ounce's and smoking weed. Shawn was quiet while everybody was looking at me.

Wally was the first to speak, he looked at me and called me by my first name. "De'Juan, if you want to keep slanging, you have to be from the hood."

"I am from the hood," I said.

Wally said, "Yeah, because you grew up here, but you have to be jumped in." What that meant was I'd have to fight three of my friends who had already been 'jumped in' for one minute to prove that I was down for the hood, and then I could continue to make money.

Shawn said, "Let me talk to him." As we walked back to his car, frantic thoughts raced through my mind. My heart was beating fast because I wasn't really a fighter, and didn't want to fight my friends. Shawn began talking, but I wasn't listening to him. I kept my hands in my pocket as we walked feeling the money. He explained me that if I'm from the hood I could keep making money.

For the love of money, I agreed, then we walked back to the circle and I announced, "I want to be from the hood."

As I prepared for my initiation, Shawn put his arm around me and whispered, "Swing first."

Wally set his digital watch for one minute as I entered the circle. My heart was beating super-fast as I balled my fists, putting them up ready for battle, while keeping my eye on Wally. As soon as his mouth moved, I struck first, attacking Donte because he seemed like less of a threat.

I was punched and kicked blows came at me from everywhere as I swung for my life. I was hit on the head so many times I felt dizzy, I let out a war scream like a crazed man.

31

I could faintly hear Wally counting down, "Ten, nine, eight."

I continued swinging for my life; the blow that hurt the most was the last one. Shawn had kicked me in the stomach, knocking the wind out of me.

I held my stomach, I couldn't breathe, then I heard "Two, one," and it was over. I fell to my knees, gasping for air.

Shawn knelt down, hugged me and asked, "Are you okay?" I couldn't answer. "Now you're from the hood," he proudly said.

Shawn helped me to my feet as everybody patted me on the back. I had to sit for a minute to catch my breath, my mouth was extremely dry, and that's when Wally handed me something to drink. I didn't even ask what it was I assumed it was water or soda. I took the paper bag and proceeded to gulp down its contents. The liquid burned my stomach I pulled the bottle out of the bag to read the label, it was an Old English forty ounce the same drink I'd often seen Bosco drinking. Then all of a sudden, the pain I felt was gone and I felt warm on the inside.

As we congregated on the bleachers, Shawn pulled out a cigarette and lit it, then passed it to me. I was already feeling good from the forty ounce, and without thinking I put the cigarette to my lips and inhaled deeply. I started coughing violently; my virgin lungs weren't ready for this. I had never smoked anything before. Everybody started laughing, and then I started laughing.

"That's some good weed, huh?" Shawn said.

"Yeah, it is," I answered. I'd never smoked weed before and I liked it.

From that day on life looked different I started to see things I hadn't seen before. I realized that we were poor, and that it was up to me to change things. I thought that since I was now officially from the hood my life would be better and I would have all the things Bosco had.

By this time, Mark had left for the last time and wasn't coming back. My older homeboys would teach me everything I needed to learn about life, and they wouldn't leave me they would love me like fathers.

CHAPTER 9

Flossing

The year was 1985 and I had just bought my first car for fifteen hundred dollars from one of my older homie's. It was a yellow 1969 Chevy Impala with a black top and the classic chain steering wheel. I had also purchased a set of brand new 5-60 tires with some used McLean wire rims from one of my other homie's.

I didn't have my driver's license yet, I had to wait until the tenth grade to get my driver's permit. I would have to park my car on the far side of the projects to avoid being seen by my mother or sisters since I couldn't let them know I had the car. I knew my mother wouldn't approve, and she'd definitely want to know where I'd gotten the money to buy the car, which of course I couldn't tell her.

My mother didn't have a car at this time she was still busing it. Every morning she would get my sisters ready for school and send them off early to catch the school bus. Well, I would slow drag, waiting for my mother to leave the house so I could then make my way to my car knowing she would be on the bus.

In the hood, a car was a status symbol of how well you were doing that's how you were judged, the more extras you had the better you were doing, well I was doing great! I was fifteen with a clean low-rider my car came with hydraulics and a banging sound system.

Even Bosco gave me praise; my name was starting to ring in the hood as a go-getter. I wasn't ashamed that my mom rode the bus because most of the mothers did, so it wasn't out of the ordinary. Now that I was making money I wanted more for my mom. She was struggling to raise three kids, and she wouldn't understand that I could help take care of her and my sisters now.

My mother started to notice all my new shoes and clothes, it was definitely getting harder to hide how I was able to buy Fila ski jackets, gold chains, Nike tennis shoes and sweat suits. Collecting golf balls definitely didn't pay like selling crack. I wanted better for myself and for her, but she would blow a fuse if she found out that I was selling cocaine.

The morning sky was cold and grey from the rain the night before. I made my way to my car without incident and left for school. I maneuverered my way into traffic and was stopped at a red light. There was a crowd of people standing at the bus stop looking cold as I sat in my car with the heat on full blast and the volume on the stereo turned up, making sure everybody saw me.

The rain started to come down and the crowd of people at the bus stop all opened their umbrellas shielding themselves from the burst of raindrops. Some people had black ones or white ones, but one stuck out from the rest it had flowers on it just like my mom's umbrella. Then we made eye contact maybe because of the loud music. I don't know but of course she instantly recognized me. A shot of panic came over me as she approached my car from the curb.

"De'Juan, whose car is this?" she screamed.

I remained composed and replied, "It's mine do you want a ride to work?" It was no use hiding any longer.

As she got into the car folding her umbrella, then the interrogation began. "Where did you get it from? and how did you pay for it?"

I considered myself a man now and able to take care of myself, she had labelled me the man of the house since I was a little boy so, I'm doing what men do, taking care of my family. She no longer intimidated me, and I was too old and big to get ass whoopins. She was going to find out sooner or later, but I hadn't realized it was going to be this morning.

I finally answered her, "the car is mine and I'm keeping it." I waited for her to respond, but instead she just stared at me without saying a word.

My mom started putting the pieces together the new shoes and clothes, giving her fifty dollars here and fifty dollars there. Golf balls and cans didn't pay like that, but the money helped her out during some rough times.

As she regained her thoughts, she asked, "Why is the car so low?"

"It's the hydraulics." I hit the switch to level the car and she held onto the door handle as the car jumped.

Her last words before I dropped her off at work were, "We are going to talk about this when I get home tonight." I was relieved that I didn't have to park the car so far away now.

After school I met up with Shawn by my car a few of the homie's were there waiting for a ride home. They all piled into my car. H-Dog sat in the passenger seat with the window rolled down. I turned the stereo on and put in LL Cool J's new tape and turned the volume way up so we could be heard and seen. I put on my hat and black shades and we were off. I would never have imagined that twenty years later I would be on a television show with LL Cool J.

School wasn't as hard as most of my homie's thought. Some of them had dropped out by the ninth grade to spend more time in the hood to slang drugs, but I enjoyed school and wasn't about to drop out. My mom would really lose it if I did, plus I liked to look good for the girls. Shawn stayed in school also; he was very smart especially in math!

We weren't bad kids we just believed we'd found our way out of poverty by selling white gold. Yeah, school slowed down the process but dropping out wasn't on our minds.

After the initial shock of the car, I started letting my mom drive it to work instead of catching the bus. After all, I was the man of the house a provider in a sense. It made me feel like an adult and powerful.

CHAPTER 10

—

First Case

Crack cocaine stock was up, everybody was making boatloads of money and the big homie's were happy. We had the whole South Bay sewed up. Shawn and I would ditch school to stay in the hood. We became pretty good at forging notes for school. We had switched the home phone numbers the school had for us with the big home girl's home phone number, so if the school called she would take care of it for us.

The crew I hung with had a system; we would position ourselves in a rotation from lookouts to salesmen. It worked perfectly, if the police came around the lookouts would yell, "one-time, one-time," and we would bolt to safety. The big homie's watched how we worked. They would drive through our area occasionally throwing up the 'hood' sign, and then we would throw it back to them, they were our mentors our teachers.

Bosco would pay extra attention to my crew, which was me, Shawn, Bam-Bam, F-Bone and Ham. Bosco and Gangsta would post up with the other big homies and watch, I guess to see who took control of the pack, or maybe they were looking for a young apprentice. I watched them without letting them know I was watching. As the never-ending sea of anxious customers waited to spend their money, I took the opportunity to orchestrate the flow of illegal commerce, our block ran like a well-oiled machine and I was heading it.

One day I was at home with a few of my homies, I had just bought five ounces of crack cocaine and was going to cut them up, but I needed a shower so I put them on my desk in my room while my homies waited. My mother came home unexpectedly early while I was in the shower, and she hadn't expected me to be home at this time. She went into my room; saw my homies and then the five ounces of cocaine sitting on the desk.

She banged on the bathroom door, yelling, "Open this damn door!"

I wondered why she was yelling, so I opened the door.

Holding up the five ounces she said, "I can't believe you brought this shit into my house! Get your stuff and get out!"

I gathered my things and left without saying a word. I was only fifteen at the time and that was the last time I would ever live under my mother's roof.

A customer was a manager for a motel in the hood, so Shawn and I worked out a deal with him to live there. It was our first place together, room number 505. We both agreed that we would continue to go to school, but this would be our home for a while.

It was a Friday night and as usual, we were supplying the need of the drug addicts. Shawn and I had just sold out; I had made thirty-five hundred dollars that night and was ready to leave.

We were waiting on Donte to sell out, so I fired up a joint and shared it with Shawn. All of a sudden the lookouts yelled, "One-time, one-time!"

The LAPD came out of nowhere it was too late to run. The police had us trapped. I wasn't really worried we didn't have anything on us but money, and money was not illegal.

Unbeknownst to us, Donte had sold to an undercover agent as we had watched him from the shadows. Those are the chances you take when you're in the game.

They even arrested the big homies that night. We were all hand-cuffed and ordered to sit on the curb. I looked up into the night sky and saw the ghetto bird shining its bright flood lights over the scene below. I wondered if we would make it on the nightly news. Sick, huh?

As we sat on the curb, an officer approached us holding up a plastic bag with a one-shot in it. A one shot is three and a half grams of cocaine or a sixteenth of an ounce, which is called a Teenager. Donte was the only one who hadn't sold out, so when the police came he panicked and tossed it toward us. When the police come, whatever you're not supposed to have you'd better throw as far away as you can, or take the case that's the number one rule.

Donte had just gotten out of juvenile detention for catching cases for dumb shit like carrying knives that were more than what the law allowed, shooting pigeons with bee-bee guns stupid shit like that. He was the only one of us on probation at that time, and if he caught a new case he was going to Youth Authority for eighteen months.

The officer stood in front of us and said, "Who wants to claim this?"

We expected Donte to man-up and take it saving everyone a trip to the station, but he didn't. In a sick way, I was curious to see what a sub-station looked like. Crazy, huh?

We were all loaded into squad cars and chauffeured to the 77th Station. Once there, we were put into separate holding rooms. Across the hall the big homies all looked pissed the fuck off, Donte sat in our cell and remained silent.

I was one of the first BGs or Baby Gangsters to be fingerprinted and have my mug shot taken. One of the big homies was also getting fingerprinted. As I stood next to my OG homeboy, I felt like his equal. "Man Power" looked at me with a pissed-off look on his face. I gave the same look, but I really wasn't pissed off for some strange reason.

Next, it was time for me to get my picture taken I was told to stand against the wall. The officer had adjusted the tiles on the booking board to reflect my name and birth date. I guess he ran out of film and he said to me, "Don't move," and I didn't. When he left the room I adjusted the tiles and put my hood's name in place of mine. When the officer returned he took a few pictures I was then instructed to turn left which I did and then turn right which I also did. After he'd developed the film he came back and was he pissed off because I'd changed the tiles! His partners were laughing at him. I thought the whole thing was funny. My picture was re-taken and then I was placed back with the homies.

Back in the holding cell, I told all the homies what I'd done and we all started laughing except Donte. He was the only one not talking. I thought this was going to be something to talk about at school and in the hood.

One of my homies "Bam-Bam" looked at Donte and said, "Nigga, you better cop to that shit."

Donte shook his head; "no I can't go to YA for another eighteen months. I just got out."

The big O.G. homie, "Man Power", yelled across the hallway, "You young niggas better work this shit out."

We all looked at Donte who looked like one of those hungry kids on commercial you see on T.V. he damn near started to cry.

I spoke up. "What if I take it? They can't do anything to me I have a clean record, and they can only give me probation."

"Man Power" said, "It's not yours Ghost."

"Donte's not going to take it; and they're going to keep us in here until the bus comes" I answered.

Man Power asked, "So you're going to take the case for that nigga?"

"Yes," I answered.

I looked over at Donte, he had a look of relief his eyes conveyed a silent thank you. See, in the streets I was told if you're going to play this game you have to play by the rules. Rule number one: ride your own beef. Donte he just looked the part, he hadn't give his life and will to the care of the game like I did. I took the oath to be true to the game. Rule number two: never snitch on anybody.

The officer returned and I yelled, "Hey, Mr. Po-lice man. That shit you found was mine."

He looked at me and said, "So you're admitting that you sold to an undercover officer and was in possession of a controlled substance?"

"Yeah, man."

I was moved to another holding cell and sent to Los Padrinos Juvenile Hall for the weekend, while the big homies missed the chain to the Los Angeles County Jail.

I wasn't living with my mom at the time, and all of my possessions were at the motel. I was sure that Shawn would take care of my things until I got out. I was arrested on February 6, 1985. On my first court date there were a lot of mothers waiting for their sons to be released into their custody. I looked for my mother in the courtroom and was relieved to see her sitting in the front of the room.

40

When my name was called, a guy I had never seen before motioned for me to sit with him. "Hi, my name is Kyle Duffy, and I'll be representing you today. Don't worry, you'll be out for lunch." That was a relief because the food was shitty in the halls.

I was given a sentence of summary probation and I was released to my mother's custody it was that simple.

My mother really didn't say much as we sat at the bus stop. I felt embarrassed sitting at the bus stop with my mom. I wanted to call Shawn so he could pick me up, but I stayed with my mom and rode the bus home with her.

When we got home, my mom made my favorite meal hamburgers and french fries. Those are still my favorites, even to this day. I knew she was pissed off, but she didn't yell or anything. She just gave me the silent treatment she had taken the day off from work to come to court, so I had to hustle to recover the thirty-five hundred dollars.

Back on the set, my name was ringing like a high school bell, I was elevated to Young Gee status and Donte was demoted to Buster status. When I walked up, all of the O.G. homies welcomed me with open arms and the homies my age did as well. Donte was nowhere to be found. I was known as a rider a stand up player in the game. It was like a ghetto parade everybody was calling my name; I was the center of attention.

Bosco drove up and motioned me to come over to him. He said, "I heard what you've done, sacrificed yourself for the homies. Niggas love you for that, come down to the apartments we have something for you." I was excited to hang with the big homies and to know they loved me.

Donte made this possible by not stepping up, but it would have been better if he'd ridden his own beef and taken the eighteen months instead of the years of being punked and humiliated by the other homies.

Anxious to see what the big homies had for me, I made my way to the apartments. I could smell barbeque in the air as I approached the back gate. I announced that I was there, and Gangsta opened the gate, Bosco was at the grill marinating some ribs, moving to the music and laughing. Man Power saw me and shouted "What up, young Ghost?"

I threw up the hood sign with a fake smile and that's when Bosco saw me.

Roger Troutman's song, "I heard it through the grapevine", was coming out of the speakers and Bosco was singing to it. Bosco told Gangsta to give him the gift. I wondered, what gift? What did they have for me?

Bosco said, "I heard they took something from you."

"Yeah, my muthafuckin' money."

Gangsta returned with a brown paper bag and handed it to me. I opened it up and there was money in it.

Bosco said, "Count it."

I did and inside was the thirty-five hundred dollars I held it up and said, "What's this for?"

Bosco responded, "That's what you lost and the homies took up a collection for you to replace what was lost. What, you don't want it?"

I was at a loss for words.

Bosco announced that the food was ready, and told me to grab a plate. I stood in line in sheer amazement that I was hanging with the big homies.

Gangsta started yelling, "Hey, hey! Wait! Let the young homie go first."

Everyone moved to the side and let me pass, I felt like an O.G. top dog, in reality I was just a puppy amongst the pit bulls.

As the day ended, I stopped by my mom's house to give her money for missing work. She didn't want it, but I left it anyway, and I gave my sisters five dollars apiece and headed out.

CHAPTER 11

—

Lost

During my run in the game, I gained a lot of respect from the O.G.'s in the hood and amongst some of my homies. The money was coming in so fast I didn't know what to do with it. I became hood famous and ghetto fabulous. I had already reached the level of Bosco and I was only seventeen years old.

There was nothing I couldn't do, I was taught how to make, cut and sell damn near every kind of drug on the street. They groomed me like a father would groom a son. They loved me, and I loved them. Each of my father figures taught me something different. I converted the word Father to Big Homie; it had the same meaning to me.

When I was a pre-teen my body started to change, I grew hair where hair had never grown before. Something weird was happening to me.

One afternoon I was sitting next to my mom and she said, "Boy, you are musty."

My body had a different smell to it, not the little kid smell, but the smell of a young man. That's when she bought me my first stick of deodorant and told me to use it every day.

Next, my voice started sounding different, when I laughed or yelled it had a lower deeper bass to it, and sometimes I couldn't control the pitch. I was sounding older, and there was a million other things happening to my body that I was too ashamed to talk about to her.

There were other things like waking up in the morning with an erection. The first time that happened, I was so scared I didn't know what to do. I thought something was wrong, but nothing hurt. I had to go to my homies and ask these kinds of questions. They told me all about life like a father tells a son, they gave me the puberty talk.

Bosco was the one that taught me one of the most important lessons like the "L" word. He said, "Ghost, you only love yourself and nobody else, none of these mother fuckers really love you," and I believed him, he had never steered me wrong.

Then I asked, "What about girls?"

Bosco answered, "You only love them with your eyes and hands never have feelings for them, and if you want to feel use your hands. Never open your heart to a woman, she'll think you're weak, keep your heart to yourself."

Shawn and I started to drift apart about this time and I had started hanging out more with the older homies, they wouldn't invite Shawn to kick it with us, so resentment formed which I didn't see. Shawn was my blood brother and whatever I got he would get no doubt.

Females to me were just toys to play with, I never had feelings for them. This was the moment that we started to drift further apart. The space that formed between us began to fill with envy, jealousy and dirty macking, but I still loved Shawn like a brother.

I wanted the money, power and prestige, while Shawn wanted a relationship. I had taken my hustle out of town by this time, and asked Shawn to come with me to get some of this money, but his girlfriend held him back and he didn't want him to leave the hood.

I was taking it to another level, I had just gotten a new connection and started taking trips to Tijuana and asked Shawn to come with me, but he refused. He'd say things like, "I got everything I need here."

I'd look around and say, "The world is bigger than the hood."

Shawn was the one who got me into the game, being ghetto rich and white folk rich are two different things. Ghetto rich means you have to continue to clock those dollars taking penitentiary chances, while white folks rich means your dollars work for you like investing or some shit like that, I wanted to be white folk rich.

44

I told Shawn, "Whenever you're ready, let me know, and I'll take you with me. We started this together and we'll end it together."

Nothing in my life was making me happy something was missing, I had plenty of money at this time my mom would say, "If I had a million dollars all my problems would disappear and I would be happy." Well, I had over one hundred thousand dollars cash and another quarter of a million in drugs, and I was still unhappy.

I thought having a lot of women would make me happy, but it didn't, the feeling was the same, I felt empty inside. The pillars I stood on were beginning to crumble.

I tried to find solace in liquor and cocaine to kill that feeling I was having inside of me. The vibration in my soul was strong and almost unbearable, something was wrong so I increased my intake of alcohol and cocaine. It looked like everything was great on the outside, but on the inside I was in pain the stronger the vibrations became, the more I drank and used cocaine to kill it.

The money didn't have the same appeal it had when I made that first six hundred and eighty dollars. It was just paper with dead white men on it. The women, they didn't really know me, I was just a guy with money who would show them a good time, that's all.

I was at home one night feeling depressed and lonely, so I turned on the television for the noise and company. I had a little box with a quarter ounce of powder cocaine in it. I chopped it up and made a few lines to snort. I folded a hundred dollar bill into a straw and snorted a few lines, then went and poured myself a gin and juice.

Sitting on the sofa, I reached for the hundred-dollar bill and unfolded it so I could see Benjamin Franklin's face, and I spoke to him. Looking around my house, I told Benjamin, "I do this shit all for you, man," but he didn't answer. He just looked at me with that 'Hmmm' look on his face. I did a few more lines and walked around feeling empty in my apartment wondering how the fuck did I get like this?

I could still feel that vibration in my chest, which meant I needed more medicine. I sat on the sofa and did more lines to quiet and tone down the vibrations, but I kept thinking, 'Is this why I sell dope, to be so unhappy?' but I knew nothing else.

Sitting on the sofa with my hands to my ears, trying not to hear what was going through my head. I screamed out loud, "Stop it! Stop it!"

This was the first time since I'd been in the game that I realized what I was doing. I was destroying families, people robbed to get high, they stole from their kids, they became homeless, they became slaves to this shit I was selling, and I became one of the slave masters, Doctor Feel Good with the magic pill. I wondered if Bosco ever felt like this.

I couldn't stop the visions I was having, I saw mothers selling themselves for ten-dollar hits. Mrs. Fontaine lost the house her husband had built to the bail bondsmen because Rod-O, their son, jumped bail. He was hooked on crack.

The hustler inside of me spoke up, he said, "If you don't do it, someone else will, so get your money man." The crack heads paid for my way of life, they bought me nice cars and clothes, they put food in my refrigerator, they made it possible for me and many others to live a life in style.

Deep down, I knew what I was doing was wrong, but this is all I knew and I had become very good at it.

I believed what was wrong was having to eat the same thing four times a week, not being able to have new school clothes and wearing shoes that were too small. What was wrong was seeing your mother work like a slave and still have nothing, that's what was wrong. The game showed me a way out of poverty. I'd been told that if you stayed real with the game, the game would reward you. Well, I was being rewarded with all the material shit, but I was never told about these feelings I was having on the inside.

I was eighteen years old now, but I felt like an old man, this was not the life I'd imagined as a little boy. The gin and juice helped drown out the vibrations. I sat back and closed my eyes and drifted off somewhere until the television started to make a buzzing sound. I sat up and spilled my drink in my lap. The gin and juice soaked through my jeans and onto the sofa.

I got up and went to the bathroom to change. I looked at the bathtub and decided to take a bath. A memory flashed of my childhood about how my mom would make us take a bath before bed. The water was always hot; too hot for my young skin. I sometimes thought I had done something wrong and the hot bath water was my punishment. I asked her, "Momma, why is the water so hot?"

She had answered, "To take all the bad stuff away so you can sleep better."

As the hot water filled the tub, the glass doors fogged up from the steam. I began to undress and automatically reached for my robe that was hanging on the door. The steam was now filling the bathroom just as the fog clouded my thoughts. I remembered the pistol I had just bought from these white dudes in a silver van. They sold guns dirt cheap and brand new still in the box. They had a large variety of handguns to choose from.

In the dope game, you have to be careful I always kept two pistols on me just in case one jammed. You need protection in my kind of life. Jackers loved to rob drug dealers because the dope dealers aren't going to call the police, so my father figures schooled me about this. They would say, "Never get caught slippin'. "Protect yourself at all times."

I got caught slippin' one time when I was in Saint Louis and that was the last time. I was making a boatload of money. I was just about sold out and I took the remaining stock of cocaine I had left to sell. One of my workers, Curtis, and his girlfriend were there with me. We were smoking weed and became hungry, so they left to get some fast food.

Before Curtis left he said, "Don't let anyone in the house."

Shortly after they left there was a knock on the door. It was two of the guys that worked for me, and I saw no harm in letting them in. We sat in the living room, drank a few beers, and then one of them pulled out a gun and said, "Where is it?"

I laughed and said, "Put that shit away," but he wasn't laughing. He raised the gun and hit me in the back of my head, and said, "Where is it?"

Now I knew it was for real. I rose up again and he struck me on the mouth with the gun. I fell to the floor and blood started gushing out of my mouth and my head. They started kicking me in the ribs, and then they tied my hands behind my back and put the gun to the base of my skull. I lay on the carpet staring at a wall outlet. I couldn't even respond to their commands anymore I was in a daze, but for some strange reason I felt at peace. I stared at the wall outlet while they viscously beat me.

That was the ugly side of the game, the side nobody talks about, I wasn't even scared I was just ready for the pain to stop.

As I lay on the carpet, the guy with the gun grabbed a handful of my hair and pressed the barrel to the back of my head and squeezed the trigger, but it didn't go off. The gun was jammed, so he beat me with it. I guess because of all the blood he couldn't grip the gun tight so the blows glanced off my skull. That's when Curtis and his girl came back with the food. Luckily, Curtis had his pistol on him, he came rushing up the stairs with his gun ablaze, and the two workers fled out the back door.

I was regaining consciousness and told Curtis to untie me. I rose to my feet but still felt dizzy, and he stabilized me. I checked my mouth and didn't feel any teeth missing, and then I checked my head. The back door was still open, I grabbed his gun and bolted out the door, I couldn't even talk because my top lip was split in two. I hopped fences and walls and I could still hear them.

The last wall was a high cinder block wall, I was getting tired and I had a hard time trying to climb it. Once I pulled myself to the top, I saw three white flashes, then heard pop, pop, and pop. The three bullets hit the wall chest level. If I had climbed over the wall, I would have been hit in the chest, I returned their fire until the gun was empty.

I made it back to the house and Curtis and some of his boys were there waiting for instructions. My mouth and head needed stitches. Curtis' aunt was an R.N, so I was taken to her house. The only anaesthesia I had was powder cocaine, and I snorted a few lines before she stitched me up. She coated the wound on my head and my mouth with powder cocaine to numb the pain.

I kept my enemies close, but my friends closer. I was becoming paranoid of some of my homeboys, and I didn't like the looks I was getting from some of them. I would never let my guard down again.

I held the brand new 357 Magnum in my hand I hadn't even fired it yet. I was holding raw power; I only wanted to use it for protection, not in anger. The running water caught my attention I returned to the bathroom and the steam had covered the mirror. I sat my drink down and wiped the mirror. I stared into the mirror, I looked like an old man with sad eyes. I thought, "I'm not supposed to be living like this, how did I get like this?" I lived better than anyone in my family, but I was unhappier than I'd ever been.

I stared into the mirror and didn't like what I saw, didn't like what I'd become. I raised the pistol to my head and squeezed the trigger. All I heard was click click. The pistol wasn't loaded, I cried as I looked at the image in the mirror. He just looked back at me and I asked, "Is this it? Is this why I sell drugs, to feel like this? Is this why I do what I do, to feel like this?" The image just looked at me and remained silent. Now I was getting upset at this time and I went to my bedroom and loaded the pistol, then returned to the mirror.

My thoughts were saying, "Do it, do it, end the pain." I wasn't the kind of person that hurts people. Deep down inside I wanted to help people, but I couldn't even help myself. I was hurting on the inside. I heard that voice again saying, 'you don't have to be in pain anymore you can end it.' I cried uncontrollably, not for Ghost, but for D.J., the little boy who had become lost.

Memories flashed before my eyes, like the time I first learned how to ride a bike, and when I became the leader of the pack, and my first day on the mound at Navy field and collecting golf balls and cans. I never needed money as a kid, just my bike and sunshine. Life was dark now; it was uncertain. I was going to funerals every other month seeing my childhood friends in caskets at the ages of fifteen, sixteen and seventeen years old, and their mothers crying hysterically, "My baby, my baby."

I turned off the bath water and submerged my entire body without caring that the water was extremely hot. I guess it was self-punishment, I finished off the last of the gin and juice, and held the pistol, I heard that voice again, I cocked the hammer back and thought, 'All I have to do is squeeze the trigger and it will all be over.' I put the gun to my head like I did in the mirror. Death seemed like an easy way out. There would be no more pain, no more needing to prove myself, and I could just rest in peace with the homies.

I thought this would be the perfect place; it would be easy to clean up, it might take a day or two before someone came to look for me. I thought about my funeral and who would be there, I thought about my mother and my sisters.

The only reason I didn't pull the trigger that night was because I couldn't kill my mother's only son.

CHAPTER 12

———

Providing

It was time to restock my inventory and supply the demand of the consumer's choice of getting high so they could leave the world's problems behind; providing a service that seemed to be never ending.

I called two of my Mexican friends to schedule a trip to Tijuana. Jesus and Sergio were both related to Ernesto the Jefe Grande. Jesus' family had moved years before any of us had gotten into the game. I was driving my 1977 Cutlass Supreme and Jesus was looking to buy the same type of car. He asked me how much I'd be willing to sell it for, I told him my asking price. Jesus knew I was in the game, so I told him that I wanted to stop working the crack houses and move on to bigger things. That's when he told me that his uncle could give me good prices on kilos. He quickly set up a meeting with his uncle for me.

When his uncle first saw me he thought I was Cuban or a Puerto Rican because of my skin and hair.

"Yo soy negro," I said in my best Spanish.

Then he frowned and said something in Spanish to Jesus, which I didn't understand.

Jesus smiled and said; "He doesn't remember you from the projects."

His uncle motioned for me to follow him, and as Ernesto spoke, Jesus translated because of our history from the projects and co-signed for me, I was in. I began selling birds to my big homies cheaper than what they were paying; I had come a long way in a short amount of time.

51

We used Jesus' truck to pick up the work, it had a special customized stash spot in it made out of lead, and it could hold up to twenty birds/ kilos at a time, but I only wanted four. Ernesto wanted to give me more on consignment, but I didn't want to work for anyone. I was told early in the game, if you work for someone they control your future, and if anything went wrong it was my loss and I didn't want to owe anyone anything.

Ernesto was one of the big dogs; his family controlled the border at that time. They were Zacatecas, a Mexican drug cartel. It didn't seem like any big deal to me at the time, and being around these kinds of people was normal to me. It was my life style and I felt comfortable. It was a business and I was just another independent vendor making sure my shelves were stocked.

Ernesto's brother-in-law was a Mexican federal agent and they raised and trained their dogs to sniff out drugs. That's why the stash was made of lead; I thought that shit was genius. As the truck was loaded and cleaned, they let the dogs go do their thing and we passed their inspection. After a few shots of tequila with a few senoritas it was time to leave.

When we crossed the border back into the United States I would always buy something from the street vendors right before the cut-off line, just to make it look like I was a tourist making it home safe.

I had a small apartment on the north side of Long Beach it was my stash spot. I got everything ready there for my trips, but I rarely slept there and it was barely furnished. There was a bed in the bedroom, and in the living room there was a couch and a TV just to play Nintendo. I was still a kid who loved video games.

I got a page from my friend Meechy, and called him back to let him know I'd gotten the keys to the car and I'd be leaving soon. Back in the day, cell phones didn't exist yet. Everyone in the game used pagers, which was the technology that was popular at the time, and home computers didn't surface until 1992 or 1993.

As I was getting things together, Shawn paged me so I went back to the phone booth and called him. He said that he needed to make some money, that things weren't working out with his girlfriend and that he wanted to move out of his mom's house. I had no problem with helping him out after all he was my brother, and I knew he would come around sooner or later.

I instructed him not to tell anyone where he was going I gave him eleven hundred dollars for expenses and told him to leave at noon, to travel by himself, also not to wear any baggie clothing. I told him not to wear a hat and to look as plain as everybody else at the bus station, and to call me when he reached the destination, then I would fly out the same day. I gave him a hug and he was off. He failed to listen to any of my rules I had one bird left that I was going to give to Meechy on consignment. I didn't like to break them down because it took too long to sell. I liked to dump them whole. I only paid ten-five for each kilo and sold them for forty thousand a pop. I could've sold them for more, but I didn't want to be greedy. That's why Ernesto gave them to me so cheap because I could dump four birds in a day. He wanted to bring them to me directly but I respectfully declined his offer. The only thing he needed to know was that I could get rid of them quickly.

I had a little bucket of a car to drive around to move the work from place to place. I didn't need anything flashy to draw the attention of the police. I had just bought a 1988 ZR1 corvette from a guy in the game who changed the VIN numbers. I paid thirty-five thousand in cocaine, which really only cost me five thousand in cash. I'd rather use cocaine instead of spending cash. I also had a 300ZX. I bought that brand new and the salesman from the dealership was strung out on crack.

As I was making my rounds, I got a page from Janna asking me to come by, I told Meechy that we were going to stop by her house for a minute. Meechy was my road dog; he wasn't in the game to get rich, he was in the game just to party on the weekends and keep a few dollars in his pocket. I told him that he needed to get real with the game or stop playing.

Janna was real cool, for a woman she was down for me. I would run some things by her and she would tell me how she felt, especially about some of the people I ran with. I respected her honesty. We pulled into the driveway and I told Meechy to wait in the car while I went to talk to Janna. She and I talked about the trip that Shawn was making for me and she flipped out. "He's not smart enough for that! Why don't you continue using your white friend as you've done before? I know you love him like he's your real brother, but he's not like you, De'Juan."

I stopped her and said, "He is my real brother."

Janna could see things that I couldn't.

On the way home, we stopped by the store to get some alcohol. I still wasn't old enough to buy it from the stores outside of the hood, so Meechy went in and bought some Hennessey. I loved that brown liquor it fuelled my flames. As we drove down my street I noticed there were more cars than usual. Sometimes I would park my car on the side street, but tonight I couldn't.

When we entered my house I told Meechy, "Don't forget to take that work with you when you leave I don't like having it in my house."

"Okay," he answered.

I took the duffle bag to my bedroom and emptied it I had some extra cash I was going to add with the rest of the cash I had in a JC Penny's bag. I never trusted banks, so there was no need for a bank account I would move the money from place to place.

I told Meechy to roll up some blunts while I made us some drinks. My buzz was coming down and it was time to get lifted. I felt better when I was buzzed it kept that vibration at a low tone.

Inside the bag was one hundred and forty seven thousand dollars neatly stacked and ready to be moved to a new location. I put the bird on the carpet so Meechy wouldn't forget to take it with him.

Sometimes my ego got the best of me as I looked into my closet I thought I needed brand new clothes so I yanked them from the hangers and threw them onto the floor unintentionally covering the kilo of cocaine. Then decided I would go shopping the next day. I still had clothes I'd never worn, but they had to go too I was going to start all new.

I tossed the JC Penny's bag back into the closet it would be safe until the morning.

Meechy called from the living room, "Ghost, you want to hit this?"

I returned as Meechy started playing Nintendo we played for a few hours, then I began to get tired and my high was coming down fast. I needed some sleep I had one blunt left and didn't want to smoke it until the morning. The Hennessey was gone by this time it had done its magic keeping the vibration low, I was tired and so was Meechy.

"Don't leave without that work," I reminded him.

Again, he replied, "Okay, homie."

Before I drifted off to sleep, I thought about Shawn being on the bus. I was happy that he wanted to finally leave the hood and see different things and make some real money. I trusted him with my life. He was always there for me, and now I could be there for him. He was my brother. Maybe that's what I needed Shawn and me together in the game it would be like the early days.

The room began to spin out of control, so I laid flat on the carpet, hoping the dizziness would leave and it did. I closed my eyes and drifted into a deep sleep.

CHAPTER 13

—

The Set Up

The telephone woke me out of my sleep, Meechy was crashed out on the couch and I was on the floor. The room began to spin and I was disoriented, who would be calling at this time I wondered. The phone continued ringing, I hoped whoever it was would call in the morning but this caller was persistent. It seemed to ring for hours before I crawled to answer it.

It was the in the early morning hours of February 6, 1990 when my life changed.

I answered the phone with an alcohol induced, "Who's this?"

"It's Ebony we missed the bus."

"Huh?"

"It's Ebony we missed the bus and we put the dope in a locker."

"What?"

"Did you hear me?" We missed the bus and the dope is in the locker."

I repeated, "What?" again.

"Do you want us to keep the dope in the locker?" she asked.

"No, bring that shit with you."

"Can we come to your house?" Ebony said.

"What?" I asked again, still out of it.

"Will you pay for the cab ride to your house?" she asked.

"Uh huh."

Shawn hadn't followed the instructions, he was supposed to leave at noon when the Greyhound bus station was busy, but instead he'd left at midnight when the bus station was damn near deserted, and he had people with him. I was too loaded to think clearly or I never would've talked about drugs on the phone. I got caught slipping again.

I couldn't tell you if it was a minute or an hour after the phone call, but I heard someone jiggling the doorknob, then bursting into my house, my first thought was, "Oh shit! I'm getting jacked."

Two big motherfuckers jumped on me, yelling, "lay down, lay down!"

I responded, "I am laying down motherfucker."

I felt a knee on the back of my head and next I was handcuffed. Meechy was lying on the couch at first they didn't see him until he moved, and then they all rushed him and handcuffed him also.

I instantly became sober and was somewhat relieved that I wasn't getting robbed. Then a bolt of fear shot through my body, Oh shit that work was on the floor in my bedroom.

I glanced at Meechy, truthfully speaking, he was soft and wasn't going to admit that it was his dope in my house, I just stared at him letting my eyes talk.

The DEA agents pulled out a picture of me and said, "Yeah, this is him."

It was about 3:00 a.m. in the morning, all my neighbours were up watching. I felt embarrassed I hadn't thought about the phone call it wasn't even on my mind. I only thought about that dope that was on the bedroom floor under all the clothes and the money.

My house was flooded with white law enforcement officers it looked like the clan was getting ready for a lynching.

Meechy and I were placed on the kitchen floor and questioned.

"Where's the rest of it?" one officer asked.

I didn't say anything.

Another officer found the ashtray with the last blunt in it and raised it up and said, "This is the root of all evil."

Meechy was still handcuffed and sitting on the kitchen floor. The senior officer asked him, "You want to go to jail?"

"No, sir." Meechy quickly answered.

The senior officer instructed the junior officer to take the handcuffs off Meechy.

I told Meechy, "Make sure you call my mom and tell her to get the bail money ready I'm going to the county."

Meechy nodded and bolted out the door I figured he wasn't going to admit to the bird in the bedroom when they found it.

The search began the lead officer walked me through the hallway as the other officers checked the closets. They tore the kitchen apart emptying sugar bowls and tasting the flour to make sure I hadn't stored cocaine there. They flipped the sofas and pulled plants from their pots. They were really tearing shit up. The bedrooms didn't have overhead lights only lamps that sat on the nightstand. A group of officers was in the guest bedroom tearing shit up flipping the beds and throwing clothes from the closet onto the floor.

As I was led to my bedroom my heart was beating so fast you could see it threw my shirt. If the officer had touched my chest, he would've known something was wrong, but he didn't. My room looked like it had already been partially searched because of the clothes on the floor. The lead officer and I stood on the clothes as the other officers continued to search.

I had a waterbed so there was no flipping that. My dressers drawers were opened and the contents were thrown next to the increasing amount of clothes that were already on the floor. I felt some relief.

One of the officers reached into the closet and grabbed the JC Penny's bag, opened it and shouted, "Bingo!"

The lead officer looked at me and smiled that's when the DEA agents came in. The LAPD officers didn't have enough time to pocket any of the cash and they looked kind of pissed off because the DEA was there to oversee my arrest.

About a year prior, I'd been pulled over by the LAPD and questioned. I had my license and I was insured, but I was still taken to the police station anyway. They said that the tags on my car couldn't be read from their police car. I had eighteen hundred dollars on me, and when they released me they only gave me seven dollars a five and two ones.

"How much is it?" one officer asked.

I responded with, "Count it your damn self."

59

I was stuck I didn't want to move from the pile of clothes that were on the ground.

After their search was complete, I heard one of the officers say, "We got a problem there are no drugs here, we don't even have an arrest warrant there are no exigent circumstances."

I didn't know what exigent circumstances meant, but it sounded like it was in my favor.

They concluded their search and then it was time for them to take me in I was relieved. I was escorted out of my house four pointed, which means two officers were in front of me and two were behind me to insure I wasn't going anywhere. I was just happy to get them out of my house.

I was put into an unmarked car that was sitting on the side street it was a white Thunderbird. We were heading to the Glass House, better known as the Parker Center.

Then it hit me these motherfuckers had been waiting for me. The phone call still hadn't registered, I wondered who had set me up. I wasn't loud; and I never had too many people over to my house, so who would have set me up?

As I sat in the back of the Thunderbird, the 3 officers started a small conversation about my arrest I remained quiet. One of my uncles was a cop, and he had told to never say anything while in the police car; just remain quiet until you have a lawyer present. These motherfuckers thought I was stupid and would run my mouth. I only thought about the bird still on the carpet, and who I could send to get it, and more importantly, who had set me up?

We arrived at the Glass House and I was promptly escorted to the booking room to be processed and fingerprinted. As we turned the corner my heart sank, I instantly felt sick to my stomach I saw Shawn, Ebony and Nisha, all handcuffed to a bench. The look on Shawn's face will forever be engrained in my memory. Rage filled my thoughts and I began to shake uncontrollably. I couldn't believe these motherfuckers had set me up. I was about to say something but decided not to. My heart hurt I wanted to rip open my chest and remove it. The officers just watched, how many times had they seen this before?

"I'm sorry, Ghost," Shawn, said.

I just looked at him.

Almost in unison, Ebony and Nisha both said, "We're sorry, Ghost."

I thought, "this no good motherfucker ungrateful coward; and here I am trying to help him eat better and this is how he repays me! Setting me up!' I couldn't believe this had to be another bad dream this shit couldn't be real, it just couldn't.

Then I thought about the phone call, and remembered, fuck! If I hadn't been so loaded I would have hung that motherfucking phone up and flushed the bird, but it was too late for that now. My blood brother had betrayed me, and sorry couldn't fix this nothing could.

I thought about what Janna had said, and knew she'd been right. I found out that he'd gone to the Greyhound bus station with some company at midnight, so they could sleep on the bus stupid shit.

Hate filled every cell of my body my hands were balled into tight fists. The pain of the handcuffs was nothing compared to the pain I felt inside. He had come to *me* for help I didn't need him for anything I'd done it out of love for him. I could have used Tim, always did as he was instructed to do, like putting on his army fatigues and getting on the bus at noon and calling me when he got there.

Ebony was the one that had made the call from the police station. She was the home girl I had helped out a few times. I'd even loaned her money to pay her rent and bought her kids clothes when their dad wouldn't. She'd even sold weed for me her life was better because of me. Now this bitch had called me from the police station with the police listening Damn! I'd got caught slippin'. That fucking alcohol! I hated it at that moment, but the next moment I needed a drink.

Shawn knew the job was dangerous when he took it, he knew if you get popped you rode the case; he knew the game and the rules.

It was my turn to get fingerprinted the officer took one cuff off and told me to put my hands in front of me and he re-cuffed me. At least then my shoulders felt much better. Then my picture was taken but this time I didn't change the tiles on the booking board.

Next, I was taken to the interrogation room still handcuffed. The officer named Fitzpatrick was sitting there waiting for me. There was a tape recorder and three sheets of paper with writing on them.

As I sat he said, "We got you."

"You ain't got shit on me."

That's when he played the tape with Ebony's phone call to me, and he sat back with a smirk on his face and watched my reaction.

I replied, "You still ain't got anything on me."

He shot back, "The IRS does."

He slid the three sheets of paper toward me to read. Each one was signed at the bottom with each of their names that dug the knife deeper my only thought was that I wanted to kill those motherfuckers. They had told the police everything, but what hurt the most was Shawn's statement. He told them that I had been a drug dealer ever since he'd known me shit; he was the one who got me into the game! He also told them that I got my drugs from the Mexicans. He's the only one that knew that. He had told them things he didn't have too. They talked about me like I was their enemy.

That shit tore me apart I guess the kitchen was too hot and he was saving his ass. Ebony's statement said almost the same thing, that I was going to pay Shawn five thousand dollars to take the dope to Saint Louis for me, but Nisha's statement really didn't say too much because she really didn't know shit.

The officer fired up a cigarette and said, "So what are you going to do?"

I replied, "Give me a lawyer."

CHAPTER 14

—

Metropolitan Detention Center

I was taken to Metropolitan Detention Center for official federal booking. As we approached the building I recognized it, but I had thought it was an office building with narrow windows. Whenever I would take the 101 freeway I would see construction workers hard at work on the building but I never thought it was a jail.

MDC was a holding facility for federal inmates awaiting trial, like the Los Angeles County jail does for State inmates. We arrived at 4:30 A.M. As I was brought through the front door, I saw a big clock on the wall with an eagle in it and a picture; next to that I saw a picture President George Bush Sr. and Vice President Dan Quayle and some other people I didn't recognize.

This was the early morning of February 6, 1990; this was the second time I'd been arrested on the same day of the month.

Once inside the building the officers started to fill out some paperwork. I stood there quietly, my high was coming down fast and I felt miserable my shoulders hurt; the cuffs were too tight, and I was extremely sleepy. I wondered how long it would be before I was released to sleep in my own bed.

The MDC officer sat behind a horseshoe-shaped desk typing on a computer. I looked around and saw that the same eagle that was in the clock was on the floor with the words "United States Federal Government Federal Bureau of Prisons" under it. On the wall there was a map of the

United States shaded in different colors to indicate different regions. I counted the prisons; there were sixty-seven federal prisons throughout the United States. That was then, now there are over one hundred sixty federal prisons.

I thought to myself, "I didn't get popped with any dope, I shouldn't be in here that long."

The MDC officer finished his paperwork and said, "We'll take it from here."

My handcuffs were taken off and a new set replaced them. I remained quiet as I was taken into an elevator with the correctional officer. He was an older white guy who looked like he'd been working there for years and preferred the night shift because it was quiet.

We rode the elevator in silence except for the noise of the cables. Then he spoke, "You'll be going to the fourth floor which is called R&D, receiving and discharge. They will re-finger print you and re-take your mug shot and assign you to a housing unit." I just nodded, facing the wall.

He said, "You don't have to do that; we can ride like regular people." I felt a little at ease with him.

The officer asked, "What'd they get you for?"

"I didn't get caught with nothing, it was my co-defendants who got popped."

He replied, "Yeah, it's your friends that'll get you all the time. I've heard that same story thousands of times, in that world you have no friends young man."

When the elevator doors opened there was another officer there waiting, I looked back at the other officer before the door closed He said, "Good luck."

I was taken to a concrete waiting room where the handcuffs were removed and the big heavy steel door echoed as it closed. The room was painted a depressing off-white with names and neighbourhoods etched into the thick painted walls. One etching in particular caught my attention, it read "God help me."

In the corner of the room was a metal toilet and sink combination with a stainless steel mirror bolted to the wall. I thought it looked unsanitary to have drinking water in the same place as the toilet.

A heavy-set black woman came to the door and opened the food trap. "Do you want breakfast, baby?" she asked.

"No, I'm good, thank you."

The truth was I didn't have an appetite I figured I'd be home by lunch.

She replied, "Okay someone will be with you to start your intake." Then she locked the door and left.

My mind drifted back to Ebony, the bitch that had set me up calling me from the police station, then wanting to apologize like I'm supposed to say, "Oh, it's okay everybody makes mistakes."

A male correctional officer interrupted my thoughts, as the key unlocked the heavy metal door, the metal against metal echoed throughout the small room. He took me to a dressing room that was filled with big blue rolling bins with letters on them, S, M, L, XL and bins with other letters.

The correctional officer reached into one of the bins with the letters "B.R." on it and pulled out a bedroll. There were two sheets and a grey wool blanket that looked itchy. The officer handed me some elastic waistband pants and a V-neck T-shirt, a pair of boxers, some socks and a pair of jelly sandals. I was taken to a dressing room and told to strip.

"What for?" I asked.

"We have to check for contraband," he answered.

"I ain't got anything on me," I said.

"It's my job."

I proceeded to remove my clothing as thoughts ran through my mind. Just a few hours ago I'd been at home chilling without a care in the world, now I was here taking my clothes off in front of a complete stranger.

I disrobed and was about to put on the government issued boxers when the officer said, "Now I have to look at your body cavities."

"What do you mean?"

"Everyone who comes in has to do this," he said.

Totally demoralized, I stood there totally nude as my mind drifted off to somewhere else, but I could hear his commands. "Raise your arms above your head."

I did.

"Open your mouth and lift your tongue." He inspected my mouth with a small flashlight. Now shake out your hair."

Again, I did as I was told.

Next he said, "Lift up your testicles."

I did that too.

I thought it was over, but he continued, "Turn around and let me see the bottom of your feet."

I rose each foot to him.

Then he said, "Bend over and spread 'em."

I paused, then bent over and did what I was told, I felt the pain of the African slaves when they were put on the auction blocks for the "***Black Friday***" inspection before they were sold. I felt less than human. This was incomprehensible, my father figures had never told me about this part of the game.

The inspection was finally over now it was time to get fingerprinted again and have my picture taken. There were only five people working on the floor the white guy who'd searched me, and a Mexican lady, two black ladies and a white lady.

As I followed the correctional officer, one of the black ladies stopped what she was doing looked up, tapped her friend on the shoulder and said, "Look girl. They are arresting babies now!"

That's when the others looked at me.

The older black woman who was standing against the wall approached me and said, "Baby, how old are you?"

"Nineteen," I answered.

She was a nice lady and kind of reminded me of an aunt.

She looked at me and said, "I'm going to pray for you, okay?"

I responded, "Okay, thank you."

"Verrett," the female Mexican correctional officer said as she told me to follow her to a small room to be fingerprinted. As she rolled my fingers across the ink and pressed them against the sheet of paper, she said, "Do you know how much trouble you're in?"

Honestly, I didn't want to hear any of that shit right now I just remained quiet as she talked and did her job.

While I was still deep in my own thoughts, the black lady was shuffling some papers and said, "He'll be going to six south, who's going to escort him there?"

The white correctional officer spoke up, "I'll take him."

Six south was the sixth floor on the south side of the Metropolitan Detention Center. There I would be assigned a room, I needed the rest I was exhausted. We went back into the elevator where I faced the wall, just to see if the CO was going to tell me I didn't have to.

He said, "You learn quick." The elevator reached the sixth floor and then the CO ordered, "All right, let's go." We exited the elevator and I was ordered to stand against the wall.

It was morning now, and as I stood in the hallway a group of inmates in a line were wearing the same thing I was wearing, which was beige pants with an elastic waistband and a beige pullover and a pair of jelly sandals, they were headed in our direction. Everything seemed to go in slow motion as my thoughts raced and my heart pumped, seeing these men dressed like me, carrying legal sized manila envelopes with the look of defeat on their faces, I made eye contact with each one of them as they walked by. I could feel what they were thinking. Every last man had the 'I fucked up big time' look. That shook me to my core! They were holding onto those envelopes as if their very life depended on it. Chills ran through my body and fear was finding its place within me.

As they walked down the hallway, it reminded me of one of those old movies where the prisoners have that last slow walk to the execution chamber, but this was no movie. I made eye contact with every man that passed I didn't see any hope in their eyes, just that 'I wish I could do it over again' look. I knew my situation was different I thought, "I'm not like them my case is different". I didn't get popped with anything, only money and that wasn't illegal, all this will be straightened out once I get into court.

The CO ran down some bullshit to me about being an inmate. He said, "When you're in this facility you're an inmate. When you're in court, you're a defendant, and when you're on the street you're a citizen, so at this moment you're an inmate."

The CO who escorted me rang the bell at the door we waited for the unit officer to open it. We were finally buzzed in, then my bed card was given to the Unit Officer and I was assigned to a room.

The inmates in the unit were just getting up for breakfast while I was getting ready to sleep. I desperately needed to get some sleep. As I looked around everybody was wearing the same thing as me except for a few guys wearing tennis shoes.

Mr. Walker was a black CO with a loud-ass voice he shouted everything he said, and it was very annoying.

"Verrett!" he said, "You're assigned to room number eleven."

I answered, "Okay," and headed to my temporary home until I could get back to my real home. I entered the room and it looked brand new. It had a bunk bed with green plastic mattresses and a porcelain sink and a separate toilet. I was glad it wasn't like the sink and toilet combination in the holding cell because I needed to use the toilet. I was also glad I didn't have a roommate. I made my bed and went to sleep, hoping that when I woke up I would be back in my own bed at home.

CHAPTER 15

—

USA vs. Me

I was awakened from my deep sleep by the Unit Officer, Mr. Walker, shouting my name as he stood in the doorway of the closet like room.

"Verrett!" he shouted, "You have been summoned to court. You have ten minutes to get ready, so meet me at the front door."

"All right." I replied.

I was still exhausted, but the sleep had helped a little. The clock on the wall showed that it was now noon I figured I should be home in a couple of hours. I stood next to the front door watching everybody. The blacks had their own section, the whites had theirs too, and so did the Spanish people. It reminded me of the map of the United States that I'd seen when I first came in a few hours ago. Everybody was separated, color-coded like that map.

The door buzzed, and Mr. Walker handed my picture card to the CO he was to take me to the fourth floor. The CO held my picture card and asked me to recite my booking number.

I responded, "I don't know it I just came in a couple of hours ago."

I had no intention of memorizing it anyway; I should be out of here soon.

I was taken to the basement of the detention center, where I was placed into the holding cells with the other prisoners. It was loud and cold as I sat observing my surroundings. The holding tanks were more like cages for animals, like the ones you see at the zoo. The only thing that was missing was a sign that said 'Don't pet or feed the animals.'

Concrete benches ran the length of each side of the rectangular holding cell. In the corner was that stainless steel toilet and sink combination if someone had to take a dump, it would be in front of everybody to see and smell. I was glad I had used the toilet in my room.

There were about sixty guys in the tank that I was locked in. There was a white guy who sat clutching his manila envelope, lost in his thoughts with that same 'I fucked up' look on his face. He had some thick-ass glasses and a bald spot, which he tried to cover up with the old up and over. He looked like an accountant or a banker.

There was also a small group of Mexicans holding hands in a circle with their eyes closed I couldn't understand what they were saying I just figured they were praying, and that's when someone called my name, "Ghost, is that you?"

I turned to see who it was; it was my childhood friend, Craig, aka C-Style. I hadn't seen him in a few years, and it was good to see someone I knew.

C-Style said, "They finally got your ass."

I didn't take offense to it that's how we talked. I responded, "Yeah homie that nigga Shawn, and that bitch Ebony set me up."

He just smiled and laughed, I really didn't see anything funny about it, but it was good to see him even under these circumstances. C-Style lived in the hood when we were younger. When it started getting crazy, his mom moved to Compton so he wouldn't get caught up in the gang life. We had a common bond he had two sisters and no father at home, and his mom worked long hours just like my mother. She wanted to give her children a better life so she figured if they moved her son wouldn't get caught up with the streets.

C-Style started gangbanging anyway I saw him at the swap meet getting his hood stitched into his hat. That's what we did; we represented our hoods on our hats, and some hoods would use NFL or NBA hats as a symbol.

We talked about the early days and what we had been up too.

C-Style said, "Yeah, homie, I just had a baby girl she's three months old." He was proud, and then he asked, "What floor you on?"

"They got me on six south."

C-Style smiled and responded, "That's the floor I'm on you must of came in early this morning."

"Yeah, and went straight to sleep."

The U.S. Marshals were getting ready to put us on the bus. I could see the chains being dragged across the floor.

That's when C-Style said; "These motherfuckers always put that black box on me."

I didn't know what a black box was it was rumoured that the black box was an invention of a former inmate. It was a small rectangular box that fit over the handcuffs. Once on, it totally restricted any hand movement. By the look on C-Style's face, I was hoping I wouldn't be black-boxed.

A U.S. Marshal opened the holding cell and made an announcement, "When your name is called, state your name and register number." I still hadn't memorized mine.

As each person exited the concrete holding cell they were ushered to an area where there about a dozen U.S. Marshals waiting to chain them up.

My name was called. "Verrett!" the Marshal yelled.

I approached the entrance of the holding cell.

"State your name and number."

"I don't know my number." The marshal said, "What's your birth date?"

I told him, and he checked his paperwork and said, "Okay."

It was my turn to get chained up this was almost worse than being strip-searched. The Marshal ordered me to face the wall and raise my left leg, then my right leg, as he put the leg iron on. The cold steel felt like it was cutting straight through my flesh as it rubbed against my bone.

Next, I was ordered to raise both of my arms as the belly chain was wrapped around my waist and adjusted to the size of my waistline. Last were the handcuffs. They were attached to the belly chain. I couldn't raise my hands any further than a few inches. The United States Federal Government now enslaved me. I hated Shawn and Ebony for this.

The Marshals ushered us into the school bus that had been converted into a rolling prison. The bus had that same eagle on the side of it with the words, U.S. Marshals. The leg irons were killing my ankles. My skin was already raw and tender and I'd only had them on for a few minutes. It was my turn to get on the bus, I took a long step and the irons cut into my Achilles tendon I winced in pain that's when the Marshal helped me into the bus.

The inside of the bus looked similar to the holding cell. The seats were made of steel sheet metal painted black with black grilled bars that secured the tinted windows. At the rear of the bus in a small cage sat a U.S. Marshal armed with his mini fourteen-assault rifle. As I looked out the window I could see the Marshals checking their weapons locked and loaded just in case someone was going to make a break for it, I guess all this drama fed their egos.

The sirens were turned on and the big steel gate began to open. We were now on the streets headed to the courthouse, I looked out of the steel grid window as people stopped and watched the show. All this wasn't necessary it only brought more attention then was needed. We were only going around the corner; we could have walked there in five minutes but not in these leg irons.

A few minutes later we arrived at the underground parking structure of the U.S. Courthouse. Once inside and secured the Marshals got into position with their guns drawn. You would have to be a damn fool to try to escape with leg irons on and handcuffed with thirty heavily armed U.S. Marshals in an underground parking garage.

We were ushered off the bus and led down a long corridor and placed into another holding cell. Once there, the Marshals removed our leg irons and belly chains and handcuffs.

The Marshal that removed my chains was a tall black man named Douglas. I later found out that Douglas was born and raised in South Central Los Angeles. Douglas seemed all right he hadn't been brain-washed yet by the system.

Since I was the youngest guy in the holding cell, he looked at me and said in a low whisper, "It hurts my heart to see you young black men coming into the system like this."

Then he asked, "Do you smoke?"

"No, I don't," I answered.

It was strange that even though Douglas was a U.S. Marshal, he still kept it real. I wondered how he escaped the game, growing up in the hood, but not getting involved. I guess it was a choice he made. He was on the white man's team, but the vibe he was giving showed love for the young black men that walked and sat in the holding cells.

Douglas asked, "What they get you for?"

"My homies set me up."

"Yeah, that happens a lot," he replied.

Another Marshal came by with a clipboard and called off some names. "Jefferson, McMillan, Mutan and Verrett."

We were escorted to the courtroom by three Marshals and were told to sit. I looked around the room it was three times bigger than the juvenile court in Long Beach. I surveyed the room looking for my mother. There were a lot of people but then I spotted her. She had a look on her face like she had been crying all night; I gave her a reassuring smile.

The first defendant called was a French guy, in the holding cell he'd been running his mouth the whole time; wouldn't shut up. Now, in front of the judge he wouldn't speak a word of English. When the judge denied his bail he began to plead in perfect English, and then the Marshals removed him from the courtroom.

The court clerk announced, "In the case of De'Juan Lamonte Verrett versus the United States of America, docket number 90-91."

Hearing my name called like that kind of fed my ego in a sick way, me against the whole United States. As I looked back at my mom, she looked scared. I thought there was nothing to be scared about. I hadn't gotten caught with anything and I would be out of here soon.

The judge asked if I had representation, then the court-appointed lawyer stood up and greeted the court.

"Good morning, your honor, I'll be representing Mr. Verrett for this hearing. Mr. Verrett was arrested and charged with Title 21 USC 841 (a) (1), possession with intent to distribute and Title 21 USC 846, conspiracy with intent to distribute a controlled substance. Mr. Verrett was arrested without an arrest warrant, no drugs were found in his home, and his co-defendants were arrested with the contraband. Mr. Verrett is not a flight risk, he has strong community ties."

It sounded very good, I thought I should be home soon and then the prosecutor stood up and opened his big mouth.

"Your honor, Mr. Verrett is a threat to his community, he is a known drug dealer. In sworn statements from his co-defendants, they implicated Mr. Verrett as the supplier of the contraband, and furthermore, Your Honor, how many nineteen-year-olds have one hundred forty-seven thousand dollars in cash in their homes? The government requests that the bail be denied."

The prosecutor made me look really bad, but the fact of the matter was I didn't get caught with anything.

The judge made his ruling. "Bail is set at two million dollars per count."

I was charged with two counts, which meant four million dollars.

The court-appointed attorney asked me, "Can you come up with four-hundred thousand dollars?"

I looked at him like he was stupid. "Hell, no!"

Back in the holding cell, Douglas asked, "How did it go?"

"They set my bail at four million."

"They'll reduce it," he said. "They always start high," that made me feel a little better.

"I think I'll try one of those cigarettes now," I said." "They're addictive."

I just wanted to get a buzz going I'd never smoked a cigarette before, actually I hated the smell but it seemed like the right thing to do at the time. I inhaled deeply, and became sick then dizzy as the room seemed to spin then it stopped and I felt relaxed.

The French guy was still crying he should have spoken English instead of trying to be slick then the stupid motherfucker might have gotten a bail, instead of bringing the 'Me no speak no English bullshit.'

Sitting next to me was this cat from Las Vegas named Willie Green; he seemed laid back puffing on his cigarette. My head was still spinning from my first cigarette.

"What's your name, youngster?" Willie asked.

"Ghost."

He nodded, and then he asked what they got me for.

I answered his question with a question, "What did they get you for?"

"White slavery."

"Oh, pimpin', huh?"

He just smiled and said, "Yeah, man."

I finally answered his question. "My homies set me up, they got popped and told them I gave it to them."

"Yeah man, the dope game ain't what it used to be like dudes can't hold their water anymore, that's why I got into pimpin'."

"That money's too slow."

"It's slow money, but fo' sho money," Willie replied.

We both laughed as he finished his smoke.

CHAPTER 16

—

Family Reunion

I guess I was sleeping hard, because Mr. Walker was shouting my name, "Verrett, Verrett!"

I came out of my coma and asked, "What's up?"

"The counselor wants to see you be at the front door in five minutes."

There were about half a dozen video cameras watching my every move. I stood at the counselor's door and knocked, a voice told me to come in and have a seat. The office was small and crowded the view was the same as in the cells. I took a seat; the counselor had his back to me while he was shuffling some papers. I had heard the voice, it sounded familiar but I couldn't quite place it. Then he turned to face me it was my Uncle James.

He wasn't my blood uncle; my aunt had married his brother. That's how we were related I remembered him from all the holiday dinners and birthdays.

James asked, "What in the hell happened?"

I told him the whole story, he even knew Shawn, he asked me if I'd spoken with my mom yet.

"Only at court yesterday," I said.

"She's been calling non-stop," he said.

"Can I call her?"

"Yeah, just press pound nine, then the number."

The phone rang a few times and then she answered. "Hello, mom…"

She cut me off, "De'Juan, I told you to stop selling that poison!"

I really didn't want to hear that now.

"It's too late for that, Mom, listen to me there's something in my house…"

She interrupted again, "What is it De'Juan?"

"It's my work I need to get it out of there, call Meechy and he'll get it."

"I'm not going to handle that poison for you."

"Call Meechy on a three-way call for me please, Mom."

I gave her the number, she dialled it and Meechy picked up. "What up, Loc?" He was hesitant to speak at first.

"Don't trip my mom's on the phone," and Meechy seemed to relax.

"Yeah, homie, go to my house and get your things take it all with you."

"Okay," he replied.

"Today, not tomorrow."

I thanked my mom and I asked how my sisters were doing she said that they were in school.

"Give them a hug for me."

Before our call ended, Uncle James said that she was on my visiting list now.

"I love you, Mom."

"I love you too, son, and so does Jesus," she said and she hung up the phone.

I asked James if he could put Janna on my list as well.

"I see no problem with that," he said and gave me a computer print-out of the list. I guess he must've heard my stomach growling because he said, "Are you hungry?"

"Hell, yes, I missed breakfast and lunch."

He shared his lunch with me.

CHAPTER 17

—

The Unit

I returned to the unit to find C-Style playing dominos with a few other guys. This was the first time I'd gotten to see what the unit looked like. The unit was a triangle shape with two tiers. In the center of the long row of cells were the showers.

My temporary home had sixty rooms with two men per room. The ground floor was called the common area. That's where the dining tables were also used to play chess and cards games and dominos.

There were four phones used for collect calls only. I noticed that only the blacks used two of the phones, and only the whites used one phone, the last phone was used by only the Spanish-speaking prisoners.

The rec deck was where you could get some fresh air. The sunlight was limited so the men followed the movement of the sunrays. A basketball game had just started and the small crowd moved to the far end of the rec deck to watch the game. I thought about Shawn, and his love for this game. I thought about back in the day when Shawn would dominate the school ground court. I loved watching him play.

My thoughts were interrupted when C-Style tapped me on the shoulder. "Hey, Ghost, I want to introduce you to the homies."

There was an unwritten bureau rule of segregation; inmates mainly for survival created it. The deepest group picked what TV room they had and what phones were to be used and what tables to sit. Everything was color-coded, separate.

I walked with C-Style; I asked him "What they get you for homie?"

"Bank robbery."

"How much time they give you?"

"Fifteen."

"Fifteen months ain't bad," I responded.

"No, homie, fifteen years one hundred and eighty-eight mother fucking months these mother fuckers gave me," he said, while holding the domino in his hand as he told the score keeper, "Give me fifteen just like the muthafucking government did," and he slammed the domino down on the table while laughing.

I couldn't understand why he was laughing about getting all that time like it was nothing.

C-Style explained, "It's part of the game, homie, I had my run and I ain't tripping, how much dope they catch you with?"

"Nothing."

"Ghost, they got this thing called conspiracy, you ain't got to get caught with some work. All they need is for a motherfucker to say you gave it to them. Half the motherfuckers in here didn't get popped with any work. It was their co-defendants who set them up. That's why I started robbing banks, if I get caught, it's on me, no co-defendants just me."

I really wasn't trying to hear he was saying, but it was true. In the drug game, there are too many ways of getting popped. Looking around the room, I wondered how many people had the same story I had. How many of their closest friends had set them up? The more I thought about it, the more I became pissed the fuck off, I wanted to get high and not feel this shit now.

C-Style introduced me to the fellas. "This is my homie Ghost we go way back!"

One by one, I met everyone C-Style knew. Zulu was a Damu, that's Swahili for blood he was from South Central; he was an all right dude. Dreamer, he was from Lynwood, I knew some of his homeboys. Then I met Sonny from Compton, Slick, Mo, Wack and Donnie-Cheese, these guys would become friends.

I told C-Style that I wanted to get high and he answered, "Don't trip, we about to put one in the air."

We all went to C-Styles' cell.

Wack asked me if I ever had jailhouse wine.

"Naw, only Bartles and James."

"This here will put you on your ass," Wack said.

He gave me a cup and filled it to the rim I took a sip just to test it, it was good. Then I took a big gulp and I felt my stomach burn. This was some good shit; I could instantly feel the alcohol doing its job.

C-Style told Zulu to watch the door to make sure the CO didn't walk in on us, then he placed seven different colored balloons filled with weed on the desk and cut one open with a razor and started rolling up some joints and handed the first one to me.

There were two air vents in the cells, one blew air out and the other sucked the air in. C-Style told me to stand on top of the desk and blow the smoke into the vent; it kept the room from becoming smokey.

That night we smoked ten joints and drank three gallons of jailhouse wine, and I felt good. Nothing seemed that bad now, I just listened to everybody's story of how they came to MDC.

I asked C-Style to give me the game on how to make the wine, just in case I had to do some time, and how to get some bud in, because if I was going to do some time I was going to do it on my terms, staying drunk and high every day.

The CO yelled, "Lock down, lock down."

I stood up and almost fell.

Zulu said, "He's fucked up!"

"I only had a few cups," I said.

C-Style said, "Nigga, you drank most of it."

We all laughed I made it back to my cell, and lay down I looked out the window at the traffic on the 101 freeway. It was only 10:00 p.m. I wished I were out there stuck in traffic instead of being stuck in this closet-like room. I looked at the city one more time before I closed my eyes. The weed and alcohol gave me comfort no worries, it wasn't so bad.

CHAPTER 18

—

Recognition

During the day the units were somewhat quiet, guys sat at their designated table's playing card games, chess or writing letters, the phones were always in constant use. There were some guys making small talk at the microwaves drinking coffee. I had a headache from the night before. C-Style was out on the rec deck doing push-ups with Zulu and Sonny, and I went to join them, not to exercise, just for the company.

"What up, ya'll?" I said.

Zulu was the first to comment about last night, "Damn Ghost! you can drink!"

I just laughed.

C-Style asked me if I still played Ping-Pong.

I answered, "Yeah."

He wanted me to play against Big Clyde Jackson.

Big Clyde Jackson was always in the TV room he basically controlled it. No one really had a say on anything, and you wouldn't dare change the channel without him giving his blessing to do so. He was a big motherfucker, 6'8 and about three hundred, fifty pounds. C-Style introduced me to him.

He asked, "Where you from?"

"I'm from Harbor City."

"I used to mess with this female in your hood named Tammy. She lived on 254th Street."

"Yeah, that's the home girl," I said.

"The first time I went down there to see her, your homies hit me up! They came out of nowhere."

"Yeah, you know how it goes down with an unfamiliar face."

"At first I thought they were going to be set tripping, but then I saw your big homie Gangsta, we did state time together, then it was all good."

It really didn't matter if you were a big motherfucker, if you got caught in someone else's hood you were in violation, and that could cost you your life. A lot of guys had been killed over things like that. Some hoods set trip, but our hoods were close to each other and he knew one of the OG homies.

C-Style interrupted and told Big Clyde that I played Ping-Pong.

"Is that right; are you any good? Big Clyde asked.

"Yeah," I answered."

Then we'll set up the table after chow, and I'll see how good you are," Big Clyde said.

"Fo sho."

Big Clyde introduced me to his cousins, Elroy and Freddie Grayson. They had a roofing business and used it as a cover for their drug business. They got popped with seventy-five kilos and three million in cash. Shortly after their arrest, Elroy and Freddie became religiously devoted Christians, holding Bible studies throughout the day.

When I walked into their cell, it looked like a paper mill; they had been fighting their case for over a year now, filing motions delaying the inevitable. They had pictures of Jesus and all his disciples at their last meal.

"How fitting," I thought.

Elroy asked if I had accepted Jesus as my Lord and Saviour, while his brother Freddie started flipping through the bible.

"No, I haven't."

Freddie said, "Jesus is the way to salvation and through Him we are free."

Free from what, I wondered he hadn't answered any of my prayers. He hadn't done anything for me, but I played along with them.

Big Clyde said that he had to make a phone call and he'd be back.

That's when Elroy said, "Run from this holy cell, Satan."

Freddie grabbed a spray bottle of water and squirted Big Clyde, saying, "I rebuke you in the name of Jesus."

Big Clyde just laughed and left the cell.

The truth of the matter was that I had stopped believing in God on Easter of 1982. I was at my mother's church in Compton when a visiting pastor came to bless all the children. The church was packed to capacity. As we were led down the middle aisle, I was nervous because I always felt different and defective in a way. I was hot and uncomfortable in my three-piece polyester suit. The band started to play their up-tempo music getting the parishioners excited. Everyone began shouting their hallelujahs and the tambourine players seemed to be in some sort of trance. People were jumping around. Even the old ladies in their big hats fanning themselves got into the action.

The other children ahead of me fell to the ground when the pastor laid his big hand on their heads. Everyone was feeling something, when it was my turn to get blessed; I stood in front of him with my heart beating fast.

He was sweating profusely as he put his sweaty hand on my forehead. "Bless this child in the name of Jesus," he said, then he pushed my head back, but I didn't fall like the rest before me. Then he did it again and pushed my head back, but still I didn't fall. I wasn't feeling what everyone else was feeling something was wrong with me.

On his third attempt, he whispered in my ear, "Just fall."

I was confused as I glanced at my mother from the corner of my eye. Her facial expression revealed embarrassment, the pastor pushed my head back again, and I went with it and just took a knee. After church was over I never wanted to go back. God was there for everyone else except me, I was broken in some way and even God couldn't fix me.

Freddie started reading the Lord's Prayer from the bible; when he came to the part, forgive our trespasses as we forgive those who have trespassed against us; that's when I spoke up.

"How am I supposed to forgive Shawn and Ebony for setting me up? I can't forgive that my life has been taken away, my whole way of life! Man, fuck that!"

Elroy and Freddie just listened I wasn't feeling anything they were saying, especially talking about God, then Elroy said, "We understand, can we pray for you?"

I saw no harm in that, we held hands and closed our eyes, but I kept one eye open as Elroy prayed for me, "Dear Lord, we ask that you strengthen this young man's heart and spirit, to open his mind to your word, to give him peace dear lord, cover him in your grace and love, in your name Amen."

I thanked them for their prayers, but I was ready to get out of there, hoping that Freddie wouldn't spray me with the spray bottle of holy water.

Big Clyde had set up the Ping-Pong table, we were to play after the 4:00 p.m. count that's when every federal prison throughout the United States takes a count of every federal inmate, and calls it in to Washington, D.C. There are five mandatory counts, the first count is at 12:00 a.m., the next is at 3:00 a.m., then 5:30 a.m., then 4:00 p.m. The last is at 9:30 p.m. we were locked in our cells until the count was officially cleared.

After the count was cleared and we were let out of our cells, it was time to put one in the air. I met C-Style in his cell and we fired one up Big Clyde was waiting at the Ping-Pong table.

The table was old and unbalanced; books had been put under the table legs to even it out.

Big Clyde had a smile on his face, "Don't take this personal, little homie," he said.

"I won't, just you don't take this personal."

The weed had me feeling good; I was ready to have a little fun. Big Clyde wasn't used to playing a left-hander, so I would use that to my advantage. For a big guy, he could move I had him moving from right to left he was good, but really no match for me, I toyed with him and after a few games he was starting to sweat. I beat him three straight games and a crowd was starting to form.

I could see Big Clyde getting frustrated, so I gave him the fourth game, then I beat him two more games. My buzz was still going strong. I had him jumping from one side of the table to the other like a dancing bear trying to return the ball. For a big guy, he had the agility of an NFL lineman. It was getting close to count time so we switched sides. Sweat was dripping from every pore in his body, and the look on his face was sheer determination.

The crowd had gotten bigger and people were leaning over the rails on the top tier to watch this youngster whoop the shit out of Big Clyde. I talked shit as I slammed his serve, Big Clyde didn't think it was funny.

That's when Elroy and Freddie walked up to me. "Don't let him intimidate you with his size Jesus and his disciples got your back."

After that game we took a break I had to pee, C-Style, Zulu and Sonny were laughing at how I had Big Clyde frustrated.

C-Style said, "You got him looking like one of those dancing bears."

We all started laughing.

The CO was also watching the game and announced that this would be the last game before lockdown. I knew Big Clyde couldn't beat me, only if I let him. His game was good, but not strong.

I told Big Clyde, "I'm going to hold you to less than fourteen points."

"Bet that."

"My money hasn't come in yet."

A white guy named Leonard Wells spoke up and told Big Clyde, "I got him covered," and he threw a roll of quarters on the table.

Leonard Wells was an ex-hippie who was in good with the blacks. He was the only white boy I had ever seen with a tattoo of a black man on his arm, it was of Jimmy Hendrix. I came to find out that Leonard got caught with twenty-seven hundred pounds of marijuana coming through the New Mexico checkpoint. When you looked at him, he reminded me of a banker or CPA or something. He was clean cut, sure didn't look like he sold tons of weed.

We started the last game I was focused on holding Big Clyde to under fourteen points. Each time I slammed the ball over the net, the crowd cheered. Big Clyde was now getting petty calling interference and time outs he damn near used every excuse in the book, and then some.

The CO called out, 'Lockdown, lockdown."

I served the ball and didn't expect Big Clyde to return it to my weak side. I switched hands without a second thought and slammed it across the net the crowd went crazy.

Big Clyde stopped and said, "You can't switch hands in the middle of a game."

His cousins corrected him "You two never agreed that you couldn't."

The point was good.

Big Clyde was breathing hard, and to be honest I was enjoying it and I knew he was too. You could see it in his eyes it was now point game my advantage. Big Clyde knew it was a lost cause, but he fought a losing battle. The score was twenty to ten, on his last serve I took a step back and swung as hard as I could sending the little white ball rocketing across the net. There was nothing he could do the ball hit him in the stomach and the game was over.

I grabbed the roll of quarters and handed them back to Leonard Wells, he told me to keep them.

I set the paddle down and walked over to shake Big Clyde's sweaty hand he grabbed me, gave me a homie hug and said, "Good game, I needed some competition."

As I was walking to my cell, I turned and told Big Clyde, "Hey homie, I shoot pool too."

He smiled and said; "I'll see you tomorrow."

I went into my cell feeling good, and then reality set in as I looked at the traffic on the 101 freeways. I thought about my family and what was going to happen in court. I started to say a prayer, but stopped and drifted off to sleep.

CHAPTER 19

—

The Thrill Is Gone

The date was February 11, 1990; it was the day of my evidentiary hearing that means the government would bring what evidence they were going to present against me in court. The graveyard shift officer woke me up at 3:30 a.m. to get me ready for court. I washed up and used the toilet I didn't want to use those metal toilets in the holding cells.

We were escorted to the basement of MDC and I was strip- searched I hated this routine, but learned to zone out and go to a faraway place. The U.S. Marshals began chaining us for the short trip to court.

Once everyone was accounted for, we were locked in and the show began. The sirens blared as the streets were blocked off I do believe that the Marshals enjoyed the attention from the pedestrians.

Looking out of the tinted barred window, I felt like a major figure that needed all this security just to get me to court. Never mind the other guys I rode with it was all about me. The Marshals were like the secret service; you know when they escort the President it fed my ego in a sick way, I had nothing else to hold onto.

Once we entered the underground parking lot of the courthouse the thrill was gone, and we were back in the florescence-lit basement, which propelled me back to reality. I wasn't Ghost from Harbor City, I wasn't even De'Juan, I was just a number 92857-012.

CHAPTER 20

—

How Do You Plead?

There were about forty guys in the holding cell and everyone took their usual seats by the color code. I sat next to this black guy wearing an expensive cream-colored suit; he looked very calm reading his court papers.

I guess he noticed that I was the youngest one in the bullpen because he said, "What's up youngster? What's your name?"

"They call me Ghost, and what's your name?" "Michael Harris."

Everybody in the game had heard of him, but most had never seen him in person and here I was sitting next to one of the biggest ballers in the dope game, a legend. He had everything from semi-pro football teams to one of the longest running Broadway plays, and a well-known black actress. It was said that he had two thirds of the United States paying him.

I didn't want to seem like I was impressed with his status, so I waited for him to start the questions.

"Where you from youngster?"

"Harbor City."

"Where you from?" I asked.

"The West side."

He sat back smiled and crossed his legs, I had to show him that I was as important as he was, I had to meet power with power or be just another follower, and I was no follower.

"What they get you for?" he asked me.

"Some bullshit," I answered.

"How about you? What they get you for?" I inquired.

"Some bullshit too" he responded.

We both just nodded looking at the floor; we would occasionally look at each other, but for no more than a few seconds. Basically, we were feeling each other out; I wasn't going to acknowledge that I knew who he was. He was just a guy in an expensive suit; I felt that he had to earn my respect. If not, he wouldn't respect me I had learned that from Bosco.

"So what floor you on at MDC?" he asked.

"Six south."

"That's the floor I'm moving also; you came in a few days ago, didn't you?" he inquired.

"Yeah, I did."

"We'll talk more back on the floor," he said.

"Yeah, no problem."

We remained quiet until the Marshals started calling names.

"Verrett," Douglas called.

I stood and approached the gate.

"Your lawyer needs to see you."

I was handcuffed and led to a small room; the room was small just enough room for one person. I looked around the room then sat on a metal stool that was bolted to the ground. There was a two-inch thick bulletproof window the kind that you see in some neighborhood liquor stores or a bank, with a thin slot to slide documents through.

I sat for a minute or two, then the Public Defender appeared on the other side of the glass with his brief case in one hand and file folders under the other arm. It looked like he'd had just enough time to review my case.

"Hello, my name is Lance Cameron; I will be representing you today," he said in his best professional voice.

"That won't be necessary; I plan on retaining private counsel," I answered in my best professional voice.

"I understand, but you have not done so yet and you are going to need representation today," he said.

Just as he was talking there was a knock on the side door and then this black man walked in and asked if he would have a word with me, "Only in my presence" Mr. Cameron stated.

"Okay, no problem," the black man answered.

"Hello, Mr. Verrett my name is Tom Woolley, Chief U.S. Prosecutor," he seemed to say with pride.

He was brown-skinned with a small square mustache. I could tell that he hadn't grown up around blacks. There was a look in his eyes as he spoke from behind the bulletproof glass.

I thought for a second that I was going to get some love because he was a black prosecutor. I figured he should know the struggles of being black in America and the shit we have to put up with and the fucked-up hand we'd been dealt always being looked at differently. I didn't see that in him I saw only shame and disgust as he spoke.

"Mr. Verrett, I'm here to offer you a deal if you give us your connections, we will give you a five year sentence, and you'll be out by the time your twenty-three."

"Fuck that! I ain't a snitch!"

"Look Mr. Verrett, we got your friends with the drugs and we got you with the money. I will use your friends' testimony against you, this is the only time I will offer this deal to you."

"Man, you got me fucked up! I don't do shit like that setting people up ratting on people," I shot back.

"Have it your way then, Mr. Verrett."

As he left the small room, Mr. Cameron looked at me like I was crazy for turning down a five-year sentence.

They didn't understand the game I gave my life to the game one hundred percent that was the side you didn't hear about in the streets. This is the ugly side of the game, the side no one looks forward too.

Mr. Cameron was talking but I wasn't listening, only thinking of what's going to happen, and how Shawn and Ebony had done me. The hate for them was growing inside of me like a virus I would get them back for this.

In the game you never do shit like setting your friends up for your mistakes. I thought back to Donte, he was weak and just looked the part; I wondered how many people had sat on this same stool going through the same shit I was going through. I thought, "I'm going to ride this out I don't know how, but I must stay true to the game."

In the courtroom I saw my family all huddled together I gave them a smile letting them know I was okay. As I glanced around the courtroom, it was filled with people I didn't recognize. The court clerk was a small man with curly hair and thick glasses and a mustache he reminded me of Weird Al Yankovic, but smaller.

He stood and made an announcement. "All rise for the Honorable John G. Davies presiding in the case of De'Juan Lamonte Verrett verses the United States of America."

That fucked me up to hear that I was going to fight against all fifty states and territories, and that's when the grand dragon himself walked in, I just shook my head.

Mr. Cameron introduced himself, "Your honor, I will be representing Mr. Verrett in this proceeding."

Then the prosecutor did the same, "Your Honor, I will be representing the government in this case."

That shit was intimidating the Judge sat high above everyone in the rectangle shaped courtroom like he was God. He had the power to let me go, or take a large chunk of my life away, and there was the court reporter. She looked like she was thinking, "Here we go again I have to record all of these lies."

Everything was in place the judge asked, "Mr. Verrett, how do you plead?"

All eyes were on me as I rose slowly then answered, "Not guilty, your Honor."

As he nodded accepting my plea his glasses hung on the tip of his nose. It seemed as if he was looking for something, then finally he said, "We will set a trial date."

The judge banged his gavel and I was done, leaving the courtroom, I smiled at my family trying to give them hope.

It was almost noon as Douglas the Marshal came to the holding cell and read some names from his clipboard. "Harris, Verrett, Sanchez."

We were done with court and were going to catch the chain back to MDC. It was always the same routine we were strip-searched, asked to turn our socks, turn our underwear and shirts inside out and shake them

94

out. It was done to make sure we didn't bring back anything we weren't supposed to. Then we were all chained up.

I boarded the bus and saw that Michael Harris had already taken his seat. He called out to me. "Hey youngster, come sit back here with me."

I shuffled my way to him and sat down we just small talked. I'd heard about him, it was like meeting your favorite celebrity and having the opportunity to hang with them, I talked to him like he was one of the homies.

CHAPTER 21

—

Street Kings

I walked back to my little closet-like room and noticed that someone had their bedroll on the top bunk. C-Style came by to tell me that one of the big homies was my new cellmate, and he wanted to introduce me to him.

On the concrete recreation deck, Michael was talking to this dude who was a little shorter than me with a beard.

"What's up, youngster?" Michael said.

"Ain't nothin'," I responded.

C-Style said, "This is your new cellie, Freeway Ricky Ross."

"What's up, homie?" I said and extended my hand to shake his in the unique way we do. "I'm Ghost."

Freeway Rick looked at me, "How old are you?"

"Nineteen."

Michael interrupted and told Rick how we met in the holding cell at the courthouse and that I was a stand-up youngster.

Rick nodded, "We'll talk after lockdown."

Michael told me to come by his cell because he'd just gotten some pictures he wanted to show me. He told me that he had an idea to start a record company for rap music and was going to call it Deff Row.

I told him that it sounded too much like Deff Jam.

Well, a few days later Michael came up with a new name, which was Death Row Records, in 1991 it became a reality.

Sonny came out to smoke a cigarette and I asked him to let me hit it a few times to keep my buzz going. We sat against the wall and watched everybody do their thing. There was a line for the pull-up bar, a half-court basketball game had just started and some Spanish guys were doing push-ups.

I was enjoying the night breeze, and then my mind wondered to the streets and everything that needed to be done. I was sure that Janna would collect the money her dad owed me for selling weed for me. My mom and Janna really didn't get along and I knew that the money would make it worse. I had loaned one of the homies some money and that needed to be collected. I wondered whom I could send to get it. I didn't want to worry about that now I just wanted to enjoy my buzz.

It was my phone time, so I called Janna, she sounded stressed out and I did my best to try to relax her. It didn't work, and all she did was cry on the phone. I told her that I got the letter and pictures, and asked her if she could come see me the next day, but I wasn't trying to be in the visiting room seeing her cry for an hour, it made me feel powerless.

My time was up and I told her that I would see her tomorrow.

Before we hung up she said, "De'Juan, I love you."

I remained quiet, I really wasn't sure what love was or if I was capable of loving someone else. Love made you weak and it was no time to be weak now, I had to remain strong at all times, especially now.

"Aren't you going to tell me you love me, De'Juan?"

"You know how I feel about you," I answered. "I have to go now." I hung the phone up and went to my cell to relax.

Freeway Rick was making up his bed as I walked in. "What's up, Ghost?" he said.

"Ain't shit," I responded.

I remembered watching his arrest on TV a few months ago. It was a big case. He was back for a lawsuit against the Sherriff's Department for letting their dogs attack him, and here we were in the same cell.

You get to know a lot about a person when you share a cell. I would have never imagined that he didn't know how to read. At mail call we would go back to our cell and I would read his mail to him. We even went over the ABC's together. Wow! Freeway Ricky Ross, a legend in the game and he couldn't read.

We had been talking for a while when C-Style knocked on the door. "Come to the dayroom," he said.

Rick and I both followed every TV was on the same channel. I was wondering what was so interesting.

The channel 7 news anchors was saying something I couldn't hear, the dayroom was crowded standing room only.

Big Clyde made the announcement, "Everybody shut the fuck up or get out!"

The room instantly became quiet.

"It is official *Nelson Mandela* has just been released from serving twenty-seven years in prison," the new anchor announced.

The whole dayroom cheered, as well as the people on the television.

The news showed pictures of Nelson Mandela before he'd gone to prison when he was a young man, and he still had that sparkle in his eyes as he stepped out of that prison.

I wondered if I would have that sparkle in my eyes if I got convicted like Nelson Mandela?

The news showed people from all around the world cheering. I wondered if anyone would cheer for me.

There was a deadly silence in the dayroom as Nelson Mandela spoke. I looked around the dayroom everyone was focused on every word he uttered. I stood outside the room; surveying the housing unit. Even the Spanish dayroom was crowded. I could hear the reporter speaking Spanish. I didn't expect the white dayroom to be crowded, but it was. Every one of us felt a connection to Nelson Mandela, no matter what color we were. He had done his time, and we were all looking at time. He looked strong and confident. I believed seeing him getting released gave everyone in prison confidence that there was light at the end of the tunnel. Nelson Mandela later became the President of South Africa. I wondered what I would do with my life after prison if I got convicted. The day was February 11, 1990.

CHAPTER 22

—

Visiting

I was on the recreation deck talking to Big Clyde when Rick joined us. We were all drinking coffee, enjoying the morning sun and the fresh air. I was starting to become pale from the lack of natural sunlight. I understood why it was so crowded in the morning. The nice breeze that swept through the recreation deck was a hundred times better than the air coming out of the vents in my cell.

The CO came out on the rec deck and told me I had a visitor.

"Is it social or legal?"

"Social."

I was escorted to the visiting room where I saw my mother looking stressed out. I gave her a big hug, and then we sat down across from each other. I asked her if she'd gotten in contact with Janna and Meechy. I knew that it was going to be an issue with Janna, so I didn't push it. She told me she'd called Meechy several times, but he hadn't called her back.

My mom had gone to my house by herself she told me that it was a mess. The plants she'd bought were dead from being pulled out of their pots. Flour and sugar bowls had been emptied on the kitchen counters and the couches were still turned over. She said that the bedroom was just as bad as the rest of the house.

"There was a pile of your clothes on the ground, and I found something under them."

"What did you do with it?" I asked.

"I flushed it down the toilet."

That was one hundred thousand dollars floating out to sea. I'd rather it was in the ocean than in evidence. I kind of knew that Meechy wasn't going to show up.

I changed the subject and asked her about meeting with my new lawyer. She had paid him from the stash money I had at her house.

I later learned that he only defended drug dealers because we paid in cash. He knew we would get convicted and would want to appeal the conviction, which meant more cash. It was a hustle I was going broke fast. It was a hard hit, but if I got out of this, I would be smarter the next time.

The visiting time was over, before my mom left she asked me about the furniture, and what to do with it. I told her to put it in storage until I got out.

She told me that some of my family members wanted certain pieces I saw nothing wrong with that.

"Okay give it to them, I'll buy everything new when this is all over."

I gave her a hug she held me tight like she didn't want to let me go.

"Okay Mom, you have to go now," I said.

She was escorted out with the other visitors and I was taken to the back room and strip-searched and taken back to six south.

It seemed like everywhere we went in this building they always wanted to strip-search you. Lift your nut sack, bend over and cough, let me see your feet.

I thought this couldn't last much longer I was ready to get high as I rode the elevator back to six south.

CHAPTER 23

Reaching Out

I was happy that she'd gone to my house to clean things up, but I was pissed off that Meechy hadn't gone with her to take the work with him. People I thought loved me were treating me like I didn't exist, and I'd only been in jail a week. Meechy was my road dog and I had treated him good. He never needed anything I always provided for him. I wanted him to stop playing with the game and get paid. I knew that the bird was a lot, but he could handle it a gram at a time I needed to make a few phone calls.

"Yo, Big Clyde, are you going to use your phone time right now?"

"Naw, homie, you can use it."

There were only four phones in the unit two were only used by blacks. You had to sign up the night before to use it the next day. You were given only fifteen minutes per call, and the calls were collect only.

I wanted to go to my uncle's office to use his phone, but decided not to. Phones calls were the lifelines to the outside world. They kept you connected I would see guys stressing over them, wondering what their wives were doing, accusing them of being unfaithful. I saw guys crying on the phones, telling their children, "Daddy will be home soon, okay."

I was happy that I didn't have any kids, and I wasn't tripping about the females either. I just wanted out and the phone was my vehicle. Using the phone and having a good conversation reminded me of sitting at home in the living room, I wasn't in jail I was just on the phone.

I dialled Meechy's phone number and the operator asked for my name the phone rang a few times and then Meechy answered.

The operator said, "This is a collect call from De'Juan, do you accept the charges?"

I heard Meechy say, "No."

I was about to say something, but the operator cut me off and said, "I'm sorry, sir, they did not accept."

I dialled his number again and the same thing happened.

Rage filled my mind and body as I gripped the phone my hands became sweaty. As I looked around the unit, I tried to rationalize an excuse for Meechy, but the feelings of rage and hate began to fill me. How could he do me like this? After all I'd done for him? I'd saved his ass from getting beat when he was trapped in another man's house fucking his baby momma. I had pulled my gun out and drawn down on those dudes.

They had said, "Stay out of this, Ghost, he's in violation."

"It is my business that's my homie," I said. A war had been caused because of him. He had called and I was there for Meechy, and now he couldn't even accept a collect call from me!

I tried another number; it was one of my aunts who wanted some of my furniture.

As the operator spoke, I heard my aunt say, "No."

I was being rejected by the very people I had helped; when she was having trouble paying her rent, she would call me. "Hey, nephew, can you help me pay my rent?"

I'd said, "Yeah, no problem." She was family.

I was the one everybody went to for help, and now they wouldn't even accept my phone calls.

I called my mother and told her what had happened I told her to give all the furniture to the Good Will.

My mother said was to pray for them.

I thought, "Fuck them! I ain't praying for them motherfuckers!"

Bitterness engulfed my entire being I noticed that it was getting hard to breathe and my chest hurt, I wanted to rip the phone from the wall.

I needed a way out and that's when C-Style walked up to save the day. He had two gallons of wine ready and seven joints that would take me away to a faraway place where I didn't have to feel or care about anything or anyone.

My thoughts became dark and uncertain even with all the alcohol and marijuana in my body, it couldn't take away the pain I felt. I really didn't care about the females either; they were just toys. The hurt I felt was like I was being eviscerated I was becoming just a shell, I thought that if I have nothing on the inside, then I won't be able to feel.

I lay in my bunk and closed my eyes, feeling the alcohol and marijuana work its magic. I floated off to a place where no one could hurt me.

CHAPTER 24

—

Slim Pickings

I was seated with my attorney Stephen Watson, as the potential jurors sat on the other side of the courtroom looking at me. I felt a little uneasy I never thought it would go this far. My family sat behind me and my mother had her bible in her hand.

It was time to pick the jury my attorney gave me a note pad and a pen.

He whispered in my ear, "The government will pick a juror and you will pick a juror, if you don't like them, you have six chances to strike them off the list use your picks carefully."

I picked a black man and the prosecutor struck him off the jury. Then the prosecutor picked a white man and I struck him off the jury. I tried to pick people of color, for they should know how the justice system treats people of color. Everyone I picked the government struck off. There were no more black people in the jury pool; I couldn't believe how this black prosecutor was acting.

The jury was selected they were all white I knew I was fucked. They were going to get back at me for their family members being strung out on cocaine the jury looked at me like getting me off the street was going to change something. I had the Ku Klux Klan on my jury, the Grand Dragon for a judge and a black man prosecuting me. None of them looked like a jury of my peers. None of the jurors looked like me, not one of them was Asian or Mexican, and they were all white.

107

My attorney called for the Batson rule, which means at least one person on the jury must be of color, but the judge denied the motion the trial date was set for May 24, 1990.

A year later the same honorable judge that sentenced me was the same judge that had sentenced the LAPD officer Stacey Koon, the one who damn near beat Rodney King to death. The so-called honorable John G. Davies sentenced Stacey Koon to less than a year for almost killing a man how honorable was that?

I caught the chain back to MDC, now back in the unit I saw my cellie, Rick, playing chess.

"What's up, young Ghost? what happened?" Rick asked.

"Man, you won't believe this shit, I got the Grand Dragon as my judge and the Klan as my jury."

We both laughed what else could I do but laugh?

CHAPTER 25

—

And in This Corner

I was finally able to wear some street clothes to court instead of the prison-issued elastic waistband pants, jelly sandals and t-shirt. Every seat in the courtroom was filled with people I didn't recognize except for my little family they looked frightened, I was surprised to see Meechy with my family, he was sitting next to my sisters; I gave him a look like "What the fuck you doing here?" then he looked sheepishly toward the ground.

The Marshals escorted me to my seat where my attorney was waiting for me; I sat and surveyed everyone in the room.

The prosecutor sat to my right, he had two assistants with him. He shot me a look, which said, 'I got you, you little motherfucker,' and smiled. I found out that there were some people, who just like to see people get convicted, and there were some reporters also; I guess because of my age. The Weird Al Yankovic looking court clerk was shuffling through some paperwork as the court reporter was setting up her stenograph machine, and that's when the room became quiet.

The bailiff made the announcement. "All rise for the Honorable John G. Davies."

The Judge entered the courtroom wearing the traditional black robe looking like the grim reaper.

If this were a boxing match it would have sounded like this: "The challenger weighing a buck O five soaking wet fighting out of the blue corner with a record of 0 and 1 and being charged with poisoning his community please welcome De'Juan Lamonte Verrett." There would probably be boos. "Now introducing the defending champion of the world with an unblemished record, please welcome the United States of America."

The judge banged his gavel, which brought me back to reality. This shit was real how was I supposed to fight against the United States of America?

I looked back at my family my mom clutched her bible, Janna looked like I was going to the guillotine, Meechy had the look of shear fright and my sisters looked confused.

I thought back to when I had first gotten into the game I was never told about this part, I really never thought it would happen to me this kind of shit happened to other people not me, and here I was in federal court about to go head up with the most powerful country in the world.

I thought about the "Rocky" movie when Rocky was going to fight that Russian and his wife said, "You can't win."

Well, I had fucked up big time I finally realized it, my heart sank to my feet; my stomach made noises and my mind raced. My life was on the line and I was powerless.

The prosecutor called the first witness, Detective Brad Fitzpatrick, to the stand. Before he sat, the court clerk asked him to place his left hand on the Bible and to raise his right hand.

"Detective Fitzpatrick, do you swear to tell the whole truth and nothing but the truth so help you God?"

He responded, "I do." Now he was under oath.

The prosecutor asked him, "What happened on the night of February fifth at the Greyhound bus station?"

Detective Fitzpatrick answered, "We were monitoring the bus station for possible drug carriers when three individuals entered looking suspicious. They fit the profiles of drug carriers. We followed them around the bus station; they seemed uneasy and in a hurry, that's when we approached them."

"And what happened next?" the prosecutor asked.

"We identified ourselves as narcotics officers and told them that they weren't under arrest and they were free to leave, that we just wanted to ask them some questions, and can we search their luggage?"

"And did they?" the prosecutor asked.

"Yes, they did and we found what appeared to be cocaine, and they were immediately placed under arrest and taken to the LAPD headquarters for federal booking."

I knew this motherfucker was lying through his teeth, taking an oath to tell the truth didn't mean shit. I looked at the jury and they seemed to believe this bullshit.

The prosecutor finished his questioning of Detective Fitzpatrick and the judge called for a cross-examination.

Mr. Watson approached the witness stand, I knew he was going to rip him a new asshole.

"Detective Fitzpatrick, you just testified that you observed the three individuals enter the bus station in a hurry correct?"

Detective Fitzpatrick agreed.

"Have you ever seen people in the bus station looking uneasy and in a hurry because they were late for their bus?"

"Objection!" the prosecutor screamed.

The judge overruled his motion, "Answer the question, Detective, the judge ordered.

"Yes, I have seen people hurry into the bus station looking uneasy because they were late for their bus."

My lawyer continued, "Then why did you stop them? Was it because the three were African-American?"

"Objection, your honor, its speculation."

"I will withdraw the question, your honor," my lawyer said.

Detective Fitzpatrick began to sweat and he was now becoming uneasy. I felt good.

"Detective Fitzpatrick, you just testified that you asked the government witnesses if you could search their bags correct?"

"Yes, and they agreed."

My attorney walked in front of the jury, "Detective Fitzpatrick, it seems out of the ordinary that three drugs carriers would be honest enough to let a narcotics officer search their bags, knowing they have a controlled substance in there don't you think?"

The prosecutor rose and objected, the judge overruled his request.

I wanted to say to that Uncle Tom, "Sit your motherfucking ass down and shut the fuck up!"

My attorney had him against the ropes, I looked back at my family they were sitting on the edge of their seats; I felt confident.

The detective was looking at the prosecutor for guidance, but found none he was on his own.

"Now Detective Fitzpatrick, you already testified under oath that they weren't under arrest, correct?"

"Yes," he answered.

"Then why did you continue to question them? They weren't really free to leave now, were they? You used the color of the law to detain them, didn't you, Detective Fitzpatrick?"

"Objection your honor it's speculation," the prosecutor yelled.

"Overruled," the judge stated, "Watch your questions Mr. Watson."

"Detective Fitzpatrick, you testified that when the contraband was found, they were then placed under arrest and taken to the police station for booking, and once there, the government witnesses told you that the drugs were given to them by my client, Mr. Verrett, correct?"

"That is correct," he answered.

"But you had no evidence linking Mr. Verrett to the drug carriers, other than them saying that Mr. Verrett was a drug supplier."

"They each wrote out a statement implicating Mr. Verrett as their supplier, so we took the steps to try to secure information about Mr. Verrett."

My attorney walked back to our table and grabbed three sheets of paper, looked at me and winked reassuring me that we were on the right path.

"Your honor, exhibit A."

My attorney held them up for the jury to see, "these are the signed confessions of Shawn, Ebony and Nisha implicating Mr. Verrett as a drug supplier. Detective Fitzpatrick, you testified that the government witnesses wrote and signed these confessions, correct?"

"Yes they did."

My attorney continued, "But all three confessions are written in the same handwriting who wrote these confessions Detective Fitzpatrick?"

"I wrote them and each defendant signed them at the bottom I told them that it wasn't fair that they should go to prison for something that wasn't really theirs, and that's when they told me that Mr. Verrett was a drug supplier, and that he was to pay them to take the contraband to St. Louis. Ebony agreed to a monitored phone call to Mr. Verrett to discuss the drugs."

"No further questions, your honor," my lawyer said.

The next witness was detective Sue Moss; she was sworn in and questioned by the government.

"Detective Moss, what did Ebony say to you concerning Mr. Verrett?"

"Ebony told us that Mr. Verrett employed her to distribute marijuana for him, and that he had been a drug supplier ever since she had known him, also that he was going to pay Shawn five thousand to take some cocaine to St. Louis for him; and when he got there Shawn was to call him, and he would fly in the next day."

"So what did Ebony do after that?" the prosecutor asked.

"Ebony agreed to make a taped phone call to the defendant to discuss the drugs."

"No further questions, your honor."

I sat in my chair steaming; I should have invited everybody from Harbor City to come witness this, but no one would have accepted my collect calls; I was sure Meechy would have spread the word. My attorney was ready to cross-examine Detective Sue Moss.

"Detective Moss, didn't you threaten Ebony with if she didn't call Mr. Verrett that she would lose her children?"

"No, I told her that she could lose her children to the state," Detective Moss answered.

"Were there any overt acts in this case?" my attorney asked.

"No, there were not," Detective Moss, said.

"Then why were you so sure that Mr. Verrett was a drug supplier? You had no evidence pointing to Mr. Verrett, is that correct?"

"We wanted to make sure that Mr. Verrett had nothing to do with this investigation…"

113

My attorney cut her off. "But he didn't. You were only going by the words of the government witnesses who were trying to put the blame on someone else. Isn't that correct? Isn't it true that even before the phone call was placed, you sent officers to Mr. Verrett's residence in unmarked cars?"

"Yes, we did," Detective Moss, answered.

"Then why would you do that without probable cause? There was no reason to send plainclothes officers to Mr. Verrett home."

"Objection!" the prosecutor yelled.

"Overruled," the judge responded.

"No further questions."

I thought back to the night I was going home and the side street was filled with unfamiliar cars. It was Shawn who had sent them to my house they didn't recognize me because I drove an undercover bucket to move my work around. I guess Shawn told them that I would be driving a corvette.

"The United States calls Shawn to the stand."

From a side door, the Marshals entered the courtroom, followed close behind by Shawn, my stomach churned and my hands instantly became sweaty. He walked in with his head down, trying not to make eye contact with anyone especially me. Everything seemed to be going in slow motion; my heart was already broken into a million pieces, and those million pieces were crushed into a fine powder, I no longer had a heart; I felt dizzy and sick.

Shawn entered the witness stand and raised his right hand.

"Do you swear to tell the truth, the whole truth and nothing but the truth, so help you God?"

"I do," Shawn answered.

As he sat on the witness stand, my mind imagined doing unspeakable violence to Shawn, I was no longer hurt I was furious.

The prosecutor glanced at me, and then started his questioning.

"Shawn, how do you know Mr. Verrett?"

"We grew up together since we were babies," Shawn answered, he looked extremely uneasy.

My mom was looking at him shaking her head, and Meechy stared in disbelief.

The questions continued; "Please tell the court about the day of February fifth."

"Well Ghost, I mean De'Juan called me and asked if I wanted to make some money and I asked him how. He then told me that he would give me five thousand dollars to take some drugs to St. Louis for him. I needed the money so I said, "yeah, I'll do it." I then asked him if Ebony could go with me, and he said, "Yes," because she sells weed for him. We were supposed to leave in the morning but we didn't. Ebony then called Nisha to give us a ride to the bus station and then we got arrested."

"Do you know where Mr. Verrett gets his drugs from?" the prosecutor asked.

"Yeah, he gets it from T.J. he goes down there and picks it up; he works with the Mexicans."

I wanted to jump up and stab him in the neck; it took all my self-control not to do so. This was my blood brother telling on me in open court.

"No further questions, your honor."

The judge said to my attorney, "You may cross examine, Mr. Watson."

"Shawn, isn't it true that you were offered immunity for your testimony?"

"Objection!" the prosecutor yelled.

Shawn looked at a loss for words; I looked at the jury it seemed that they didn't care they just wanted to get me off the streets.

"Yes I was," Shawn, answered.

"No further questions, your honor."

The assistant prosecutor motioned for the Marshals to bring in three portable tables the courtroom became silent.

I glanced at Tom Woolley; he had a smirk on his face, and I wondered why the tables were being brought in.

My attorney jotted down something on his note pad, but I was focused the scene just a few feet from me. They put the tables together and banged them. The jurors jumped at the sudden noise, and then they brought in three boxes and began to empty their contents onto the tables.

The jurors watched as the Marshals pulled out small bales of money and neatly stacked them next to each other. The jurors eyes widened then a few of them looked at me.

The prosecutor sat in his chair leaning to the side, biting his fingernail and he smiled at me. Everything seemed like it was all planned out. The Marshals placed the three kilos of cocaine on top of the money and left the room.

I wanted to sink into my chair, the scene that had just played out destroyed any chance I had of winning. If the jury had any doubt about my innocence, that was smashed. They looked at me like I was public enemy number one.

I could almost hear their thoughts, "Lock him up! He's guilty, he's guilty or he wouldn't be here."

I was done, finished, any hope of going home was out the window.

The jury was still focused on the drugs and money. The prosecutor delayed getting up, giving them more time to hate me. The courtroom was still quiet, and then he got up.

I leaned over to my attorney and said, "This shit looks bad, doesn't it?"

He just tapped me on the shoulder and answered, "We can get them on appeal."

I stared at him, then closed my eyes and put my head down. I felt the crushing weight of the world on me. This couldn't be happening to me. Darkness was invading, I thought about how close I had come to pulling that trigger in the bathtub. My momma was here to witness her only son's conviction, this was too much, and the darkness overwhelmed me.

I felt myself rising; I opened my eyes and stood, "Your honor, I want to plead guilty."

The prosecutor stopped talking and all eyes were on me.

"Your honor, I want to plead guilty," I repeated.

My attorney tried to get me to sit down, but I pulled away from him.

The judge ordered all the attorneys to approach the bench.

I began to breathe rapidly, I felt like I was going to hyperventilate. I looked back at my mom and she was already crying. Janna ran out of the courtroom crying, my sisters held my mom and Meechy wept.

My attorney and Tom Woolley approached the bench, but I couldn't hear what they were saying my stomach was in knots. I couldn't believe what I had just done but I had to stop it. I knew if you lost the trial you

116

would get more time, and the way it was going down I was going to lose.

The judge called for a fifteen-minute recess I was led into the judge's chambers with three U.S. Marshals, my attorney and the three prosecutors. The judge sat behind his desk my attorney and I took the only two seats left.

"So, Mr. Verrett, you want to plead guilty correct?" the judge asked.

"Yes that is correct, I do your honor."

The lead prosecutor looked at me while he talked to the judge. "Your honor, I offered Mr. Verrett a deal, but he turned it down."

"You wanted me to set people up!" I shot back.

My attorney wanted to say something, but I cut him off.

"Your honor, I am a first time non-violent offender I should be given the mandatory minimum of ten years."

The prosecutor interrupted, "Your honor Mr. Verrett is far advanced for his years, and the severity of this case doesn't trigger the mandatory minimum."

"What does the United States offer Mr. Verrett now?" the judge asked.

"Since Mr. Verrett didn't take the first offer, the government will offer a two hundred and thirty-five month sentence."

Just hearing that shook me to my core.

"This will be the last offer take it or leave it Mr. Verrett. We will get a conviction on this case, and the government's case is strong. The United States has three of your friends that will finish their testimony against you, and I am sure the jury will find you guilty. Then we will push for the maximum sentence of two hundred and ninety seven months."

I told him to give me some time to think and waived him off.

Mr. Woolley was offended by my gesture and said, "Mr. Verrett, the offer is good for sixty seconds."

He pulled his sleeve up and started counting, "Fifty three, fifty-two, fifty-one..."

I looked at my attorney for guidance as the clock ticked and he gave none. My heart was beating louder than his watch. I was sure everyone could hear it.

"Twenty-six, twenty- five..."

This was crazy, I thought. "A nineteen year old boy given sixty seconds to decide whether he wanted to spend twenty years in prison?"

I closed my eyes and clenched my teeth.

"Fourteen, thirteen, twelve, eleven, ten, nine..." He continued counting down. "Six..."

"Okay!" I shouted. "Okay. I will take the deal."

The government had won.

The judge asked me, "Are you making this freely?"

"Yes your honor, I choose to accept the deal freely." I thought, "How in the fuck is this freely? If I didn't take the deal I was going to get almost thirty years.

I looked at my attorney I had paid this motherfucker thirty-seven thousand dollars to plead guilty to two hundred and thirty-five months!

I thought about what my mother had said, "Jesus will find a way."

Shit, Jesus couldn't even help himself get off the cross nobody could help me get off this cross I was on.

Tom Woolley looked at me and smiled, his smile was like a knife turning in my gut. I didn't even have enough power to get angry and I felt paralyzed. Two hundred and thirty-five months in prison seemed like an eternity. I tried to add it in my head, but my thoughts wouldn't let me calculate. I knew it was almost the same amount of time I've been alive. I would spend my entire twenties and most of my thirties in prison. I was overwhelmed with despair. I couldn't even summon tears. I was really a little boy who had become lost, my soul wept for this little boy named De'Juan.

Tom Woolley broke the silence. "Your honor, I will have my assistant draw up the plea agreement."

My attorney tried to comfort me; I shrugged away from him I didn't want to feel anything. I needed to get drunk, getting smashed to oblivion.

The judge was looking at his calendar to schedule my sentencing hearing. "Let's see, how does January third sound?"

Everyone checked their calendars; it looked good, they all answered.

We entered the courtroom and took our seats. My family looked uneasy.

The judge made his announcement, "Ladies and gentlemen of the jury a guilty plea has been entered in this case. I thank you for your services and you are now dismissed."

My family looked shocked they probably wondered what had happened in the judge's chambers.

"Your honor, may Mr. Verrett embrace his family?" my attorney asked the judge.

"Yes he may," the judge answered.

As I stood up, the U.S. Marshals surrounded me as if I was going to try to run out of the courtroom. I gave my mother a hug and she held me tight for a few seconds. I tried to break her grip, but she wouldn't let go.

"Let me go, Mom, let me go," I said.

I was starting to get upset; maybe because I was being filled with emotions I pulled away from her I had to be strong and show no emotions. My little sisters were crying I looked at them and told them that everything would be okay. Then Meechy, his eyes blood shot red I just gave him the homie hug and we hit the hammer. That's a handshake that we use not the normal handshake. It is a balled fist and we just tap each other's fist.

The U.S. Marshals escorted me out of the courtroom and back to the holding cell in the basement of the courthouse where I sat, deep into my thoughts.

CHAPTER 26

—

Game Over

I made it back to MDC and was escorted to my unit, six south. I was headed to my cell when Big Clyde and Elroy called out to me.

"What happened, young Ghost?" Big Clyde asked

"I stopped it I plead guilty."

"You did what?" he said as if he hadn't heard me the first time.

"Yeah, homie, I plead guilty to two hundred and thirty-five months."

"Man, that shit is crazy," Big Clyde, replied. "They can't do that."

"Well they did, and what's crazy is losing the trial and getting twenty-seven years that shit is crazy."

Big Clyde and Elroy just looked at me.

C-Style and Zulu walked up, "What's cracking, Ghost?" they both asked.

"Nothing homie, I just plead guilty to two hundred and thirty-five months."

They were momentarily at a loss for words.

"Where it at?" I asked "I need to put a few in the air right now."

"Don't trip I got you homie," C-Style responded.

C-Style gave me a nice sized joint for me to smoke by myself.

I asked Rick, "Do you need to use the bathroom because I'm going to be in there for a few minutes?"

"No homie, go ahead and handle your business I can wait."

I stood looking at myself in the mirror as the smoke drifted around me. I took another deep pull from the joint and filled my lungs, then exhaled. The weed was doing its magic I thought about all that would happen during my time in prison. People would be getting married and having babies, and well off into their careers and there'd be high school reunions. I wondered how many homies would be killed, I thought about my sisters; they would be grown women probable married with kids themselves. I wondered about my mother, how would she hold up with her only son being locked up for twenty years. What would the streets look like? How would I live life after doing all that time? Would I make it or would I lose my mind? Would I become that person that Hollywood portrays as mean and bitter?

Millions of thoughts ran through my mind, it was too much to think about I laid on my plastic mattress, floating like the smoke and faded away.

I was woken up by the Unit Officer yelling, "Count time. Count time!"

It was now the four o'clock stand up count, which meant mail call and chow was only an hour away. Rick looked at me he wanted to say something, but I guess decided not to.

After the count was cleared, everyone surrounded the CO's desk and waited to see if they were receiving any mail. I stood on the tier as the names were shouted out.

"Williams," the CO called.

"Pass it back," the guys yelled.

"Verrett," the CO called.

"Pass it up," I answered.

I opened the manila envelope. It was a copy of the plea agreement I thought, "Damn, they sent this shit fast."

Elroy asked if he could speak with me after chow.

"Fo sho" I answered.

I knew he was going to do that Christian thing, but I saw no harm in letting them pray for me, so I played along with it. Freddie was sitting at the desk reading the Bible when I entered the cell. My eyes were still red from the marijuana, so when he looked into my eyes, I bet he thought I was crying. Shit! I wished I could cry, I felt like my soul had been taken away.

Elroy instructed us to join hands and to close our eyes. I thought about the first time they'd prayed for me. Their intentions were good.

Elroy began. "Dear Lord, heavenly Father, we come to you for guidance and protection from the evils of this world. Lord, we are lost sheep trying to find our way back to you and stay in your grace. This young man, De'Juan, he lost his way. Lord, help him find his way. I ask in your name Lord, in the name of the Father, the Son and the Holy Ghost, Amen."

I was headed back to my cell when C-Style, Sonny and Zulu called me. "What's up, Ghost?"

"Nothing, just going to lie down," I responded.

"All right, I feel you," Zulu answered.

I thought, "Don't nobody know how I feel right now!"

"I'll get with ya'll in the morning," I said.

"How did I get like this?" I asked myself, looking out of the bullet-proof window, watching free people on their way home.

I grabbed my Walkman, put on my headphones and tuned in the Art LaBoe radio show. The song that was playing was by Ron Isley's, "How Can You Mend a Broken Heart?"

My heart was broken I felt like my soul had been ripped from me. I thought about all the fucked up choices I had made I should have never given them that work. I should have stayed using Tim. I should have listened to Janna.

It would take me sixteen and a half years to understand that it *was* all about the choices I had made. My heart would mend, but I couldn't see it then. My eyes became heavy I heard Rick come in.

I heard the CO yell, "Lockdown," then I drifted off to sleep.

CHAPTER 27

—

Paying the Piper

It was the day of reckoning I wasn't looking forward to this day, and my stomach was in knots. I couldn't think clearly or focus on anything; today was the day I would be sentenced to twenty years. That didn't even sound right, but I had to get used to saying it. I had to accept it this was the jagged pill I had to swallow.

I was up before the CO came to my cell I was by myself again. Freeway Rick had already been transferred, and I had already prepared for the day.

"Verrett, you have twenty minutes to get ready."

The time was 4:15 a.m.

"Okay," I answered.

I watched to make sure the CO went back to his office, and then I stood on top of the desk and fired up a joint. I took a deep long hit and held it as long as I could, then blew the smoke into the vent. I chained-smoked two joints. I washed up to get the smell off me and made a cup of coffee.

I sat on the top tier looking around the unit; it was quiet except for a few guys that were going to court with me. I had been here a month shy of a year. Things had changed for me; C-Style, Sonny and Zulu had already been transferred. Big Clyde and his cousins, Elroy and Freddie, were still here prolonging their sentencing.

I went to the recreation deck to smoke another cigarette; I never smoked them on the streets, now I was buying cartons from the prison store.

The CO came to the rec deck and asked me if I wanted to eat I declined I really didn't have an appetite.

Deep into my thoughts, trying to imagine how it was going to happen I was brought back by my uncle's voice.

"De'Juan, how are you doing?" he asked.

"I'm good," I replied."

"I need to talk to you," he said.

We sat at the dinner tables he was concerned for me.

"What are you doing here so early?" I asked.

"I knew it was your sentencing day; ask for a request to be sent to Terminal Island since you're a first time non-violent offender, okay?"

"All right," I answered.

"And keep your head up nephew."

The CO called for us I could tell he wanted to give me a hug, but instead we shook hands and I was off to court.

We were strip-searched I had become used to it by now I wouldn't even say anything. I would just stand in the booth, strip and go through the motions and stand there totally nude and wait to be issued my street clothes. Even putting on the leg irons, belly chains and handcuffs didn't bother me anymore. I recited my name and number before they even asked. I didn't even look out of the windows as we rode up Spring Street with the sirens blaring and the lights flashing it had lost all its glamour.

I had learned how to walk in leg irons so they wouldn't cut into my Achilles tendon. Douglas, the U.S. Marshal, was waiting for us to remove the custom-made prison *bling, bling*. Douglas was all right; he made it as comfortable for us as possible. As the chains were removed, he pulled out some cigarettes. I needed one to keep my buzz going I wasn't going to feel it when the judge gave me my time.

Douglas said in a low whisper, "You don't know you're hunted until you in the trap."

I puffed on my smoke, listening I wondered how Douglas hadn't gotten caught up in the street life. He had lived in South Central, and I wondered what made him different. Then I thought about Trenton

Holmes. He had lived in the projects with me and he didn't have a father either he had three younger sisters. Trenton would play basketball with us, then leave and go home. He wouldn't even smoke or drink with us. He wouldn't rep the hood to save his life. I wondered what did they do to not get involved. Both of their lives were better than mine right now. They had chosen not to be involved and I had chosen to be involved. That was the difference. I came to realize that there were a lot of homies who lived in the hood, but they had never involved themselves with the negative activities in the hood. Trenton sold tacos and burritos and I sold kilos. I never heard of anyone getting two hundred thirty-five months for selling tacos. In those funny uniforms and hats, he helped to provide a service of feeding people while I provided a service of feeding people's addiction.

I would see Trenton at the bus stop and ask him, "Hey Trenton, want a ride?"

He'd say, "Naw, man, I'm going to catch the bus. Thanks anyway."

Now I would be the one on a bus chained up like an animal. Crazy, huh?

Douglas gave me some real stuff to think about. I found a place on the concrete bench and sat thinking. The cigarette enhanced my buzz. My head was starting to spin and I felt a little at ease. Then my name was called.

"Verrett," Douglas said.

My stomach instantly became uneasy a shot of fear enveloped my entire body.

"It's time to pay the piper," Douglas said.

I began my slow walk to the courtroom.

I took my seat next to my attorney I gave my family a quick smile. My attorney gave me a pen and piece of paper, but my hands were so sweaty I couldn't even hold the pen my hands stuck to the paper.

The Uncle Tom prosecutor gave me a sarcastic smirk I wanted to spit in his face.

My stomach began to make noticeable noises; my attorney patted me on the back for comfort.

"All rise for the Honorable John G. Davies," the court clerk announced.

The entire courtroom rose to their feet as the judge entered.

"You may be seated," the judge said.

"In the case of the United States of America versus De'Juan Lamonte Verrett, docket number 90-91-JGD."

The judge asked, "Has the pre-sentencing report been filed, and are there any objections?"

"Yes, your honor," my attorney answered.

"Mr. Verrett was placed in criminal history category six when he should have been in category one. He has no adult convictions. His prior conviction was when he was a juvenile, we ask this court to grant the motion."

That's when Uncle Tom Woolley stood up, "Your honor, Mr. Verrett committed the instant offense within the five-year period. Mr. Verrett was fifteen years old when he was convicted of the juvenile offense. Under federal rules of procedure 3b1.1, it states, if a defendant commits the instant offense within five years of serving a previous offense, it can be used as a prior."

"The defense motion is denied."

I never thought that by taking that case when I was a kid it would ever come back to bite me in the ass, that juvenile case had put more time on my sentence.

"Is there anything else?" the judge asked.

"Nothing further your honor," my attorney answered.

The judge then went into his long speech about how he was mandated by Congress to hand out this Draconian sentence to me. He said that his hands were tied.

"Mr. Verrett, the world you entered is unforgiving in the eyes of the federal government. If this were a state case you would have had a better chance of winning with the representation you have, but this is the United States of America. You were offered to join us, but you didn't. You can't beat us, Mr. Verrett. That is why you didn't win."

My mind raced as the judge spoke, my mouth became dry I placed my shaking hands on my lap to hide them.

The judge asked, "Is there anything you would like to say before I hand down your sentence?"

"Yes there is your honor, I feel that this is an injustice it was made to look as though I was caught with the drugs. I was taken out of my home without a search warrant. The only witness for my defense that the officers came into my house without a search warrant was somehow put on the government's witness list. I couldn't call him to testify on my behalf. I was put under duress to plead guilty, my constitutional rights have not been protected."

I spoke for as long as I could to prolong my sentencing, my mind drifted because I was high, but there was nothing I could say to not get sentenced.

"Very compelling speech," Tom Woolley said with the look of distaste on his face as I finished.

"Mr. Verrett," the judge said, "I see no other reasons why we should depart from the original agreement. Therefore, I hereby sentence you to a term of twenty years of imprisonment to be served in the custody of the Federal Bureau of Prisons."

The judge banged his gavel and it was done, my life was in the care of the Bureau of Prisons now. When he banged his gavel a part of me died right there. I looked back at my family; my mom burst into tears and fell to the ground she couldn't even stand on her own.

I looked at Tom Woolley he was unbending about the way he felt about me. If he had really known me, he would have known that I wouldn't have chosen this life style.

I was taken back to the bullpen where I saw some of the other guys who were sentenced. This guy named Cliff; he was sentenced to twenty-five years, and I saw Michael Harris and his crew.

"What's up youngster? What they give you?" Michael asked.

"twenty years," I answered.

Michael didn't seem as hurt as me.

I asked him, "You getting sentenced today?"

"I already did," he answered.

"What did they give you?"

"Life and twenty-seven," he responded.

An old man who called himself Uncle Claude was given ten years. He sold more heroin than anybody I knew of, but he went in with a doctor's note and a cane, playing the role of an old dying man. In the unit, he would talk shit with the best of them and play dominos all day and night, but in that courtroom he was a fragile old man.

There was a father and son team Antonio and Dominic Cervantes. They were selling speed in Hawaii and making tons of money until Antonio's friend got greedy and made a run by himself and got popped; then he set up Antonio and his father Antonio was sentenced to fifteen years and his dad got ten.

Leonard Wells came back with twenty years for twenty-seven hundred pounds of marijuana. Everybody who got sentenced came back with a boatload of time. I watched Michael and wondered why he seemed calm. I guessed that he had accepted the ugly side of the game and was cool with it.

I caught the chain back to MDC and made it to the floor. I was ready to get fucked up and my high was gone. I had that feeling like after you have a surgery when the pain medication wears off, you know that pain Well that's how I felt, and I needed some medication; that night I got supremely fucked up.

Elroy and Freddie wanted to pray for me, but I wasn't in the mood to be prayed for. They left my cell saying, "Jesus loves you De'Juan."

"Yeah, right," I thought, I wasn't about to become religious like most of the guys did in here. Elroy and Freddie were converting new arrivals daily and had a nice following. I didn't need Jesus to comfort me all I needed was my wine and weed and I'd be all right.

CHAPTER 28

—

Gladiator School

It was February 28, 1991 I was awaked at 3:30 a.m. Today was the day that I would be going to prison. I had become somewhat comfortable in my little cell at MDC, but it was time for the next stage.

"Verrett," the CO whispered as he opened my cell door. "You have twenty minutes to get ready."

"All right," I answered.

I washed up and gathered all my letters and pictures. The commissary bought food I would leave at Big Clyde's door with a note.

I had two joints left and smoked them to get the edge off. I stood looking at myself in the mirror and I noticed that my mustache had gotten darker. A year ago, it was barely noticeable. I had a few new lines on my face, probably from spending long hours with my eyes closed tight trying to look within myself to understand how I became like this.

I looked around my closet-sized cell to make sure I hadn't forgotten anything. Everything I owned was in a small transparent plastic bag. I thought about all the material shit I had on the streets. None of that shit mattered now. I was reduced to a bagman. The homeless people I saw on the streets as I looked out of my jail cell window all had it better than me at that moment. I wished I were with them. At least they were free.

We were taken to the basement of MDC, strip-searched and chained up as the Marshals called our names to get on the bus. I was sitting on the cold concrete bench thinking this would be the last time I would be in Los Angeles for eighteen years. I felt small and powerless.

"Verrett," the Marshal called.

I shuffled to the front of the gate.

"Name and number," the Marshal ordered.

"De'Juan Verrett, 92857-012," I answered.

He checked his paperwork and nodded and I entered the bus.

There were no sirens this time as the bus pulled onto the freeway and headed north on the 101 freeway. I sat next to the window looking out at people as they were headed to work. I saw school buses filled with kids smiling and laughing. I thought to myself, "When I get out, all of those kids will have finished college and have jobs and will be married with children of their own."

I tried to memorize everything I saw. I would focus on something and close my eyes as if taking a picture, trying to burn everything I saw into my memory. I saw some Cal-Trans workers planting trees. By the time I got out those trees would be fully-grown and home to hundreds of birds. I saw some young guys with their girlfriends in a 64 Chevy Impala. I thought about when I used to travel this highway early in the morning coming from a hotel with a female, and Meechy was in the back with her friend. I closed my eyes and drifted off, letting the marijuana take me.

The bus jerked as we pulled off the freeway. There was a sign that read 'Do Not Pick up Hitchhikers.' We were close to the prison now. As my heart raced and my hands became sweaty, I was sure that everybody on the bus felt the same way. Then I saw the prison. My stomach bubbled and made noises, but the roar of the bus' engine drowned the noises out. We drove down Klein Boulevard. There were two prisons one on my left and the big one on my right.

The bus stopped in front of the big prison. The Marshals exited the bus and got into their position. I looked at the medieval-looking prison and my heart began to beat faster. It was very intimidating. In the front was a gun tower with a prison guard pointing a machine gun at the bus and all the other guards had their weapons drawn.

Everyone on the bus was quiet. The only thing you heard were the chains. We were all uneasy.

The Marshal opened the steel gate and made an announcement. "When I call your name, give me your number."

I closed my eyes, hoping that he wasn't going to call my name.

"Sanchez," the Marshal called out.

The Spanish guy stood and recited his number then exited the bus.

Then the Marshal called the next name. "Verrett," he called.

A shot of panic engulfed me; my stomach churned as I opened my eyes and recited my number before I exited the bus.

There were about twelve of us standing next to the bus. We were all patted down and led into the prison. In a single file line, we were escorted to R&D (receiving and discharge) to be processed. The gate was closed and I heard the bus' engine start and fade off as it drove away. I looked around only to see miles upon miles of razor wire and gun towers every fifty yards.

As we shuffled, I saw shapes behind the bars watching our every move.

One of the COs said, "That's one of the housing units and some of you will be living there."

It looked like Frankenstein's castle. I was waiting for a bolt of lightning to come out of the sky and strike the building with a mad scientist screaming, "It's alive, it's alive!"

The shadowy figures behind the rusted bars reminded me of lost souls trying to find their way toward the light.

Once inside the receiving building, the chains were removed and the process began. We were ordered to stand against the wall and remove our clothing. I was used to this routine by now. My mind would automatically shut down. My feelings were turned off.

I became like a robot just following the commands, "Open your mouth, shake your hair out, lift your nut sack, bend over and cough."

This was the part of being in prison. This is what my life consisted of. This would be a part of my life for the next eighteen years. I was angry inside and I was angry at the world. I was angry at God, I was angry at my mother, I was angry at Mark for leaving me when I was a kid and I was angry at Bosco because he'd never told me about this shit.

We were given some institutional clothing and ordered back into the holding cell. The next step was to see the prison psychologist. It was time to do my prison intake assessment.

"Mr. Verrett, I'm going to ask you a few questions," he said.

"All right," I responded.

"Do you feel hopeless?" he asked.

"No, I don't," I answered. To be honest, I did, but I wasn't going to tell him that. I would give the same answers I gave at MDC.

He continued, "Are you scared?"

"No," I responded.

"Have you cooperated with the government in any way?"

"No," I answered.

"Do you feel like harming yourself?" he asked.

"No," I answered.

"Is there any reason why we shouldn't put you in with the general population?"

"No, there is no reason," I answered.

The last question was, "Do you have trouble sleeping at night?"

"No, I sleep soundly," I replied.

"Well, okay," he said as he finished his paperwork. Then he escorted me back to the holding cell.

Next was the doctor to do an initial physical.

"I see you're asthmatic," he said.

"Yes, I am," I responded.

I had been told at MDC to say that I was asthmatic in order to avoid the difficult jobs.

We were then all escorted to have our picture taken for our prison I.D. cards. The only other I.D. card I'd ever had was my driver's license, and I had only had that for three years.

The intake process was complete and I was assigned to K-Unit. The staff members called it Kilo Unit. I thought, "That's what I'm in here for, kilos."

I remembered a movie called the *Falcon and the Snowman*". This was the prison one of them had escaped from. I wondered how he did it with all the security. This place was a fortress.

As we prepared to be escorted to the housing units, I was curious to see if I knew anybody.

The butterflies in my stomach began to flutter as the CO called a few names. "Armijo, Thomas, and Verrett," he called. "Come to the front."

I maneuverered my way to the front of the line, "These three are going to SHU he said.

"Special Housing Unit?" I asked. "Why am I going to SHU?"

The CO answered with a lame excuse. "I'm just following orders."

We were all handcuffed and led to the dark side of the prison. All this was a mistake I thought, but then I thought about that punk ass Tom Woolley.

As we were walking to SHU, the CO looked at my paperwork and said, "You were born in 71?"

"Yeah, I was," I answered.

"Don't worry, you'll only be in there for seven days. It's called a Captain's review."

I felt a little at ease knowing that I wouldn't spend my entire sentence in SHU.

Special Housing Unit resembled what I had seen on TV, except this was real. There were no spoiled actors with trailers here, no catering trucks, and no re-takes. Before we entered the cellblock, I tried to summon all the anger and hate that was within me to show on my face.

The CO yelled, "Pop the gate," and the heavy metal gate opened.

Walking down the aisle with my bedroll in my handcuffed hands, I saw guys lying in these tiny cells. The bunks took up most of the width of the cells. They were just bigger than a storage closet with a toilet and sink combination.

We stopped in front of cell number eleven, which was already occupied. The CO ordered him to cuff up before the barred gate was opened. I stepped into the tiny cell. It was so small that he had to move to the rear of the cell, and then our handcuffs were removed.

We made our introductions.

"What's up? I'm No-Good. Where you from?" he asked.

"I'm Ghost from Harbor City," I answered.

He smiled. "I know some of your homeboys. You smoke?"

"Yeah, I do," I replied.

He gave me a pack of Camels, non-filters, and I fired one up.

"How old are you, homie?" he asked.

"How old do I look?"

He rubbed his chin and smiled. "About fifteen."

135

We both laughed.

No-Good schooled me to how it was done in here. He said that we had a lot of homeboys on the yard, but the Mexicans controlled it because they had the biggest dope sack. He told me that the COs bring the food three times a day, and we shower only twice a week. This was going to be a long seven days. The cell was so small I could touch both walls and I'm not a big person.

We passed the time away by playing chess. No-Good had drawn out a chessboard on the ground, and we used tiny pieces of paper with the letter K for King and Q for Queen. I liked the game because you had to use your brain.

At night, it was loud. The Cubans made the most noise. No-Good told me that they were there permanently because they couldn't go back to Cuba. He told me that they had TVs in their cells. I couldn't see how, due to the size of the cells.

When you're in a cell, you get to know a lot about the person.

"Why they call you No-Good?" I asked him.

"Ever since I was a kid, I was curious about everything. I would always find something to get into, sometimes good and sometimes bad. I had millions of questions that were never answered. I was curious about everything, homie, from girls to drugs to how the world worked. Ya feel me?" he said as he puffed on his cigarette.

I felt the same way.

"My pops, I don't know him even to this day, so the big homies groomed me. I started to get into all kinds of shit, and that's how the name came, No-Good, because I was always up to no good."

I had learned a lot from No-Good. I felt a connection to him because we had the same story and the same outcome! We both had questions that were unanswered and we sought advice from the big homies. We thought we had found the answers in the streets. There were millions of young men just like us – blacks and whites, Hispanics and Asians. No matter what race we were, we all had one thing in common. We all lacked experience.

My week had passed, and my name was called.

"Verrett, roll it up!" the CO yelled.

I told No Good that I would see him on the yard. I was cuffed up and escorted to my unit.

CHAPTER 29

—

The Block

I was just a pup on the yard with the big dogs now. You know how a puppy acts when he's around the vicious dogs? Well, that was me. I quickly learned how to posture and put on my mask at a moment's notice. Every inmate I saw was Shawn and I hated him. I used that hatred and bitterness to disguise my fear.

I was put in a cell with a guy who called himself Insane. He was just a bit shorter than me, brown-skinned with a muscular build.

"What up, homie" was my greeting to him.

"What's up?" he answered.

I placed my bedroll on the top bunk.

"Where you from, homie?" he asked.

"I'm from Harbor City."

"Right, right," he said as he nodded.

We made small talk as I made my bunk, then I was taken to meet the homies. They gave me a care package of shower shoes, soap, and a couple of packs of Top Ramen, some coffee and a knife. I was told to find a stash spot for the knife, as I held it in my hand looking at it, I made a silent prayer that I would never have to use it on anyone. I thanked the homies, and then Insane escorted me back to the cellblock.

I asked Insane, "Do you have a knife?"

"Everybody has one. You need it in a place like this. "How much time you got?" Insane asked.

"Eighteen and a half years."

"How much you got?" I asked.

"Fifteen. This is my second fed case. I took the deal."

I thought to myself, "This is my first fed case and I got more time than him, and this was his second."

We all went by our street names instead of our government names. His real name was Walter Ruiz. He was Belizean. I didn't know that Belize had black people. His parents came to the United States when he was five years old and moved to South Central Los Angeles.

Insane told me that it was hard being a black kid that only spoke Spanish in a black neighborhood. He was teased until he got older. Then he began to do some crazy shit.

"All I wanted to do was to fit in, then I started banging and got the name Insane because of the shit I used to do," he revealed to me. Insane was the perfect name for him for catching a second fed case.

I told him how I got my name, Ghost, and he laughed.

"Yeah, homie, that is a perfect name for you."

"How many kids do you have?" he inquired.

"None," I answered.

"How about you?"

"My girlfriend just had my first son when I got arrested. I have two daughters by another female. Homie, I fucked up. You're lucky you don't have any kids. You really don't think about it until you're taken away. I thought I was doing it for them, but it was only for me. My baby girls don't even know me. When I got out the first time I took them to Disneyland and bought them clothes and toys, but that was it. I had to raise my girls in the visiting room, and now I'll have to do the same with my son. He'll be fifteen when I get out. There will be no one there to teach him how to be a man. That shit hurts homie, and the killer part of it is, I wasn't born here and I'm going to get deported back to Belize when I'm released."

I felt for Insane. Life was insane for him. He had a lot on his plate. I knew if he had to do it different he would. The choices we make can affect our future. None of us here could see it at that time. I was in a place where we were all infected with bad decisions.

How could I learn to make good choices and decisions in a place where men who made bad choices surrounded me. I had no role models on the street and there were none in here. I had looked on the outside for happiness. The money didn't make me happy. Alcohol and drugs didn't make me happy. I thought women would make me happy, but they just drove me crazy. Nothing on the outside of me could make me happy.

I would learn many years later that change is an inside job. Freedom is an inside job tolerance, patience and happiness its all *an inside job*.

When you're in a cell you open up and show the real you. Once you step out of your cell, you have to become another person. The mask automatically comes on and all feelings are hidden.

I flipped through Insane's photo album and he pointed out his kids. Like a proud Daddy, he told me about them.

I was happy I didn't have any kids. I could see the pain on Insane's face as he spoke. I wondered what it felt like to be called Daddy, to have a child run to me with unconditional love and hug me. I remembered times when I would run to Mark and just hug him, happy to see him, fighting with my sisters to take his shoes off when he got home, to see him in the stands at one of my baseball games, and teaching me how to ride a bike.

In the visiting room, I would see kids run to their fathers screaming, "Daddy, Daddy!"

All that toughness would just melt away.

One of the older homies told me, "The most painful thing in the world is raising your kids in the visiting room and watching them grow up in pictures. Be grateful you don't have any kids, young Ghost."

The funny thing about all of this was to hear gangstas talk about how they would want to be part of the PTA (Parent Teachers Association), helping their kids with homework, which was some real life stuff, meaningful.

Living with another man for years, you really get to know him. You become like brothers. No egos, no posturing, and you can let your guard down. It's like a light switch. I learned to turn it on and off without thinking about it.

When we left the cell, it looked like everything was good like we got shit on lock, and like nothing bothers you. When you're in a cell, you talk about shit you wouldn't dare bring to the yard. Everything was all about reputation. It was everything.

I met most of the homies who were running things. I was told that the Mexicans had the yard on lock because they had the biggest dope sack, and they formed an alliance with the Aryans. There was a lot of drama, but it was peaceful on the yard at this time. I learned that the controlled shifted from one race to another, and the Mexican mafia controlled the flow of commerce. Stamps were currency, which was paid to the workers, and the big dollars went to the Captains via wire transfer.

The money was sent to a family member, and that family member sent a postal money order with your name and number on it and mailed it back to the prison, then it was placed on your books. With drugs came money, and with money came power and control. I watched and learned how things were done.

When it was time to go to the commissary or the prison store I would buy zoo zoos and wam wams, better known as junk food, like potato chips and candy bars.

I still had the recipe for making wine that C-Style had given me back at MDC. I bought a six-pack of 100% orange juice and a box of sugar. One of the homies named Dolla-Bill worked in the bakery, which is where I bought some active yeast, a raw potato and some raisins. I smuggled everything back to my cell and put it all together, found a stash spot and let it cook for a few days.

The weekend arrived and it was time to get fucked up! The wine was ready. My mouth started to salivate in anticipation. I had two gallons of penitentiary wine. I needed this.

We sat in the cell playing dominos and drinking wine. I had finished my first cup and started my second before Insane was halfway done with his first. We had hooked our headphones to a makeshift speaker box made out of a Cheese It box and plugged it into our radios.

I was making wine every other day to make sure I had enough to get me through the week.

"Damn, homie," Insane said. "You drink damn near every day."

He didn't know that it was my coping tool. It kept me sane. I couldn't feel. It was my escape.

I began to start selling wine to the homies and was making a lot of stamps. One day Insane told me that it was looking bad that I had a lot of people coming and leaving our home.

I understood. I didn't want to bring heat on the house, so I paid one of the homies to distribute the wine for me. It was a good hustle. I felt useful again, providing a service.

My name was spreading that I had *The Bomb* wine. I was making fifty books of stamps a week. I would always keep a reserve of fifty books of stamps tucked away in my legal paperwork just in case I got transferred and I needed money. With the stamps, you could buy anything you wanted, like cocaine, heroin, weed or a knife.

Insane only drank on weekends. He would pour himself a cup and flip through his photo album looking at his kids with a smile on his face, and tell me a story of what they did when the picture was taken.

There were some of the homies who were broke and nobody sent them anything. I would save a gallon just for them. It really didn't hurt my hustle. They only wanted what everybody else wanted some relief, and in turn they loved me and would be on stand-by if I ever needed them. My rep was growing in just a few short weeks.

One day I was called into the counselor's office. I hoped nothing was wrong.

"What's up?" I inquired.

The counselor was a tall white man with a red face who wore some cheap prescription glasses. He looked like an alcoholic, but he was all right, a veteran of the Bureau of Prisons.

"Mr. Verrett, you were never supposed to be here. You are getting transferred to the FCI (Federal Correctional Institute) across the street sometime this week," he said. "It's protocol that we lock you up in SHU because of your security level."

Fuck! I didn't want to go back in there and just sit. I had shit happening.

He continued, "Since you will be leaving this week, I'm going to let you stay on the yard."

"Thank you," I said and left his office.

I had heard stories about the FCI that you can stay on the yard until 11:00 p.m. and that you could have sex in the visiting room, and there was less life threatening drama on the yard. It was more laid back.

At the Pen, you always had to have someone with you. You showered with a group. As you went in, your homies would stand guard. The yard would close at 7:00 p.m. There was a CO everywhere no matter where you were on the yard, and someone was always watching you.

The Bureau of Prisons had smart people working for them, or so I thought. They were trained for damn near everything from chaining you up, to doing your paperwork, and somebody fucked up on my paperwork. It was going to be tough to tell Insane that I was going to be transferred to the FCI.

I planned to tell him after the 4:00 p.m. count over a few cups of wine, which should ease the blow. We had become tight in the few weeks we'd been cellmates. He was a good dude. We started drinking and that's when I told him.

"Damn, homie, I got some news today from the counselor," I said.

"What happened?"

"These motherfuckers are going to transfer me to the FCI. I was never supposed to be here. Someone fucked up on my paperwork."

I saw disappointment in his eyes as he sipped on his wine.

"That's cool," he replied. "You don't need to be here anyway. You've been handling your business since you been here. Niggas love you already, so when did they say you leaving?"

"Sometime this week," I answered.

The next day, shortly after breakfast, I was called to report to R&D. Insane was already headed to his work assignment. I quickly wrote a note and placed it in his phonebook where I knew he would find it. I looked around the tiny cell one last time. I saw a few of the homies and shook their hands and then I was escorted to R&D.

CHAPTER 30

Lower Level

The Federal Correctional Institution at Lompoc looked like a college campus, except for the barbed wire surrounding the entire facility.

Seven of us were transported in a white van with tinted windows. Of course, we were all shackled, but it didn't bother me. I was thinking about the stories I had heard. As we pulled to the rear of the Institution, I could see guys playing tennis and walking the track. There were no gun towers with guards with itchy trigger fingers ready to shoot at a moment's notice, only two perimeter trucks circling the outside of the institution.

We arrived at the rear sally-port entrance the guard shack was manned by a CO with a military style buzz cut who was wearing Oakley reflective sunglasses. He went through the motions of checking the paperwork, and then permitted the van to pass the heavily secured gate.

One of the redneck COs boarded the van. He looked just like the one in the guard shack. They all had the same haircut. I thought that they all must go to the same barbershop.

"When I call your name, state your name and number and exit the van," he shouted.

I was called last.

"Verrett!" he yelled.

"De'Juan Verrett, 92857-012," I answered, then exited the van.

We were ordered to stand against the van for a light pat down. The CO doing all of the shouting looked no more than twenty-eight years old. He was an ex-military brat that couldn't do anything else but work in a prison. He acted tough, but his eyes revealed that he was soft.

I got used to doing the prison shuffle in leg irons. I became good at it. We were led to R&D and placed in a holding cell where the chains were removed.

Next I was strip-search; it was now routine for me just another part of prison life.

"Show me your hands, open your mouth, shake out your hair, lift your nut sack, turn around and show me the bottom of your feet, bend over and cough, and what size do you wear?"

I had become used to this. I remember the first time this happened I felt traumatized.

"Hell, I ain't ever seen my own ass," I thought, and here I am ordered to show it to complete strangers. I had learned to turn off my feelings and keep them turned off.

The intake was always the same. The psychologist would come in and ask the same questions,

"Are you depressed? Can you sleep? Do you feel like hurting yourself or others?"

Next was the PA (Physician's Assistant). They all seemed to be from the Philippines and they were some mean little bitches.

"Mr. Barrett," she said.

"It's Ver-rett, not Bar-rett," I said, and she shot me a dirty look.

"You are asthmatic, yes?"

"That is correct," I answered.

I filled out all the paperwork. I checked the same boxes as before. They even wanted to know which hand I wrote with, and I would give the wrong answer. I wouldn't let the enemy know everything.

We were waiting for the old man with the cane to finish talking to the doctors. He had all kinds of complaints. He needed a lower bunk. He wanted to know when the rest of his medication would arrive and what about his diet because he could only eat certain foods, and that he was a diabetic and he needed a shot. Every one of us in the holding area hated him.

That shit was funny a heroin addict with a gang of tattoos wanted Kosher meals, shooting all that dope had fucked him up.

Before we could hit the yard, we had to be interviewed by a case manager. Mitchell Gates was mine.

"Mr. Verrett, I'm your case manager," he said.

"Hello," I responded in my best professional voice.

The questions began. "Are you affiliated with any gangs?" he asked.

"No, I am not."

"So you don't know any gang members?" he said sarcastically.

"Yes, I know some, and I know some U.S. Marshals also. Now does that make me a U.S. Marshal?" I asked.

"Then I will put no," he replied. "You will be housed in A unit."

"Okay."

"You have a lot of time. I have a son your age."

I didn't want to be reminded of that, I already knew how much time I had. I didn't need him to tell me that.

"Is that all? Are we done here?" I asked.

The intake was finished and we were led to the prison laundry to receive our institutional clothing. We marched in a single file line while being escorted by two COs. The inner compound did not look like a prison. The grass was freshly mowed. I thought about the time when I used to mow lawns as a kid. Everything looked clean, not like at the pen.

The compound seemed relaxed; everything seemed laid back, and the CO started telling us about how the inmates act here.

"There is nothing that happens here that we don't know about. The difference between here and the USP is that the inmates here tell us everything."

I took that as a reminder that there are a lot of snitches here.

I saw a few of the homies from MDC.

"What's up, Ghost?" it was Zulu and Wack.

They told me that C-style was here and that he worked in the laundry. With the homeboy working in the laundry, I was going to get all new clothing. When homie hits the yard, everybody who knows him will be there waiting to greet him.

"What up, Ghost Loc?" C-Style said with a big Kool Aid grin on his face.

145

"What it do, homeboy?" I replied.

"Don't trip. I got all new shit for you. I saw your name on the roster. I knew you were coming in today."

I was given brand new boots, jackets, boxers and t-shirts, all Dickey brand. Most guys who weren't known would be issued used clothing and blankets. That's just how it was done.

"I got a job for you working here with me," C-style said. "I already told the foreman, and he was cool with it."

Working in the laundry department was a plush job because you had access to all the new khakis, boots and T-shirts, but before I could start work, we had to go through an A&O (Admissions and Orientations) where you sit in the gym, and all of the department heads come and lie about how they care for you and if you need anything just ask. All the new arrival had to sit through this.

The AW (Assistant Warden) was the first to come in with a big fake-ass smile as he greeted us.

"Good morning, gentlemen," he said, and then went on with his speech. It only took him five minutes and then he was out the door.

Next was the Education Department. The motherfucker looked old and tired, way past retirement.

The old lady with a beehive hairstyle like in that movie, *Grease,* spoke first. "If you need a GED, we offer you the opportunity to earn one here. It is important that you have that when you're released."

I thought, "Ain't that a bitch? I will spend half my life in here. What good is a GED?"

All the Unit Managers came in next. They ran the units. They discussed the role of the case managers and the counselor's. The case manager reviewed your progress and every six months you would go to team, which consisted of the Unit manager, Case manager and Counselor. If you had something coming like a transfer to a higher or lower institution, the case manager would do the paperwork.

The Counselor's job was to process your visiting list and assign you an institutional job like the kitchen or laundry. They would also assign you to what bed you would be sleeping in. That's why it was called Unit Team. Some of the Unit Teams didn't play for you to win. They played against you I would later find out.

146

This shit was getting boring. Some of the guys were asking some dumbass questions like, "Are there conjugal visits? What if I win my appeal?" Stupid shit like that.

During a break, we all agreed that we wouldn't ask any questions, just sit and let the staff come and go, and be done with this bullshit.

I was assigned to A-3 west, the third floor of A building. I lucked out because C-Style and Zulu also lived there. I had the top bunk next to the window, which was all right with me. I made my bunk and put all of my clothes in a small locker, which I would live out of for the next eighteen and a half years. My whole life was in that box; everything I valued, from pictures to soups.

I really didn't like the dorm setting. It was too open with no privacy. You could hear a conversation clear across the dorm, radios playing, people coughing, sneezing. Chess was a big thing too. You would always hear someone yelling, 'check', or someone shuffling a deck of cards, and someone was always passing gas, and someone was always walking around dragging their feet just constant noise it was going to take some time to get used to this.

I was assigned to work in Food Service at 4:30 a.m. This was a mistake. I'd never been up to go anywhere to work at that time. I was supposed to work in the inmate laundry with C-Style. I wasn't about to crack eggs all morning or wash dishes. That was not going to happen.

Inmates are paid nine cents an hour to work eight hours a day to perform various duties from working in the kitchen to the factory. The government-run factory was called Unicor. They made everything you could think of from circuit boards used in military tanks to office furniture. Unicor also made inmate clothing and soldiers' uniforms and they would pay the inmates less than slave wages. Unicor put a lot of small businesses out of business. The work was top grade, built by bank robbers and drug dealers. I came to find out that Unicor was on the New York Stock Exchange. Prison was big business and someone was making a killing.

I had just gone to sleep around 2:00 a.m. when the CO tried to wake me. I had been getting high and drinking all night.

The CO tapped me on the shoulder. "Verrett," he said.

"What's up?" I asked.

147

"You are assigned to work in Food Service."

"What time is it?" I asked.

"Fifteen after 4:00 a.m."

I felt like I had sand in my eyes. I had only been asleep for two hours. There was no way I was going to get up and crack eggs at this time in the morning.

When the CO left; I rolled over and went back to sleep. The alcohol and weed brewed in my system and I wasn't going to do nothing but sleep.

The CO returned. "Verrett, it's time for work!" he shouted.

"I ain't going anywhere," I shouted, disturbing the other guys in the dorm

"Are you refusing to work?" he asked.

"Yeah, I'm refusing to work at 4:00 in the morning." That's when the CO called the lieutenant.

The lieutenant was head of all the Correctional Officers. They had the authority to lock you up in SHU and at this time of the morning I didn't care. I just needed to sleep.

"Verrett, are you refusing to work?" the Lieutenant asked.

I explained to him that I was supposed to work in the inmate laundry, and that my counselor already had the paperwork. Because of the commotion at 4:20 a.m., the entire dorm was awake and watching. To save face, the Lieutenant told me to cuff up, and that I could rest in the hole. At that point I didn't give a damn. I felt miserable. My high was coming down fast and I needed sleep.

When I was placed in the holding cell, I laid on the cold plastic mattress. The room began to spin out of control. I felt sick and was about to throw up. I crawled to the toilet and threw up everything. When I was finished, I was still trying to get that taste out of my mouth. The Lieutenant was leaning against the bars, smoking a cigarette watching me; He had a look of compassion in his eyes like he had been through this before, on his hands and knees throwing up in the toilet.

"Everything okay?" he asked.

I tried to play it off. "Yeah, it must have been something I ate," I answered. I wasn't fooling him.

"I see that you have a lot of time," he said.

"Yeah, I do" I replied.

"It's going to get harder if you do it like this," he said.

I thought, "What the fuck does he know? He can go home after his shift is over. I have to be in here until 2007 and it's 1991. He doesn't know how I feel."

"I'll tell you what I'm going to do. I'm going to let you sleep until my watch is over. Your counselor should be in by then, and if it is true that you're supposed to work in laundry, I won't send you to SHU."

"All right," I answered and lay on the plastic mattress and drifted off into my alcohol-induced coma.

The Lieutenant kept his word and I was released from the holding cell. My counselor said that the paperwork somehow got screwed up.

C-Style warned me that I had to slow down on drinking and smoking because of the random drug testing. If you got a dirty test the BOP (Bureau of Prisons), would transfer you to another institution anywhere within the United States. I didn't give a fuck about being transferred. Every prison would have drugs and alcohol and prison is prison whether it's in California or New York. I didn't care. I was going to do this time the way I wanted too! I needed it to numb myself. When I got high I wasn't in prison. I was just hanging with the homies. I would smoke some weed and walk the track with the homies. It reminded me of walking in the hood. I could hear laughter. I could hear the cars driving by with the homies yelling my name as they drove by. "What up Ghost?" they would say. I would put on my headphones and listen to the Art LaBoe station. I wasn't in prison. I was in my own world. Did I care about getting transferred? Not really.

CHAPTER 31

—

Let's Play Ball!!!

Sports were a big deal in prison, just as they were on the outside. Whenever the NFL season started, the PFL (Prison Football League) started. When Baseball season started on the outside, it started on the inside and the same with the NBA.

It was a sunny Saturday afternoon when I met up with C-Style, Zulu and Sonny on the yard for our afternoon Pow wow. We took our place high on the bleachers so no one would smell the aroma of the marijuana, plus we could see everything.

Baseball season was in full swing; the field was filled with guys wanting to try out to make it on a team. It reminded me of my days chasing pop flies, playing catch to warm up our arms and stretching. The guys seemed as though they weren't in prison. They were just on a baseball diamond having fun. I thought about Kyle and the Navy Field. I thought about how I had to prove myself to Coach Stevens just to play. I hadn't played baseball in years, but I knew I still had it in me.

It was highly competitive on the inside prison leagues; point's spreads were created just like in the free world. You could go to a bookie and place your bet just like in Las Vegas. On the weekends, there were poker tournaments and black jack tournaments. Gambling was big on the inside; playing the game of chance, and we were all in here for taking that chance.

There were two leagues for baseball, the A league, and the B league. Today was the try-outs for the A leaguers. There were a lot of guys who were really good. Some had played semi-pro ball and college ball. They had just got caught up trying to make ends meet and got arrested and messed up their chances of going to the pros.

There were also a lot of poor college students who were having a rough time financially, and made a bad decision to be a mule to make a few dollars and had gotten arrested and ended up in prison.

Talent has its price even in prison. You would sell your services to the highest bidder. There were two "A" league coaches that owned their teams. Motel Lou and Hector Diaz were the owners of the top "A" league teams, and they were arch-rivals. They would pay top dollar to stack their teams to win the prison pennant and bragging rights.

Motel Lou was a black dude with a baldhead who had a handlebar mustache, some big eyes with a country accent and he chewed on a soggy cigar and yelled at everybody. His team was called the Hit Squad.

Motel Lou loved baseball. He couldn't play worth a damn, but he could sure coach. I learned that he was the prison chess champion three years in a row, and I guess he would use that talent and apply it to the ball field.

Motel Lou got his name from having sold tons of cocaine out of the string of motels he owned throughout Texas. He had five years in on his twenty-year sentence.

Hector Diaz was Motel Lou's arch-rivals on the field. Hector had won the championship two years in a row. He was serving a twenty-five year sentence for bringing marijuana and people from Mexico into the United States through a tunnel in Douglas, Arizona.

They both loved the game of baseball, and off the field you would see them occasionally walking together smoking soggy cigars and drinking coffee. They respected each other on and off the field. When they played against each other, if the umpire made a call that the other didn't like, they would go crazy arguing and kicking dirt. You would think that someone would pull out a knife or something, but it was part of the game.

Motel Lou was thrown out of the game and had to leave the field, and was suspended for a game. It was the playoffs. He must have had a lot riding on it.

152

Let's Play Ball!!

Hector and Motel Lou had a lot of pull with the recreation department. They were able to buy uniforms for their teams through the SPO (Special Purchase Order). I wanted to be a part of that.

I was feeling good. It was a hot sunny day and I had a good buzz going.

"I'm pretty good at baseball," I said, surveying the field.

Sonny answered sarcastically, "Pretty niggas don't play sports." Everyone laughed.

"Fuck you, nigga. I play that shit for real," I shot back defensively.

I passed the joint to C-Style and headed to the field.

"Where are you going, Ghost?" Zulu asked.

"To try out," I answered and Sinbad followed.

Sinbad was a short buffed out dude. He was just a bit taller than a midget. It didn't make sense for someone to have all that muscle; it could interfere with hitting the ball, but he was extremely fast. He was on the track team in high school. He had dominated the Jessie Owens Track meets, and he was fast. He had gotten a scholarship to go to college for a major university, but made a bad decision to make some quick cash and he'd gotten arrested at LAX airport.

I approached the guy with the clipboard.

"What up? I want to try out," I said.

He looked at me as though he was sizing me up, and responded, "The B league try-outs are tomorrow."

"I'm not a B league player. I'm an A plus player," I shot back.

"Okay, what position do you play?" he asked.

"All of them," I replied.

He was looking at me like Coach Stevens looked at me, and then he insulted me and asked, "Can you catch?"

Sinbad saw that I was getting upset. "Don't trip, homie. Fuck this, let's go."

I wasn't about to go anywhere. Just because I wasn't as big as the players on the field didn't mean that I wasn't as good. I was better than most of the guys on the field. He was looking at my baby face and judging me without seeing what I could do. It was easy to underestimate me by my appearance.

I was told, "Never throw an alarm clock in a grave yard, just leave them sleep."

153

"Okay, let's see if you can hit," he said.

I smiled and grabbed a bat to loosen up. I looked up to the bleachers and saw C-Style and Sonny watching. Motel Lou and Hector were on opposite sides of the field talking.

I hadn't had a bat in my hands for some years and it felt good. I wrapped my hands around the handle and squeezed. My heart started to beat fast. I thought about Kyle and the tennis ball, and instantly became relaxed. My breathing returned to normal.

I heard Sonny yell from the bleachers. "Don't strike out, Ghost!"

I just gave him the bird.

For a brief moment, I wasn't in prison. I was transported back to Harbor City Park on a hot sunny day. I remember one summer when it was the All Stars game. We were playing a team from Palos Verdes and I arrived at the game late, so Mr. Moore, my Harbor City coach, was upset with me and sat me on the bench.

It was the seventh inning and we had our last ups to bat. We were down three to one with two outs and the bases were loaded. I was up to bat; the pitcher knew that he was going to strike me out because I was smaller than the rest of my team.

Before I stepped into the batter's box, Mr. Moore said, "They don't know what you can do! Take any pitch you want."

The umpire called, "Batter up!" and I stepped into the batter's box.

My mom was in the stands with my sisters. Everyone was quiet except for the fielders chanting, "Hey batter, batter, hey batter, batter."

The pitcher looked confident as he read the signs from the catcher, then went into his wind up and let it go.

The umpire yelled, "Stee-riike."

I just wanted to see how hard he could throw. It wasn't even close like Kyle's pitches, and the coach of the other team told his outfield to play in closer.

I looked at Mr. Moore and he gave me the go-ahead sign. I was going to take the next ball deep. The pitcher went into his wind up. I focused on the ball. I tightened my grip and swung hard. All you heard was the sound of the aluminium bat crushing the baseball. It felt good as the ball soared.

Mr. Moore started screaming, "Go, go!" as the base runners started advancing.

I hit the ball deep to left center. The outfielder didn't expect me to have that much power and they couldn't recover quickly enough. The runners started coming in. I hit a triple and we won the game, four to three. My mom jumped from the bleachers, screaming, "That's my son, that's my son!"

I was given the MVP trophy.

"Okay, you're up," he said.

Motel Lou and Hector were now watching as I stepped into the batter's box. I chose to bat on the right side. The pitcher threw one at me; it was high and inside. I was waiting for one low and inside. The next ball I foul tipped. I had to settle down and relax. I stepped out of the box and took a few swings. I was tingling inside as I remembered how much I loved this game.

The next ball was what I used to call a cheeseburger. I swung hard and the ball took off like a comet. Everyone watched it go over the double razor wire fence. I knew I had their attention now. Hector and Motel Lou stood there in disbelief, as I went to the left side of the batter's box.

"He's mine, he's mine!" Motel Lou screamed across the field with that soggy cigar in his mouth.

I looked into the stands. C-Style and Sonny were shocked as Hector Diaz and Motel Lou both raced toward me.

"Youngster, can you do that again?" Hector asked.

Motel Lou cut it. "He's mine, Hector!"

They were fighting over me.

"Let him hit again," Hector said.

I adjusted my stance. I smashed the first ball and it flew over the right field fence.

In disbelief, Hector asked, "Where do you get it from youngster?"

I didn't want to tell them I learned using a broomstick.

"I don't know," I answered.

The truth was, I had spent many days swinging a broomstick hitting tennis balls. I felt good inside and it wasn't the weed, it was something else.

I dropped the bat and headed for the bleachers. Hector and Motel Lou both followed me.

"Youngster, I want you to play for me," Hector said.

"No, he's going to play for me," Motel Lou argued.

I told both of them that I'd think about it.

"Damn, homie you got power," C-Style said.

"Yeah, you know, I been playing ball my whole life," I looked at Sonny and said, "Pretty niggas do play sports," and we all laughed as we watched Sinbad sprinting around the bases.

Prison is political. You have to play the game of politics. When you played sports some of the teams were mixed - blacks, whites, Hispanics and Asians, but that's the farthest it went. In the chow hall there was a section only for your race. If you were black, you sat with the blacks, and the whites sat with the whites. Even the punks had their small section and they lived together.

Later that day I was in the dayroom watching rap videos when Motel Lou walked in.

"What's up, youngster?" he said.

I just gave him the head nod.

"Youngster, I need to talk to you."

"About what?" I asked curiously.

"Let's go outside so I can hear. You youngins always have that damn rap music blasting out of the speakers."

I followed Motel Lou to the front on the unit and fired up a cigarette as he spoke. He still had that nasty soggy cigar in his mouth. It looked disgusting and he was spiting every few seconds, taking my focus off what he was saying.

"Youngster, you got a lot of power, and you can hit on both sides. There is no doubt that you can also play any position. I'll give you one hundred dollars to play for me for the season, and five dollars for every home run. You'll be paid after every game, win or lose."

"That's all?" I said. "Hundred dollars ain't shit, and five dollars for every home run? I play that shit for real, Lou."

I put out my cigarette and began to walk away.

"Hey, wait, wait! How about five hundred for the season and ten dollars for every home run paid after the game?" he said as he extended his hand.

"Deal. I'll give you one hundred percent on the field," I said and we shook hands.

To be honest, I would have played for free because I loved the game, and standing in that batter's box brought back those feelings that I had almost forgotten about. Motel Lou had the biggest sack on the yard, he was making thousands per week, and five hundred dollars was nothing. He wouldn't even miss it.

I had to get back into playing shape and lifting weights would give me the extra strength I needed. C-Style and Zulu worked out on the weight pile together. Zulu was a beast on the weights. He would grab dumbbells that weighed almost as much as me, and just toss them around like they were nothing. C-Style was strong, but not as strong as Zulu. I figured it was time to put on some size.

On the weight pile, it was all egos and testosterone. A lot of guys would spend all day out there lifting ridiculous amounts of weight, grunting and making high-pitched sounds. The whites worked out with the whites, the blacks with the blacks, and the Hispanics with the Hispanics. Everything was color-coded.

The weight pile can be intimidating for a beginner and I wasn't really the weight lifting type. I was strong, but not weight lifting strong. C-Style and Zulu had been lifting for a while. We started on the flat bench. They started the warm up with one hundred; thirty-five pounds and they made it look easy.

Now it was my turn I lay on the bench and gripped the bar. The moment I lifted the bar out of the rack I knew it was too heavy, but my ego wouldn't let me stop. I lowered the bar, trying to make it look easy. It felt like a million pounds. I couldn't control it and the bar came crashing down on my chest. My shoulders cracked and then popped. I tried to keep my composure, but the bar was crushing my rib cage. Zulu grabbed it with one hand and placed it back in the rack.

I wasn't fooling Zulu or C-Style or myself. My ego was shot down on my first day on the weight pile and I had messed up my shoulder.

C-Style said, "Just warm up with the bar, homie."

I couldn't even warm up with the bar. It was too heavy, plus my shoulder hurt, I decided that the weights weren't for me, at least not for now.

CHAPTER 32

—

Family Time

The last time I saw my sisters was the day I was sentenced. A year had passed and I was excited to see them. It was about a three-hour drive from San Pedro to Lompoc.

I heard the announcement over the PA system. "Inmate Verrett, report to the visiting room".

I entered the visiting room and saw my family sitting by the vending machines.

"De'Juan!" my youngest sister screamed and rushed to give me a hug, as my mom and other sister watched. I knew by the look on my mother's face that this was killing her, her only son in prison.

"Do you want something from the vending machines?" my mother asked.

"Yeah, some hot wings," I answered.

Something was wrong. I knew it by the way my mom was acting. I knew my being in here hurt her, but it was something else. I was concerned about my sisters; I was the man of the house. I protected my family.

My sisters were maturing fast and I wasn't there to keep the wolves away. My youngest sister was only fifteen years old, but she looked older than her age. I didn't want my sisters to be like most of the females I knew, having babies too young and by different fathers. I wouldn't be there to shield them. Both of my sisters sat very close to me. It hurt me to not be there for them. I had to hold back my emotions and remain strong.

My youngest sister asked, "Are people in here forever?"

I pointed to an Asian guy sitting with his wife. He looked harmless, but he was one of the biggest heroin dealers in the United States, and was now serving a life sentence. He was sitting with his gorgeous wife eating microwavable noodles.

"When are you coming home, De'Juan?" my youngest sister asked.

"Soon," I responded.

"When?" she insisted.

That's when my mother interrupted with, "The Lord Jesus will find a way."

I didn't want to hear any of that. If Jesus couldn't even find a way to get himself off the cross, now how could he help me, but I chose not to say what I was thinking. I just wanted to enjoy the day with my family.

The visiting room was crowded on the weekends. The outside visiting was great. The guys who had kids would sit in the grass and play with their kids and the setting didn't seem like a prison setting.

Every month the inmates were given forty visiting points. On the weekends for every hour you spent in the visiting room it was double, and on the weekdays it was one for one. My mom would come and spend the whole day with me. I appreciated her driving two hundred seventy-five miles, but I also wanted to spend some time with my girlfriends. I didn't know when would be the last time I saw them. Some of them knew how much time I had and I lied to the others.

I had asked my mother if she could come every other Sunday, and she agreed. There was no reason to go out of her way to be here every week; she would burn herself out. The visit came to a close. It was a good day. We had taken some pictures, we had laughed and now it was time to say goodbye.

My sisters started to cry. "We want you home big brother" they said with teary eyes.

I couldn't do anything but hold both of them tight. Next was my mother and she went into her prayer mode.

"Cover him in your blood, Jesus. Protect my only son," she said as she squeezed me.

"Okay, mom, you have to go now."

I didn't like it when she did that, making a scene, and it made me feel weak, like everybody was watching. I didn't want to feel anything, especially any emotions. As they left I told them that I would send the pictures when I get them back.

That night I called Kimberly to tell her that she could come up the next weekend. Kimberly was half black and half Italian. She was five foot two with cinnamon skin tone and curly black hair that flowed down her back. She had one of the greatest asses ever and she loved me.

Kimberly was down for me. She would do anything I asked, but she didn't know how much time I had. I lied to her and told her that I only had eighteen months to do, so I was going to get as much as I could before she found out. Kimberly lived in the valley, and she didn't know anybody I knew, so the secret would be safe for a while. I felt bad lying to her, but she brought anything I needed and I had promised to marry her when I got out.

Kimberly took penitentiary chances just to make me happy. She would bring me a dozen balloons filled with weed, but I looked forward to the quick sex. We would sit at the picnic table and straddle the bench, and then Kimberly would lift her dress and sit on my lap and bump and grind. It was true about what they said about the FCI; the guards were laid back.

When we spoke on the phone I told her that I had received the pictures. "Do you like them?" she asked.

"Hell yes, I do," I replied.

She had sent me some pictures of here wearing lingerie. It was a big deal to have them. I would only show them to my close homies. A week prior to that I had proposed to Kimberly and she had accepted.

I had been told when I was a youngster that all females planned their weddings from when they are little girls, and I was going to use that to lock her in so she would continue to run for me, keeping her interested. I knew that Kimberly really loved me. I liked her a lot, but I didn't love her enough to marry her.

It was 1992 and I wouldn't be going home until 2007. I couldn't tell her that I would be damn near forty when I got out. If I had she would have left a long time ago. There was no way she would stick around for fifteen years, so I had to keep the game going.

When I would use the phones, I could hear the guy next to me arguing with his wife. "I know you're fucking someone. Why didn't you come for a visit? Where are my kids? Why didn't you answer the phone?"

It must be hard to know that your wife is fucking someone and you're in here for ten years. I didn't need to go through that kind of shit. The only thing I wanted was for her and the rest to bring me some weed and sex. I didn't care about anything else. No woman would wait that long. I knew I wouldn't.

About eleven months had passed and now Kimberly was starting to ask questions about when could she send my release clothes. I would tell her that my mom was sending them. She would get pissed off and say, "I'm your fiancé. It's my job to do that.". I would try my best to avoid that conversation with her.

I was on the weight pile with C-Style and Zulu. I wasn't working out, just hanging with them, when I heard my name called over the PA system.

"Verrett, report to the counselor's office."

I was just about to fire up a joint.

"I'll be right back," I told them.

I entered the counselor's office. I knew it wasn't anything serious because if it were then I would have been called to the chaplain's office.

"What's up, Mr. Jones?" I asked.

"Your fiancé just called."

A shot of panic ran through my body as I sat down in front of his cluttered desk. His office was filled with awards he had received during his twenty-four years working for the BOP. He had a bronze trophy of a Big Mouth Bass that'd he caught from one of his fishing trips hanging on the wall. Papers were stacked everywhere, very disorganized. The fan in the corner gently ruffled the stacks of paper and he used staplers as paperweights.

"What did she want?" I inquired.

"She wanted to know when she could send your release clothes," he answered with a smirk.

"You didn't tell her how much time I have, now did you?" I asked, already knowing the answer.

"It's public information. I had to tell her. November 1, 2007."

"Man, you just fucked up my relationship."

"You can't blame me. You're the one who lied to her, and I told her the truth," he shot back.

The truth was she wouldn't be coming back to visit and bringing the supplies I needed.

"She said to call her. She sounded very upset."

"You don't think," I shot back.

Before I called, I thought about who would replace Kimberly. I walked back to the weight pile where C-Style and Zulu were waiting to hear what had happened.

"What did he say?" Zulu asked.

"Man that motherfucker told my girl when I get out. She called up here to see when can she send my release clothes, and he told her that I don't get out until 2007 isn't that some shit?"

They finished their work out, and then we headed toward the track. I needed to get high before I called her.

I called Kimberly and for thirty minutes she screamed at me, cursing me the whole time. I couldn't do anything but listen. I thought that the relationship had run its course. She would have found out sooner or later. That was the last time I spoke with Kimberly. The next time would be seventeen years later, using a social networking program called Facebook.

CHAPTER 33

—

Bad News

The CO announced that the count was clear. That's when everybody on our floor would prepare for mail call. That was an important time for us, when we received something from the outside world. It felt good to get a letter that smelled of perfume sealed with a kiss. Pictures are a big deal in prison too. They keep you updated of the ever-changing world.

Birthday cards, Father's Day cards, Christmas cards, are all important. Some guys who didn't have anyone writing them would go the chapel and order cards, which were sent to the mailroom, then sent to the units. Basically, they sent themselves mail just to stand in the crowded hallway with everyone else, it was sad.

Mail call began and my name was called. "Verrett" the CO yelled.

"Pass it back," I answered.

I had received two letters, one from Kimberly and one from Tisha. I opened the letter from Kimberly first. She had taken some suggestive pictures of her wearing a G-string with her ass facing the camera lying on the bed, and another picture of the clothes she had bought for me to wear when I got out. I received the pictures the same day she found out that I would be going home in fifteen more years, I slipped the Kimberly letter under my sheet to look at later.

I opened Tisha's letter no pictures, just a short letter. She knew how much time I had. Tisha was cool, didn't want a relationship, just wanted to kick it, party and have great sex. I could call her anytime of the day or night. If I wanted to see her, she would stop everything she was doing just to be with me. We would smoke a few joints and then she would crave powdered donuts.

What I liked about Tisha was that she knew that I didn't want a girlfriend.

She said to me one night after sex, "Ghost, you the kind of nigga that can't have just one girl."

I respected her. She didn't want to lock me in, just wanted to have fun.

As I read her letter, she apologized for not writing, and that she was sorry about my uncle Pat-Bone getting killed. I had to read it again to make sure I read it correctly; she said that my Uncle Pat-Bone was dead. It couldn't be. I had just talked to him a few days ago, right before my mom came to visit.

Then it hit me. That's why my mom was acting that way, putting extra care on everything. She knew that he was dead and didn't tell me. I had to find out in a letter from Tisha. I was filled with rage; I hated my mom for not telling me that my uncle was dead.

"What's wrong, Ghost?" Troy asked

I was lost in anger and didn't hear him.

"Hey Ghost, what's wrong?" he asked again.

I was clutching the letter in my hand as I headed for the phones. I had lost my uncle and my girl in the same day.

I called my mother. "How come you didn't tell me?" I demanded.

"I didn't want to upset you," she responded.

"What do you mean, upset me? You knew he was dead when you came up here. What, you didn't think I was going to find out?" I said angrily.

"I didn't want you to get into any trouble," she said.

I was furious with my mother. She talked about me not getting into trouble, that's why she didn't tell me. I was a young man, but still a man, and by not telling me she always kept me in that little boy place, trying to protect me. She really didn't know me. I could handle the sentence they gave me. I could handle myself in the streets. I could handle bringing dope across the border, tying people up. I survived being kidnapped, and she didn't want me to get in trouble.

166

I just hung up the phone. This was too much for one day. I needed to get drunk to kill this feeling. I went and found C-Style. He was getting a tattoo in Chinese that meant 'Trust No Man'. I thought it should read, 'Trust No One' instead.

I was in pain, but not physical pain. I hurt inside but I couldn't find the exact spot. I would miss my uncle, and I will always remember our last conversation.

Pat-Bone was his hood nickname. He was a big dude. He had some big ass twenty-four inch arms, and he was well respected in the hood. I remember when I was a little kid; he took me with him to his girlfriend's house. I loved being with him. They gave me a box of Captain Crunch and let me watch TV as they went to the back room to talk.

I filled my stomach with cereal and went to sleep. I was awakened hours later. "Come on Dee, we have to go," he said, gently nudging me.

I guess we were late because he was walking fast. I tried my best to keep up with his long strides.

"Uncle Pat, what took you guys so long?" I asked.

"We were talking," he answered.

"About what?" I asked.

He smiled and said, "You ask a lot of questions nephew."

I just smiled.

"I'll tell you when you get older," he said as he put out his hand and gripped my little head. His fingers were by my nose and his fingers were stinking.

"Ugh, your fingers stink. Why your fingers stink?" I asked him.

I grabbed his other hand and smelled his fingers. They didn't stink like his other hand.

He smiled and said, "When you get older, you're going to love that smell."

I thought I would never love anything that smelled like that.

I thought about our last conversation before he was killed. I had called my Grandmother's house and he answered.

"What up, Unc?" I said.

"Hey, nephew, how are you holding up?" he asked.

"Oh, you know. I'm holding it down," I answered.

"Nephew, I got to lace you on some things. I know you staying down for yours up in there, but I got to tell you some thangs. It's fucked up that your homeboys snitched you out, but that's the side of the game. They didn't hold the oath, like you did."

I just listened.

"Nephew, you were doing way too much and the motherfuckers hated that, this young nigga balling out of control. You made OG niggas look bad."

I just laughed.

"Now you're seeing the ugly side of the game. You must stay true to it, and stay strong through it all, and when you come home, you can keep your head up. Your young ass will walk through the valley of death, and you will come out unharmed, I know it. I knew you were strong ever since you were a little boy."

I had never heard my uncle talk like that. I had the phone pressed tightly to my ear as he spoke.

"There are three rules that you must live by while you're in there, and if you live by them, niggas will respect you, and look to you for guidance."

Rule number one. Don't fuck with any homosexuals and don't hang with anybody who does."

I interrupted, "I don't get down like that."

"I know you were a young player out here and I know you got them females busting down the door to see you, but I had to say that," he added.

Rule number two. "Don't steal or fuck with anybody who steals."

"I ain't ever been a thief," I said.

"I know that, but I just have to say this shit. Rule number three. Don't run with big groups. You are a leader. Sit and watch who's who and listen, then take your spot. Ya feel me?"

"Yeah, I got you," I answered.

"All right, let me get off Grandma's phone, and send me a picture. I love you, Dee."

"I love you too, Unc. See you when I get home".

I found out how my uncle was killed. In the rival city, a group of youngsters had to put in some work before they could be initiated into their gang by doing a drive-by. They drove through where my uncle lived and saw him walking to his house. They knew he was an OG by his size and they would get a lot of Hood Points for killing an OG.

They drove up to him and fired twice, hitting him in the chest, killing him instantly, and sped off. My uncle died on the streets I used to play on as a kid; the same street I had walked with him that night when his hand was stinking.

The youngsters were caught and were given a sentence that was half of mine. They would be out before me. They killed my uncle and got less time for taking a life. I resented the justice system.

My grandma was devastated. Her youngest son was violently killed. I wanted to kill everything they loved, their mothers, their sisters and brothers, even their pets, and I wanted their families to feel the pain my grandma was feeling, the pain I was feeling. I would settle it when I got out.

That day I felt dark on the inside. I couldn't trust anybody. Yeah, I didn't tell the truth to some people, but my mom couldn't tell me about my uncle getting killed. I changed. The only one I could trust was me. It was going to be all about me! I would apply what my uncle told me. Just listen and watch.

I became an expert on words, especially when I used the phone. I listened closely to what I heard. I could tell if someone was lying to me. I could tell when they were hiding something from me. I listened to the stress in their voices. When someone was trying to bullshit me, I would know and quickly cut them off. I changed. I changed everything about me. I became bitter and unbending and angry, and the boatload of time I had to do didn't make it any better.

C-Style and Zulu were my road dogs, and they saw the change in me. They began to talk.

"What's up with Ghost?" some would say.

"I think the time is getting to him," some would answer.

To be honest, it was partly true. The time was a big part of it, and I felt like I was by myself! In a world that didn't have any sympathy for weakness, I learned the skill of being uncaring for anything or anyone. I was mastering this newfound craft. This vibration that was inside of me was tormenting me, and I fought it off with drugs and prison wine. I had to numb myself, never let the real me show.

I learned how to wake up in the morning bitter and angry, resentful for everything and everyone. Smiling was a thing of the past, an old memory. Evil thoughts consumed my being. C-Style and Zulu looked me at differently. What they saw in my eyes was a volcano waiting to erupt.

I began to drink heavily. I would sit in the dayroom and just listen. Being silent and present made people wonder what was going through my mind. I had noticed that the shot callers always remained silent as they watched and listened. I made a mental note of that.

The death of my uncle had triggered something in me. I heard his words for the next fifteen years.

"You're a leader, Dee," he said. "You're a leader."

CHAPTER 34

—

Dayroom Drama

After the 4:00 p.m. count our unit was released to go to the chow hall. I didn't have an appetite and decided to sit in the dayroom and watch television instead. I wanted to be by myself for a while, and the only place where I could find quiet was in the dayroom.

I was flipping through the channels when a group of old men came in to play cards. My brief moment of serenity ended as their card game started. They all began to smoke those nasty smelling cigars. The smoke quickly filled the room. I became instantly irritated. I just shot them a dirty look, which didn't seem to affect them.

The shuffling of cards and the loud talking overpowered the volume of the television. They seem to be having fun and I was miserable. It should have been the other way around. I should be having fun, and those old men should be miserable, but the noise finally got to me.

"Hey ya'll, could you guys keep it down? I'm trying to watch TV," I said.

They all looked in my direction in unison and dismissed my request like it didn't matter and they resumed their game. That pissed me off.

The noise seemed to get louder. It was like they were doing it on purpose, just to get me angry. I didn't want to get crazy with four old heads, but they were disrespectful, and disrespect was disrespect no matter if you were young or old.

"Hey, I'm trying to watch these videos," I said.

Now I had all of their attention. The game had stopped and all eyes were on me. Bennie The Fox was the old Jewish gangster. He had all white hair that was combed perfectly, and not a hair out of place, even his beard was all white. He sat in his chair facing me, twirling a tooth-pick in his mouth, holding his cigar.

"Ain't it past your bedtime, youngster?" Bennie asked sarcastically as the other old men laughed.

"Yeah, it's past his bedtime. Look at his eyes. They're red. He looks tired," Lawrence Livingston added.

Lawrence Livingston was an old black man who refused to cut his afro. He resembled Fredrick Douglas in a way. He was super old school. He was serving a forty-three-year sentence for cocaine trafficking. Lawrence Livingston was a big name in the Midwest. He still owned a lot of property in Tulsa, Oklahoma.

"How old are you?" Vinnie Cratacci asked.

Vinnie Cratacci was an Old Italian gangster from New York who was ratted out by one of the soldiers in his family. Later I found out that a book had been written about Vinnie. He'd had a wild life. He'd been going to jail ever since he was my age, and now he was this old Mafioso playing pinochle in a dayroom.

"Old enough to be in here," I shot back.

"Youse think that something to be proud of?" Bennie asked, puffing on his cigar.

"I just turned twenty-one."

"Youngster," Bennie said. "I've been in here for twenty-four years, while you were still in your Daddy's pants".

"Congratulations. What do you get? A prize?" I shot back harshly.

That got Bennie's blood boiling, "Youse got a smart mouth on you, you infant."

Bennie acted like he was going to get up and whoop my ass. He briefly forgot that he was almost eighty years old. He still had fight in him and I silently admired that.

Lawrence had to hold him back. "Hold up, Bennie. Relax. He's just a baby. You know how babies are. He knows not what he does."

Then I added, "Yeah, relax Bennie, and take your medication."

That really burned him up and lit his fire. I just smiled.

172

"Youse disrespectful infant!" Bennie shot back.

"I'm disrespectful? You motherfuckers are disrespectful. I just wanted to watch some TV and you all come busting in here smoking me out with those nasty ass cigars, talking loud. You motherfuckers are disrespectful."

"It's past your bed time, infant. Take your young ass to sleep," Bennie said.

"Check this out," I said as I stood up. "Two things are going to happen," I announced.

They all froze still as if they were in a picture.

"We either are going to fight right now or…"

They all stopped what they were doing. Lawrence stopped shuffling the cards. Marcus and Vinnie both put out their soggy cigars and Bennie carefully placed his cinnamon flavoured toothpick on a napkin. Then, like it was staged, they all took off their glasses in unison.

"So what's number two, infant?" Bennie asked with a devilish grin.

"Number two is… you old motherfuckers, are going to show me how to play this game," I answered.

I would not get any points for whooping four old men. They seemed to like me talking shit to them. It got their blood pressure up, and the thought of getting my ass whooped by these old men would ruin my reputation as a young gangster. There was no respect in that.

They all started laughing, and then Lawrence stopped and became serious, as he rubbed his chin in contemplation.

"Lookie here, youngster," Lawrence finally said, "You can't whoop all of us."

Bennie interrupted, "Let me get him. I still got some fight in me."

Back in the day, Bennie was a triggerman and an enforcer. I could still see the old scars on his face. He was instantly transported to his ripping and running the streets days, but that time had passed. Now he was just an old man in bad health with a life sentence.

Lawrence broke the odd silence. "Okay, young man, I am not going to cut you," he said, as he pulled out a razor and placed it on the card table. I was shocked that this old motherfucker had a weapon on him.

"Bring your chair over here and we'll teach you the game," Lawrence instructed.

I sat down next to Bennie. He was still growling, twirling his cin-namon toothpick in his mouth, and trying to stare a hole through me.

My time was different after the altercation with the Four Horsemen. I respected each of them. They were all different, not only in race, but in personality. I learned something from them, and I became a regular card player, and Bennie The Fox was my card partner. He always had a cinnamon toothpick for me and Vinnie. I learned to play an Italian lawn bowling game called bocce ball. Marcus, he was a book reader. He stayed reading something, and he told me to feed my mind, to learn something.

Lawrence Livingston, he actually taught me how to shave. I was in the bathroom one day washing up, and he was in front of the mirror with shaving cream all over his face.

"When are you going to clean up that peach fuzz?" he asked.

My beard was starting to grow in patches by this time. I had never shaved before.

"Do you know how to shave?" he asked.

I hesitated at first because I was embarrassed.

"No, I don't," I answered.

"Here, let me show you. See, first you have to get your whiskers soft by putting a hot rag on your face, then spread the shaving cream, not too thick, nice and even, now long strokes."

Lawrence had become very knowledgeable in the law. He thought he could help me give back some time. I told him everything about my case, and there was nothing he could see to help me. The only thing that could help was if Congress changed the law to help first time non-violent offenders.

In 1992 a bill was introduced to Congress that would reduce sen-tences for someone like me. There was a lot of commotion surrounding the bill. Some politicians were for it and some were against it. It was costing taxpayers thirty-seven thousand dollars a year to keep us in here, and we were going to be in here for decades. Most of us were young black and Latino males who didn't see another way out of the ghetto, and drugs seemed like the best available option.

The proposal was in every newspaper and on all the news channels. It looked like it might actually happen. Guys were recalculating their sentences. I was too. I thought if it went through I would be home in a two more years. I could do that easy.

The prison law library was crowded; inmates were filing motions. It was like a law firm, typewriters were buzzing, there were lines at the copy machine, and people were talking about how they would get to make their kids graduations and about how life was going to be different this time around.

The announcement was made on November 1, 1992. Every day-room was filled with standing room only. That was the day we had all waited for. Every TV was on CNN waiting for the long-awaited news.

The anchor for CNN was a sexy woman named Lynn Russell. She was beautiful and smart. She had brunette hair and high cheekbones and spoke with intelligence and I had a crush on her.

As she read from the teleprompter, the entire prison population became silent. "Our next story, the proposed bill that would release thousands of first time nonviolent offenders, was shot down in Congress today."

The silence was deafening. Everyone in the dayroom was lost for words, and no one said anything as Lynn Russell went to the next story.

"Fuck those motherfuckers!" someone yelled.

You could feel the tension on the yard. I was devastated like every-one else. Anger filled me, just as every dayroom was filled with men whose hopes had been crushed.

The dayroom quickly emptied, just as quickly as it had filled up. No one was in the law library except for the guys who worked in there. Trashcans began to overflow, filled with useless motions and our hearts were broken. I needed to get high. I needed to escape that feeling I felt.

I sat on the bleachers of the recreation yard. I wanted to be by myself and that was the only place I could be isolated. I inhaled deeply, letting my lungs fill with the marijuana. A few seconds later, I was feeling the THC, but the pain was still there. I would spend all of my twenties and half of my thirties in prison.

I watched the people on the yard. They began congregating and something was being planned.

CHAPTER 35

—

Up In Smoke

Normally during the work week more than three hundred prison staff members ran the prison, and during the weekends it was less than half that, for an inmate population of seventeen hundred.

Since the crushing announcement that Congress had struck down the Bill that would reduce first time nonviolent offender's sentences, tension on the yard grew. The system had to pay.

Nothing was going right. I had just found out that Janna was married, her husband was in prison and was about to be released. This news fucked me up because I had trusted her. I was getting bad news damn near every week. First Kimberly found out how much time I had, then my uncle got killed, now Congress had shot down the Bill that would send me and many others home, and now the only female I ever trusted was married! Life was fucked up for me.

Bitterness became my companion and hate became my motivation. Something had to be done and someone had to pay for this. I walked back into the housing unit and saw some inmates praying. I became angry, and I thought, "God isn't here! And if there was a God then why would He do this to me, or to us?" I thought praying was for the weak. None of my prayers were ever answered, so what's the use? It was a waste of time.

The word on the yard was that something was going to happen, and the weekend would be the best time to strike back, since less than half the prison staff was working. After the 4:00 p.m. stand up count, we were released to go to the chow hall for dinner.

I was sitting in the chow hall when the transformer blew. The entire prison instantly became covered in darkness. Everyone waited for the backup lighting to kick in, but it didn't. Only the emergency lights worked. Then it began…

The prison was in a total blackout. The screams and yelling started. Next I heard windows being shattered. I told C-Style, Zulu and Sonny that we had to get out of the chow hall. Outside it was pitch black and we could barely see a foot in front of us. The glowing emergency lights that were mounted over the front doors of the units guided us.

Then I smelled smoke. Something was on fire. It was mattresses. The thick smoke from burning mattresses filled the night air. Fiery rolls of toilet paper lit up the smoke-filled sky as they rocketed across the yard. It reminded me of one of those old medieval movies I'd seen when I was a kid, where the enemy was attacking the city trying to breach the fortified walls. The only difference was that here the enemy was faceless. We were our own enemies.

We made our way into the housing unit. I was on extra guard. People were running through the hallways with their faces covered. Everyone was bumping into everyone. The bathroom where Lawrence had taught me how to shave was filled with guys setting toilet paper rolls on fire and throwing them out of the broken windows, cheering as the fiery bombs hit their targets.

We passed the counselor's office. The door was wide open and I saw some hooded figures breaking open the file cabinets, pouring baby oil over all of the files. The desk drawers were ripped open and all the contents were thrown on the floor. One of the hooded guys told everybody to get out of the office because it was going to go up in flames. He sprayed baby oil over the entire office as another hooded figure coated the sprinkler head with peanut butter. The peanut butter protected the glass on the sprinkler system so the temperature would remain cool. Therefore, the system wouldn't know that the office was on fire.

The match was lit and the entire office was engulfed in flames. I never knew baby oil was that flammable. I stood in the door way watching the blaze in a semi-trance, not believing that this was really happening.

178

Everything was on fire, the chair that Mr. Woolley sat on, visiting list print-outs, all the miscellaneous piles of paper that were stacked in the corner, all of Mr. Woolley's awards for his years of service, pictures of his family and his coveted trophy of that big mouth bass that hung on the wall fell to the ground in flames. Everything was gone. Nothing would survive. All of our prison files were reduced to ashes. I guess the guys thought that burning the prison files would give us a clean slate, a new beginning. Broken hearts and dreams fueled the flames, not the baby oil.

"Come on Ghost, we must go" C-Style said, taking me out of my trance, pulling me away from the flames. "We gotta pack our shit because when this is over they are going to ship out all the young blacks," he explained.

The unit was partially emptied, except for a few old men standing next to their lockers guarding their valuables. Everything that meant something was now in a 3x4 metal box, and we were all only one-step away from homeless people.

At the far end of the hallway, we saw someone with a flashlight heading in our direction. At first I thought it was a CO, but they wouldn't be that stupid to come into a burning building with a couple hundred crazed inmates. As the light came closer, I could hear my name being called.

"Ghost, Ghost!" the figured yelled. Out of the shadowy smoke-laced hallway the homie Sonny appeared with a big smile on his face.

"What's up, homies?" was his greeting.

"What up?" we all answered.

"Man, the whole institution is on fire motherfuckers is running around tearing shit up out there. Now they're trying to get into the commissary. Let's get down there before everything's gone," Sonny suggested.

We made our way out of the burning building. By this time the Ghetto Birds, or helicopters, had arrived, circling the chaos, shining bright lights that barely penetrated the dark plumes of smoke.

"Everybody cover their faces," I commanded. This was a precaution just in case the Ghetto Birds were filming. The havoc that surrounded us reminded me of a war torn city during the Second World War. Housing units were on fire, and some inmates became instantly homeless. A

179

group of punks was huddled next to a tree in the courtyard crying hysterically. The one who called himself Reesie Cup (I will never eat those again) was trying to calm the others. He stood looking at the burning building, crying. All of his possessions were lost.

The old men were trudging their way to the bocce ball area. I could see the look of disgust on their faces even through the smoke. The four old men that had befriended me sat watching everything unfold. I was glad that I had my face covered.

There was a large group of masked men standing in front of the commissary. The commissary was the prison store where you could buy everything from batteries to tennis shoes, from ice cream to cigarettes. There was a two-inch thick glass window that separated the looters from their prize.

There was a big guy trying to smash the window using a concrete ashtray, which wasn't working. He was having a hard time and tiring himself out, but the glass was too strong.

"Let the homeboy, Ghost try," Sonny yelled, and everybody looked in my direction.

"Nigga, why you saying my name!"

Everyone's face was covered and it was hard to know who was who.

I told Sonny to get me one of the big bocce balls. He returned with one and I placed it in the net laundry bag. I told everyone to step back, I swung the bag as hard as I could, hitting the glass window square center with an echoing BOOM. I swung a second time, and the window started to crack. The masked men cheered. I didn't care what was behind the window. The prizes that were only two inches away didn't motivate me. I only needed to lash out, release the pain I was feeling inside. I swung again and again, and then the window came down.

Zulu stood in front of the window and pulled out an ice pick, warning the masked men not to enter the commissary.

"My homies go in first!" Zulu announced.

No one was going to contest his demand. He was a big ole motherfucker, and he had an ice pick in his hand, ready to use on the first person that disobeyed his order.

C-Style, Sonny and Dreamer went inside first, then Zulu. I went in last. Zulu went straight for the sweats and tennis shoes. Sonny went for the cigarettes and batteries. C-Style filled his bag with cans of tuna and chicken, while Dreamer filled his bag with hair care products and shaving razors.

I really didn't need any of this stuff. I already had most of the shit in my locker, and I stood there just looking around. I didn't need any more zoo zoos or wham whams, better known as potato chips, honey buns and candy bars.

C-Style said, "You ain't gonna take nothing, Ghost?"

Zulu chimed in. "Ghost a baller he doesn't need any of this shit."

"They have your favorite ice cream," C-Style offered, throwing me a pint of Rocky Road ice cream.

"Come on," I said. "We've been in here too long."

The men on the outside were becoming restless waiting for their chance to do some free shopping.

The yard looked like an atomic bomb had hit it. Every window in the institution was broken, flames raged in the chow hall and the education department. Even the barbershop building was reduced to a pile of burning nothingness. It was only a matter of time before the prison authorities rallied their troops and took back the prison.

My high was coming down and reality was starting to set in. I needed to get away from here. I mean my body was here amidst this insanity, but I could transport my mind back to Harbor City, or in the safety of my home, to the park where I played baseball or to the golf course where I collected golf balls. I thought about Bosco. When I was being groomed, I was never told that this is what happens when you're in prison. I was in a mad house. The year was only 1992. I would have to live in this kind of environment until 2007.

Angry men were running around taking out their frustration and making the system pay, while the Old Heads sat watching all the mayhem unfold, shaking their heads. The looks on their faces revealed their thoughts, but they remained quiet and calm. I saw power within them, an acceptance of circumstances and life choices. I felt only glimmers of that power when I was still and quiet. I felt uneasy most of the time, maybe it was due to the inexperience of my youth. I had no positive male role models. Shit, I learned how to shave in prison. That was the first positive thing I had been shown and it was by an old man I met in prison.

When I wasn't high or drunk, I didn't know how to keep the noise in my head quiet. The drugs and alcohol helped me to not to feel. I had become dependent on them to soothe the savage beast that was between my ears.

We all sat under a big tree away from the commotion. The helicopters were still circling, shining their bright lights on the inner compound.

A thunderous voice came from the bullhorn. "If you are not involved in the disturbance, walk to the softball field."

I saw the Old Heads slowly get up and head in that direction. I told the homies it would be best if we followed them. Everyone gathered their prizes. I pulled my beanie down and pulled up my bandana, blending in with the slow procession of senior citizens.

Lawrence recognized me, and gave me a look of disappointment.

"You youngsters have fucked up a good thing," he said.

Marcus, Bennie, and Vinnie chimed in, "Yeah, youse infants messed everything up."

I remained silent I didn't have any smart comebacks. Lawrence knew I was in internal pain. He put his arm around my shoulders like a grandfather would do his grandson and guided me to the softball field.

"De'Juan," he said, "You have a lot to learn. It's going to be a long and bumpy road for you. You have to find yourself, even in this kind of environment."

I just nodded in agreement.

The news helicopters were now flying overhead, capturing live footage of the mayhem below. This would all be over soon. We followed the slow procession of old men to the open field. One thing about the Old Cats they all seemed to have one thing in common. They were old and didn't have time for the prison politics. The four Old Heads were a perfect example. They all understood each other, and they played cards together and even went to the medication line together.

It was getting late and cold outside. The voice on the bullhorn continuously made the announcement, "If you are not involved in the disturbance, report to the softball field."

The flames began to die down and the smoke was beginning to thin out. There was a group of masked men armed with fire extinguishers standing in the courtyard, spraying the contents into the cold night air, which blocked the view of the helicopters and their cameras.

Watching the drama unfold from a distance, it looked like a real life war movie. Buildings were burned. Every window was broken. Glass was everywhere and everyone had become displaced.

"This is going to be our last day here," Zulu said.

"It will definitely be mine," I said. "Yelling my name out like that."

"My bad, homie, my bad," Sonny admitted, while taking off one of his shoes and removing a plastic bag which contained a dozen smashed joints.

"Damn, nigga! You been holding out on the sack," Zulu said.

"I'm a bank robber," Sonny said. "I ain't doing good like you guys. Don't no one send me money. I ain't got a female coming to see me. I'm broke! That's why I've been selling weed for Motel, Lou."

"Damn, homie. You could've been slanging for us," I said.

"Yeah, I tripped out homie!" Sonny admitted.

I understood how Sonny felt he was struggling to make ends meet, tired of depending on the three hots wanting to fit in, tired of doing without, he always wore the prison-issued uniform, while I had three different pairs of sweat suits. He wore only the prison issued boots, while I had three pairs of tennis shoes. He was trying to keep up and look the part. the Jones, it was called.

In the hood, it was the same thing. In order to get out of the poverty stage, fast money was the way out. It broke the cycle. It gave the illusion that things would get better if we had the right clothes and drove the right car, so the drug trade, and taking penitentiary chances, was our ticket to the good life, so we thought.

For most of us in the hood, education was the last thing on our minds because it took too long. Twelve years was long enough to be in school, and most of us didn't make it that far. We believed that the fast money would give us a better life. Well, it did for a short time.

Sonny was just like me, and thousands of others who got caught in the trap, wanting a way out of poverty, never thinking of taking the education route to a better life. I thought about the next generation that would follow in, our footsteps. Generations after generations of young men, and women following the path that would lead them straight to prison, we paid a big price just to look the part.

"Damn, homie! You ain't got to lie to kick it with us," I said.

"We all from the streets," C-Style added.

"I'm keeping it real and one hundred percent, homie. Everybody knows I'm broke," Zulu said.

We busted into laughter.

Dreamer added, "I braid all of the homie's hair. That's my hustle and I ain't ashamed either."

Dreamer got popped with six grams of crack cocaine and was sentenced to a decade of time. The crack was equal to the weight of six five-cent coins. He would spend ten years of his life in prison as a result. His arrest history gave him more time than the drugs, petty cases like stealing tennis shoes from the Foot Locker shoe store, clothes from the Gap, dumb shit like that. He just wanted to look the part, the Jones syndrome.

The softball field was becoming filled with inmates. I instructed my little crew to the far side of the field to finish off the last of the weed. If I was going to be transferred, I was going to sleep through it.

Lawrence, Vinnie, Marcus and Bennie didn't seem to be worried about anything. They didn't seem attached to anything. They'd been through it and seasoned to the game. I knew I was going to get transferred, and I would miss those four old men.

Lawrence was an unbending businessman who'd made his fortune in Tulsa, Oklahoma. He'd made millions in the drug game and bought a lot of property, then sold it to developers. His grandson got popped for a drug case and set up his own grandfather.

When the feds popped Lawrence, they got him with his hands dirty. He was sentenced to one hundred and forty-three years for flooding the mid-west with cocaine.

Vinnie was an old gangster, a true Mafioso. He still had a baby face that he was known for, and a high-pitched voice. He was a good old dude. There was a book that had been written about him.

Marcus Cole, he reminded me of Fred G. Sanford from that old TV show called *Sanford & Son*. Marcus followed the same path his father had. His father was a gangster and died a gangster's death in the United States Penitentiary in Marion, Illinois, which is a twenty-four hour lockdown facility. Marcus told me that his father died of a heart attack in an eight by six concrete cell.

Now Bennie, he was an old Jewish gangster from New York, who loved to play pinochle, talk shit and chew on cinnamon toothpicks. He was always grooming himself. Never a hair out of place, always clean cut. His hair and thin Abraham Lincoln-style mustache had become pure white during his twenty-five years in prison. He still had that intimidating stare. I had gotten to know Bennie, and would sometimes catch him staring into space. When he would snap out of it, his eyes revealed his pain and regret of things he'd seen and the things he would never see.

We joined the four old men on the bleachers.

"This youngster right here," Lawrence said, pointing at me, "He has the potential to be more than he is, but he believes that he can be no more than he is, so that's all he will be."

"He's lazy," Bennie said.

"Yeah, he is lazy," Vinnie, concurred. "All he wants to do is smoke that reefer and stay drunk."

"That's a damn shame," Marcus added.

The truth was, I believed that I was a gangster, a G from my hood. I believed that I could do no more than what I'd been groomed to do. All of my homies in my hood believed the same thing, and that repping the hood would protect it, and that selling drugs would give us a better life.

That belief had caused destruction in my neighborhood and created poverty. I looked around and saw hundreds of young and old men who believed the same lie.

Bennie looked at me with sad eyes. "Infant, I wish I could have believed in something else in my early days, but I believed in the wrong things, and by believing I was doing the right thing, I will spend the rest of my life in here. Believe in something good, Infant. Believe in something good."

Those words hit me like a Mac truck. What did he see in me? I felt it on the inside, but I didn't know what to do with it. I just remained quiet and so did the homies.

The Goon Squad was preparing to take the yard back. I could see them from the top of the bleachers, and there were hundreds of them in attack formation. In a sick way, I was enjoying the view from my perch.

A small legion of the Goon Squad advanced toward the doubled razor wired fence. At the command of their leader, they began to launch canisters of tear gas into the inner compound. We knew that it was over then, but there was still a large group who resisted. They would not surrender.

The Goon Squad entered the compound from the north entrance. They looked impressive from a distance, all lined up in formation. Five men across, and six rows deep in each legion I counted close to ten groups. They reminded me of the Roman soldiers I'd read about in history class, preparing to conquer another kingdom for the Roman Empire. In this case, it was the Bureau of Prisons Empire.

Some of the masked inmates fought back by throwing the canisters of tear gas back at the sea of black uniforms. The Squad was in full riot gear. They were equipped with plastic shields, bulletproof vests, gas masks, helmets with face guards, and those dreaded nightsticks with the little metal balls on the tips, which was used to separate the ribs. That must be painful. All their combatants wore were prison clothes.

As the Squad advanced, a small group broke off and marched in our direction. As they came upon us, I became disappointed, for they did not look very impressive up close. Most of them were old and out of shape. I recognized some of them. The foodservice foreman led the small group. His black uniform was too small for him. H looked uncomfortable and sweaty.

In his group was Ms. Castro, a sixty-something year old secretary in riot gear. Now what could she do? She wouldn't be able to stop nothing or nobody. Most of the rundown soldiers looked tired or hung-over. Half of them removed their helmets and fired up cigarettes. This was a joke and killing my high.

I guess they had someone working on the transformers because the prison sky lights began to glow orange. This was the sign that it was all over. The darkened prison became filled with bright light.

My little crew knew that we would be transferred as soon as order was restored. Lawrence, Bennie, Marcus and Vinnie, all looked at me, and they all knew I would be shipped.

Shortly after the power was restored, the fight was over. It was now just after midnight. I was dog-tired, my high was on crash mode and I was cold. Then half dozen greyhound-like buses drove into the prison.

The Goon Squad was now back in control of the prison. The entire perimeter was now manned by legions of guards dressed like Ninja Turtles with long nightsticks. The Commanders, or Suits, as we called them, surveyed the damage. The Warden looked pissed off to the tenth degree. His prison was destroyed, and it looked like an atomic bomb had hit it and you could still taste the charred remains of what was once called home to fourteen hundred inmates.

The sun was beginning to rise in the east. We had been out doors for several hours by now and the morning chill ran through my bones. I fired up a cigarette and inhaled deeply and let out a big cloud of smoke. I knew this would be my last day in California.

The day watch lieutenants led small groups of armed guards who carried shot guns loaded with salt rocks, and definitely would not hesitated to use them. I knew the guards were itching to use them.

We were put into bullpens and were separated into groups. The four old men were placed in the holding cell across from me with the other Old Heads. For a brief moment I felt a sadness engulf me as I stared through the Plexiglass window.

Lawrence saw me lost in my thoughts, staring into space, and then he finally got my attention. He raised his palm to the window, and closed it his hand into a tight fist. I understood what he was saying.

We were called out of the holding cells in groups of ten and strip-searched. Yeah, the same old routine shaking out your hair, opening your mouth, lifting your nut sack, and bending over and showing your ass. We were issued traveling clothes, a V-neck t-shirt, elastic waist-band pants and jelly sandals, then the ankle chains, belly chains and the handcuffs.

We were loaded into one of eight Bureau buses and headed to Vandenberg Air force base where a 737-jet airplane awaited. The staff called it Con Air.

CHAPTER 36

—

Con Air

As the plane came into view, I thought about the last time I was on an airplane. I was flying back from St. Louis in the first class section on a TWA flight, drinking Wild Goose, eating steak and flirting with the pretty flight attendants. This would be one of the many times that I would travel across the United States on Con Air airlines.

The Air Marshals were getting into position, forming a perimeter around the airplane with their guns drawn, as the buses stopped at the rear of the plane. To be honest, I was nervous. My stomach started to make funny noises and my hands began to sweat. I quickly glanced around the bus and saw the same look on the faces of the other men. We all felt the same way, but nobody admitted it.

The feeling of powerlessness had overtaken me, and I'm sure the others felt the same way. The Lieutenant boarded the bus and made an announcement,

"When I call your name, give me your registered number and birth date, and then exit the bus."

I was one of the last inmates called. As I exited and stood against the bus, I said a little prayer, holding the chains in my hand like they were religious beads, trying to focus on something other than getting on this airplane. The paperwork was transferred from the prison staff to the Air Marshals, and we were ordered to board the plane.

We shuffled in pairs of twos as if we were entering Noah's Ark. Once inside the belly of the plane; I sat by the window.

I looked out of the window, and thought that there was too much security. No one was going to come and try to free anyone, especially not at a military base. It would be suicide.

The plane was fully loaded. It was time to leave. I felt uneasy inside. I needed to stretch to shake my nervousness, but the chains wouldn't allow me this simple pleasure. Next, a voice came over the cabin intercom, as the Air Marshals went through their safety instructions.

The plane was in total silence as we watched and listened the last instruction brought sheer terror to every cell in my body.

As the marshal pulled out some bolt cutters, the voice over the intercom announced, "In case the plane loses all power, the Marshal is instructed to cut all restraints."

I prayed even harder this time, without showing it. Fear had set in, and I didn't have anything to help me with it, no wine or drugs. I had to face this fear sober. I closed my eyes and thought about my days as a child. I tried to summon pleasant memories when the days were simple and innocent. I wished I was a million miles away, not on an airplane chained up, and headed to an unknown destination.

The plane's engines began to hum and the marshals took to their seats. As we taxied to the runway, I thought about what the Pastor of the church had said during a sermon, "A reverent prayer of a righteous man availed much."

I knew deep down I was good. The core of me was good. I felt a little relief. We were cleared for take-off. The plane gained speed and we were airborne. As the plane climbed, I could see the entire valley and them the ocean. It looked beautiful. I briefly forgot about the chains and that I was on Con Air. I closed my eyes and said a silent. "Thank You."

CHAPTER 37

—

Valley of the Sun

I was awakened as the plane landed. My prayers were answered. I was on the ground again. I automatically wanted to stretch, but I was quickly reminded of my restraints. Looking out of the window, I saw a sign that read, Welcome to the Valley of the Sun. I heard an inmate say that we were in Phoenix, Arizona.

I was wondering when they were going to feed us. I hadn't had anything to eat since that ice cream the day before. On Con Air they didn't feed you like a regular airline, no steaks or Wild Goose, no one caters to you. You were told to just shut up and don't say shit.

I thought we were going to shuffle in a single file line through the airport with the regular people. I was wondering how the marshals would do it. Would they draw their weapons and heard us like cattle to the buses?

The plane continued to taxi past all of the terminals. We headed to the far end of the airport. Then the buses came into view. There were about fifty armed U.S. Marshals waiting for us, with an additional twenty or so prison staff. I could tell the difference by their uniforms.

The back of the plane opened as the U.S. marshal made an announcement. "When I call your name, stand up and give me you register number and date of birth."

The entire plane became deathly silent. I was one of the last inmates called to exit the plane. It was the same routine as before. We went through the preliminary searches, and then we were ordered to stand next to the bus.

"We in Phoenix," one guy said excitedly. "I got some homeboys here," he continued.

As we boarded the bus, one of my cohorts asked the prison staff, "CO, when you think our property will get here?"

"I don't know. You have a fifty-fifty chance of getting it," he replied.

Another CO spoke up and finished the answer.

"When you get processed into the institution, the counselor will contact the previous prison and let them know where you are, and they should send it."

I was hoping that my property would reach me. I took the necessary precautions of putting everything into a bag with my name on it. I appreciated that this CO was giving it to us straight. Most of the time they just lied to you to keep you quiet.

I thought about my letters and pictures, especially the ones of my uncle smiling. I really didn't care about the material stuff; I could buy new tennis shoes and radios. It was the things that came from the streets that I cared about the most.

We were now approaching the prison. There was a big sign on the highway that read, Do not pick up hitchhikers. When we turned onto black canyon road, another sign read, Federal Correctional Institution, Phoenix.

The prison looked like a college campus, except for the double fence with razor wire. The grounds were well manicured and cactus decorated the landscape. It looked like a resort from the outside, very clean, and it seemed peaceful in a strange way.

The BOP guards got into position as they had rehearsed thousands of times. Armed vehicles blocked off the entrance road to the institution. The showing of force ruined the brief moment of serenity I was having.

The weapon-wielding prison guards lined up in their strategic positions in full body armor with their AR-15 assault rifles. Riot pump shot guns were at the ready just in case someone was dumb enough to try to make a run for it. How far could someone running with leg irons and handcuffs connected to a belly chain get? It was beyond me, but it was their protocol to put on this show.

Once everyone was in position and the perimeter was completely secured, the front gate opened and the lieutenants came out to inspect the new arrivals. The senior lieutenant with the flattop and handlebar mustache was calling the shots. He stepped forward and gave a visual inspection of us.

"Take them to R&D and take off the cuffs and leg irons," he ordered.

The lieutenant's name was Pierfax, he reminded me of the Marlboro Man since he was smoking a cigarette. He was a tall man, about 6'5, a big red neck cowboy type. His face was deep red, maybe from the Arizona sun. He seemed peaceful and laid back. I later learned that he was a few months from retirement.

Once inside the prison, the landscape changed. Cameras watched our every move, there were one-inch thick steel bars mounted on window seals with bullet-proof Plexi-glass for windows, and heavy steel doors were always being slammed with an echoing *boom*, reminding you that you are locked up.

The intake process at Phoenix was the same as the other institutions I'd already been in. It was a big relief to have the chains removed. Being handcuffed with leg irons on for ten hours could drive any man or woman crazy, and I learned to focus my attention on pleasant memories rather than the cold steel chains that restrained my movement.

I had been locked up for two years and had already had three different addresses. The politics were the same. Segregation was alive and well in prison, and the blacks had their section on the yard and in the chow hall and the whites and Hispanics did too. The only thing different in Arizona was that there was a bunch of Indians that were added to the mix.

I had never seen an Indian up close. They all had long black hair and wore bandanas like in the movies. They were the only ones allowed to wear them. I was tripping off them because they seemed so different from us and didn't seem to fit in. In today's culture, I wondered who their leader was, what voice did they have and who spoke for them? They hated the white man. Well, that was no different from everybody else who hated the white man. Who didn't?

I learned that they had their own communities called reservations, which were on government land and poorly funded. Since most of the

Indians lived on the reservations, they really didn't interact with the outside world, and even in prison they didn't interact with the rest of the population. They were into their own culture, and most of the time I would hear them speaking their native language they fascinated me, they had unity and they knew their history.

Religion was a big deal in prison. Guys found God fast, especially if you didn't have a clique to be a part of. The Indians were given an area of the prison where they could have a sweat lodge. Only the Indians were allowed to go into the lodge. It was called Indian Territory. Indians don't like to be called Indians. Native Americans are their proper title.

I befriended a Native American who had the longest name I'd ever heard. His first name was Standing Yellow Horse and last name was Rides Like the Wind. Imagine that on your driver's license. He was a cool dude and he loved R&B music.

I asked him what tribe he was from, and he responded. "I'm Apache."

"Where are you from?" he asked.

"From Los Angeles."

"I want to go there one day."

"Yeah, it's cool," I added. "So you like R&B?" "Yeah, I do," he said.

"You ever heard of a group called Red-Bone? I asked him.

"No, I never have."

"Well, Redbone was a Native American R&B group in the 70s. They had a big hit called "Come and Get Your Love," I told him.

"No shit!" he responded. "What's your name?" he asked.

"They call me Ghost."

"I'm Standing Yellow Horse, but you can call me Yellow Horse."

"All right, Yellow Horse. I talk to you later."

We were housed in Yuma unit. This was the receiving unit for all new arrivals. I would call this home until a bunk was available in Mohave Unit, which would be my permanent residence during my stay in FCI Phoenix.

I hated Yuma unit. The rooms were only made for two men, but they squeezed three men into one cell. I was there for two weeks before I was transferred to Mohave unit.

CHAPTER 38

Cell Block M

I was moved to Mojave unit and assigned to cell number 153. This would be my new home for a while. The inside of the unit had the same triangle design as MDC with cells on the upper and lower tiers. The center of the unit was called the common area. There was an old pool table, which had seen better days. The fabric was faded and worn out with two big holes exposing a smooth black surface. I could see why the table had holes in it. The pool cues were broken and they looked like spears instead of pool cues.

Lining the outer section of the common area were four picnic-like tables. Each table was occupied by a different race. Some were playing chess and others were playing table games.

I stood by the stairs watching everything and thought to myself, "I have to spend the next fifteen years in this kind of environment." I felt heavy, and then despair engulfed my entire being. The urge to get high overpowered my thoughts. That's when I met Hopper and Fishbone.

"What up homie? Where you from?" they asked.

"Harbor City," I responded. "Where ya'll from?" I asked.

"We're from L.A. too," they answered in unison.

"What cell they got you in?" Hopper asked.

"In cell 153."

"Oh, that's homeboy Bull Dog's cell," Fishbone said.

"Where is he?" I asked.

"Here he comes right now," Hopper said.

"What up, Loc? Where you from?" Bull Dog asked.

"From Harbor City," I responded with authority.

"Right, right," he replied.

"They got me in the cell with you," I told him.

"It's all good," he said. "How much time you got?"

"Eighteen years and ten months," I answered.

"Damn, homie! They broke you off, didn't they?"

"Yeah, they did," I said.

He just shook his head.

Bull Dog was about my height and dark-skinned with a foo Manchu mustache and a fluffed-out afro. I could see in his eyes that he was just like me. This is not what he imagined his life to be. On the inside, he was in pain just like the rest of us. The rule was to never show who you really are outside of the cell.

After the introduction was over, we shook hands, not the normal handshake, but our own handshake, and then he pulled out a key and opened the cell door.

"What you doing with a key?" I asked.

"They give us keys to our cell here. You'll get one too," he said.

"No shit! That's some civilized type shit." I responded.

As we entered our cell, I threw my bedroll on the top bunk.

"You smoke?" Bull Dog asked.

"Hell, yeah," I replied.

"Come and let me introduce you to the rest of the homies."

We entered the TV room, which was filled with young black men my age and older. Some were watching rap videos on one TV and soap operas on the other a small table in the corner was occupied by four guys playing dominoes. On the other side of the TV room, a guy was getting his hair braided.

That's when Bull Dog made the announcement. "Hey, we got a new homie."

Everyone turned to look at me I noticed that the room was mixed with Crips and Bloods. The Crips and Bloods population was the largest in the entire prison. It gave the blacks strength and power. It was amazing to see so many black men getting along with each other. The

196

Blue and Red flags were respected, but the common banner was that we were all black, and we had to stay united, if not, then we would be conquered and the ceded land on the yard that we called ours would be taken from us. There was very little Set Tripping, which means that a Crip or a Blood would start politicking like they were on the streets, but that would be quickly squashed before it got out of hand.

In the chow hall, we had our own section. Just like the other prisons, you had to be black to sit there, and the other races had their sections too. By sitting together and sharing space and talking, which led to playing dominoes, which led to doing things together, we learned that we had shared similarities, and the common denominator was that we were black. This shed new light on the Crip & Blood issue. It was a belief in a color. It was a belief that we had to represent our hoods. It was building a reputation; it was gaining respect. That's why we were killing each other. I would learn later that it was all wrong but for now this was the life I must live.

A few months passed and I had found my position amongst my peers. It started on the baseball field and grew from there. One weekend the Warden had authorized an acknowledgement ceremony. He had authorized award certificates and bean pies for the most improved behaviors. My cellie was to receive an award for the most changed attitude and earning his GED.

The award ceremony was bootleg, but it gave encouragement to the men. Some of the men who received their bean pies ate them on the spot. When Bull Dog received his he wanted to take it back to the unit. The Warden had authorized in a memo that the awardees could take them back to the housing units. The Warden left before the ceremony was over, once he left, the night lieutenant entered the chow hall smoking a cigarette, followed closely by his Yes Men.

Lieutenant Lynch was his name. He was the kind of man who wore a white sheet at home. Evidence of his favouritism was the tattoos of lightning bolts on his arms, and this evening he had his sleeves rolled up to show them. His presence disrupted the entire ceremony.

Lieutenant Lynch stood in the doorway and asked, "Where do you think you're going with those pies?"

The chaplain quickly pulled out the warden's memorandum showing the names of those who were authorized to take the bean pies back to the unit. Lieutenant Lynch ignored him. With the warden gone, Lynch was now in charge of the prison, and he could do anything he wanted until the morning.

"Nobody will be taking food out of the chow hall," he announced.

The chaplain's face revealed a combination of frustration and uneasiness, while trying to maintain his composure. Pointing to the memorandum, he said, "The warden authorized the named inmates to take them back to the housing units."

Lynch didn't even look at the memorandum and he wasn't listening to the chaplain. He just puffed his cigarette with a devilish grin on his face.

"Look, Chaplain, the warden is not here. I'm the officer in charge until 6:00 a.m." he said.

The chaplain saw that he was getting nowhere with Lieutenant Lynch, and asked the food service foreman to place the bean pies in the refrigerator until the morning.

"Yeah no problem the food service foreman answered.

"That will not happen," Lynch shouted. "There will be no saving of the bean pies."

The tension in the chow hall was thick as fog the chaplain was doing his best to calm the situation. The hall was filled with a hundred black men that were starting to get upset, and then the mumbling started. I looked around the hall. Everyone was tense. Fists were bald into tight balls and I noticed that the guys' breathing had changed. Hate filled the hall it was like handling TNT.

"Dump 'em," Lynch ordered.

"What do you mean, dump them?" the chaplain asked.

"Throw them in the trash what part of that don't you understand?"

In front of everyone, he started to throw the pies into the trashcan as the chaplain and food service foreman watched in sheer terror.

We had reached our boiling point.

The chaplain quickly jumped onto a table. "I will straighten this out tomorrow, please remain calm, please!" he said.

The chaplain was a good man and well respected. He did his best to accommodate everyone, but he was powerless at this time.

The Old Heads were actually holding back the crowd of angry black men who wanted to charge forward and kill Lieutenant Lynch.

"Don't worry, we'll get more pies tomorrow," the chaplain shouted on top of the table.

It wasn't about the bean pies. It was about the disrespect. The older homies joined the Old Heads trying to calm down the growing anger. The chaplain had tears in his eyes. He was in complete disbelief of what this professional BOP officer was doing.

The chow hall quickly emptied as we silently walked back to our assigned housing units. Everyone was thinking in their head – something had to happen.

The Bureau of Prisons gives authority and power to people who abuse it. No wonder there are riots and guards get killed. The guards that treat the inmates like human beings are protected during such times. Only the asshole guards get attacked when the opportunity presents itself. BOP employees like Lynch create a dangerous environment for the prison system.

Once we were back in our cell, Bull Dog fired up a joint. It was much needed. We needed to relax and go over the night's events.

"That motherfucking Lieutenant is a cold piece of shit," I said to break the silence.

"Yeah, it didn't make any sense throwing all those pies away like that he just punked us," Bull Dog replied.

He passed the joint to me and I hit it deep, filling my lungs, and then blowing the smoke into the vent. I lay on my bunk feeling the effects of the marijuana and listened to Bull Dog talk.

"Hey, Ghost," he said. "Did you ever imagine you'd be here, doing all this time?"

"Naw, homie I didn't," I answered.

"How did you feel when the judge broke you off all that time?" he asked.

"Shit, just like I feel right now, high as a muthafucka," I said and we both started laughing.

"You are different, homie," Bull Dog said, "The homies talk about you. We see it in you."

I knew it wasn't the weed talking. I was being told the same thing from different people on the streets and in here.

"You got a good heart Ghost, and keep it that way. I'll holla at you in the morning," and he was off to sleep.

I lay there in the darkness listening to the birds chirp, wondering why I didn't see what people saw in me. Even convicts saw something in me. Why didn't I see it? Something on the inside of me was strong and it spoke to other people. Why didn't it speak to me, I wondered.

The vibration I felt was at a low tone. I liked it better that way. It made me feel weird, almost vulnerable. I wasn't in a place to have feelings; they had to be tucked deep away and forgotten about. I didn't need them. The only help I needed was my wine and weed to get me through this time because God wasn't there.

There was a light knock on the door around 3:00 a.m. It was a CO

"Washington, you have a UA," the CO said in a light voice.

"Okay," Bull Dog answered and began to get dressed.

The BOP can issue a random drug test at any time. Most of the inmates would use in the cells after lockdown. Where there is a pro there is always a con. You could beat the drug test by drinking a lot of water, which flushed your system. The CO didn't notice that Bull Dog was putting on three pairs of socks.

The holding cells didn't have any sinks or toilets. The COs would give you all the water you wanted to drink, and then lock you in the empty room. Once your bladder started to fill up, you just took a sock off and peed into it, then another sock, and another one, watching the color of the urine change from dark yellow to clear white, and when it looked like water, you were clean. Your system was flushed.

Bull Dog grabbed his coffee cup and finished the last of its contents. He grabbed my water jug, which still had cold water in it, and then he left.

When I awoke for breakfast Bull Dog, wasn't there. I thought maybe he was in the TV room watching the news. I entered the TV room and saw Fishbone and Hopper looking confused.

"Have ya'll seen Bull Dog?" I asked.

"No, we haven't. We're looking for some of the homies," they said.

A lot of the homies were missing. Other homies came out of their cells asking the same questions. Everybody was confused. It was almost 6:30 a.m. and the chow hall would be closing shortly. We went to the front door, but it was locked. Fishbone went to get the CO to unlock the door, but he was locked inside his office. Something was definitely wrong.

Looking out the front door window, I saw a line of water jugs on the ground.

"Hopper, come look at this," I said, pointing to the jugs.

We were on lockdown status. Only the lieutenants could open the door.

Then the announcement came over the PA system. "Mojave Unit, get ready for the morning meal."

As we exited the unit heading for the chow hall, the walkway was lined with coffee cups, water jugs and other personal items. It was evident they'd been told to drop them. The front of the other housing units looked the same. Personal items lined the walkways. I knew they'd been cuffed and taken away.

The administration told us nothing, but the homies who worked in the chow hall gave us all the information we needed. The prison system is like the Internet. Word can spread fast from one prison to the next.

One of the homies named Drac, who worked the morning shift in food service, had seen everything go down. He provided the needed information. The food service morning shift started after the 3:30 a.m. count to prepare breakfast for fourteen hundred hungry men.

As we entered the chow hall all of the administration personnel was there. The mood was quiet and no one spoke loudly. Standing in line, I made eye contact with the homie, Drac, as he was spooning watery eggs onto my tray.

"What up, Loc?" I said.

"They kidnapped all the homies who got an award last night and a few fuck ups," he mumbled. "We had to make one hundred and thirty sack lunches this morning."

As the line progressed he gave more information to the next homie in line. By the time we all sat down, we knew everything we needed to know. I really didn't have an appetite and neither did the homies Love or Hopper.

The information we gathered was that the homies had been put on a bus headed to El Reno, Oklahoma, which was the transit center the BOP used to transfer inmates eastward.

"Two minutes," the lieutenant yelled, letting us know to finish our morning meal.

Back in the unit, we were instructed to go the TV rooms where the warden was making an announcement. He apologized for the events that had happened and that his instructions were not followed.

Nobody really wanted to hear that shit right now and saying sorry just wouldn't fix it.

It was time to pack all of Bull Dog's property. All the homies did that for their cellies. That's just what you did. I took down the pictures of his kids that were taped to the inside of his locker and carefully placed them in his photo album. I took the batteries out of his radio and put them back in his shaving bag. I folded his sweats and placed his tennis shoes on top of them. I kept all of the donuts and cookies since the CO would throw them away anyway. I placed stamps in his phone book to pay for the pastries and I wrote my home address in his phone book with a note.

I made sure that his phone book was tucked between his sweats. An inmate's phone book is his link to the outside world. If you lose that, then you don't have anything. It is the most prized possession an inmate can have. Then I put his property by the door for the CO to take.

I knew that when Bull Dog received his property he'd be grateful that all of his belongings were there.

CHAPTER 39

—

Striking Back

I was watching CNN news when my favorite newscaster, Lynn Russell, came on with a story that caught my attention. There was this young white girl from Florida crying in front of Congress complaining that prison inmates were automatically given Pell Grants.

She said, "Criminals could go to college, but she could not. It's unfair!" she cried. A stream of tears ran down her face. The cameras zoomed in on her as her family tried to console her.

Before it was over, her closing comment was, "Do I have to commit a crime in order to get a Pell Grant to further my education?"

That was all that was needed. The Pell Grant Program for inmates was terminated shortly after that.

The Education department had set up about sixty computers that could be used by the inmate population. The whole world was beginning to use computers. The intention was to train inmates how to use them and learn the programs in order to be useful in the workplace once they are released.

Most of the population was excited about the computer-training course. To qualify for the computer class, an inmate had to be eighteen months away from his release. Everything was a go and the classes filled up quickly. Excitement and hope filled the education department. If a guy could become proficient in the use of these new computer programs, they would not have to revert to committing crimes. I saw the excitement in their eyes. I saw hope. They even stopped hanging in the TV rooms and they read their books preparing to start class.

Everybody knew that education was the key to the future. Once they were released with this new skill, they could compete in the workplace, and didn't have to return to a life of crime of selling drugs or robbing banks. They could become law abiding citizens.

The future looked good for them, but for the rest of us who still had a boatload of time remaining, it was still the same – get high and get drunk, lift weights, play dominoes, write letters and talk about our war stories.

When the termination of the Pell Grant program for inmates was announced, it was a sad day for the inmate population. You could see the change in the homies who were enrolled in the class.

An unheard negative vibe floated around the prison yard. The system was against us. I went to the recreation yard and met up with the homies walking the track. Everybody's mood was negative and I couldn't blame them. There were inmates huddled in their assigned places on the yard. I finally spotted Drac, Bear and Love and joined them.

"It's going down on Saturday after the noon meal," Bear said.

"The motherfuckers got to pay for this shit. They keep fuckin' with us. First they kidnap the homies, now they cancelled the computer classes. How much can we take?" Hopper said.

Everybody on the yard had the same feeling. Hearts and dreams were broken. The Machine had teased us, and it was time for the Inmate Empire to strike back. Saturday had arrived and business was as usual. Inmates were being called for their visits, housing units were called one by one for chow, and the recreation yard was filling up. Lines formed at all the ice machines, preparing for another hot Arizona Saturday in August. The time was about 11:00 a.m. and the temperature was already close to ninety-five degrees.

The word on the yard was that after the noon meal it would begin. Our unit was released for chow, and as we walked toward the chow hall I had noticed that some of the homies were heading back into their housing units. It was clear that they didn't want to be a part of it.

The ones who walked back to their housing units were the ones who seemed the most thugged out. They wore their prison khakis sagging, and always talking about how gangster they were, and they always frowned and looked like they don't give a fuck about nothing or nobody, and there they were, heading back to the housing unit. I lost respect for every last one of them.

The Crips and Bloods united for one goal – to take over and burn FCI Phoenix to the ground, sending a message to stop fucking with us. The ten-minute move was announced over the PA system. That meant that you have ten minutes to get to the housing units or the recreation yard before the inner compound closed.

During the ten-minute move hundreds of inmates filled the inner compound moving in different directions. It resembled the 405 free-way at rush hour. The move was over and there were still hundreds of inmates on the compound. The signal was when the announcement came over the PA system, and just like clockwork it happened.

"All inmates clear the compound," the voice over the speakers said.

That was the cue. The OTB and OTC were instructed to stay on the inner compound and divert the compound officer's attention. The letters OTB and OTC stood for Out of Town Bloods and Out of Town Crips. Those were guys who claimed Los Angeles neighbourhoods but were from states other than California.

When the Los Angeles drug trade took its business eastward to America's small towns and cities, these small town guys were fascinated by the Los Angeles gang culture, and the females loved the guys from Los Angeles. The Crip and Blood culture was different from the east coast gangs such as the Vice Lords or the Gangster Disciples. Those gangs had only one leader who called the shots, but they were organized. Crips and Bloods are independent but they're unorganized.

Most the OTC and OTBs were put on the set in prison and proved their allegiance to the Blue and Red flags.

"This is a direct order. Clear the compound," said the voice over the PA system.

"Fuck you," one of the inmates shouted.

Then it started. A large rock was thrown at the chow hall window, shattering it upon impact. Then the rest of the men joined in as a hail of rocks hit their targets. The chow hall was showered with stones. The inmates inside the kitchen ran for cover. The compound officers darted inside the lieutenant's office for safety. The yard went crazy. Half of the prison population was in frenzy, like sharks that smell blood.

The education bungalow where inmates took their GED test was set on fire. A group of masked inmates had broken the windows and poured baby oil on the curtains and lit a match. I knew what baby oil could do. Within seconds, the building was engulfed in flames. I watched in disbelief and the flames rose upward as a large group of men cheered.

A housing unit was next to the bungalow and the wind shifted, fanning the flames toward it. The flames reached the roof. The unit officer had locked nearly two hundred men inside a burning building.

Within a short time, the roof started to cave in. The inmates inside couldn't get out through the windows and I heard them screaming. "Help! We can't get out!"

The flames roared with a vengeance, and the combination of the fire and the ninety-five-degree dry heat made it almost unbearable to stand outside.

I saw the homie Shadow stick his head out of the window. I covered my face for protection from the smoke. This fire was moving fast, and the wind didn't help either. If something wasn't done quickly they would all burn to death, the flames roared like a forest blaze. They couldn't climb out of the small security window, only their screams escaped.

I ran up to the window to look inside, and saw Colombo standing next to Shadow. Colombo was a big motherfucker, about 350 pounds. He was from Washington. D.C. The roof began caving in on the west side of the building and time was running out. I told Colombo to use all of his weight to break the door down from the inside. Luckily, this was a bungalow door and not the regular steel doors because if it were, there would be no hope in saving them.

Colombo rammed his big body against the door, boom, boom, boom!

The homie Shadow, yelled out to me. "We can't get out! We can't get out!"

I quickly ran to the front door.

"Colombo, bang on that motherfucker as hard as you can!" I ordered him.

The smoke was starting to come out of the windows. The men inside were fighting for fresh air. They screamed in sheer terror as the building started coming down around them. I grabbed a fire extinguisher, but it was used up. It was up to Colombo to save the men.

Colombo couldn't fail in his mission to break down the door. I used the butt of the fire extinguisher to weaken the doorframe and it started working. The frame was starting to give.

"Harder, Colombo, harder!" I yelled.

As Colombo slammed his body against the door, all I could hear was a thick boom, boom, boom sound! I could feel the sense of desperation as he slammed against the door. Finally, the doorframe started to give.

"Harder, Colombo, harder!" I yelled.

With one last try the door fell to the ground and the two hundred frantic men ran into the clearing, gasping for air.

Every man inside the building was safe, just as the entire building collapsed. We all just stood there watching the flames consume the building.

"Everything is gone," one man said.

"All my shit is burned up," another added.

There was an ache in my heart. I felt for the guys who lost all of their personal belongings, pictures of their children, phone books, legal work, One guy was sobbing uncontrollably as one of the older men tried to console him.

"Ghost, you bleeding, homie" Shadow said.

I scanned my body, but didn't see any blood. "Where?" I asked.

"Your hand, homie" he said, pointing to the cut on my hand, as blood oozed from a lacerated vein.

Shadow found a first aid kit and dressed my wound,

"Keep pressure on this until it stops bleeding," he said.

"How do you know about this?" I asked him.

"Oh, I was going to be a paramedic before I caught my case," he answered.

"What happened?" I asked.

"I started making a few dollars and dropped out. I wish I could do it all over again," he said.

It was a well-known fact that most of us in here had other dreams for ourselves than drug dealing or robbing banks. Somewhere we just gave up got caught up in the immediate gratification. We were fooled by the glitter and gold. When did we stop believing?

Havoc and mayhem filled the prison. Commotion was everywhere. We headed toward the education department, and there I met up with Hopper, Fishbone and Love.

"What happened to your hand?" Love asked.

"I cut it on the window trying to get Shadow out of that burning building," I answered.

As we entered the education building, it looked like a bomb had exploded. Every window was broken and smoke filled the hallways. The law library was in shambles. Men ran up and down the hallways with their faces covered, screaming. We walked down the corridor and stopped in front of the computer room. Every last donated computer was destroyed. Tears filled my eyes, not from the smoke, but from the broken dreams that lay in ruin on the floor.

I really didn't care about the computers being destroyed because I still had fourteen more years left on my sentence. I felt sad for the guys who expected to get into school and learn these computer skills that was greatly needed for them to find a good job once they were released.

"This shit was fucked up," I thought. Thousands of men and women who would have never thought about going to college had the opportunity to better themselves before they were released, and here comes this little white girl crying in front of Congress because she couldn't get a Pell Grant. If her father or brother was locked up, she would want them to have an education. If it was someone she knew who needed to learn a skill or trade, she would have fought for them, but instead she caused hearts to be broken throughout the prison system. Hope was dead and gone in here.

"Come on, Ghost," Hopper called.

He was enrolled in the ceramic course in the recreation department and wanted to check of his projects. My hand continued to bleed, so we went to the back of the recreation department to find some fresh dressing. Ms. Lopez was a recreation officer and she had gotten trapped inside the building, so she hid in the storage room. When we entered the kiln area we saw her. The look on her face when she saw us revealed a deathly fear. There was no staff anywhere to protect her she was alone with fourteen hundred crazed convicts.

"Ms. Lopez, what are you doing here?" I asked her.

"I didn't hear anything," she said, as if pleading to a parent.

She didn't have anything to fear. She was a good woman and she was lucky we'd found her instead of some of the other inmates. Now we had to get her to a safe place.

The front entrance to the education department was out of the question. The inmate population controlled the inner compound. The only thing we could do was take her to the back of the recreation department where there was an emergency exit door so that's where we took her, and we could provide her protection.

"Ms. Lopez, do you have your keys to the emergency door?" I asked.

"Yeah, I do," she replied nervously.

I told Ms. Lopez to put on my jacket and beanie. Hopper and I escorted her down the hallway to the emergency door and we got there without incident. Ms. Lopez fumbled with putting the key into the lock. She was extremely shaken by the events. She couldn't say a word but the look on her face said enough. When the door opened she turned and gave us a nervous thank you smile and was off to safety.

We left the education building and headed to the recreation yard. It was total mayhem and reminded me of those movies of war-torn Germany during the Second World War. Buildings were reduced to rubble and chards of glass coated the pavement. Smoke filled the hot Arizona sky as helicopters circled the prison's air space. The prison staff had rallied their troops and attempted to enter the prison through the front gate. The only problem was that the adjoining building to the recreation yard was occupied by inmates who were on top of the roof, armed with sodium bicarbonate fire extinguishers, while others were armed with forty-five pound weight lifting plates as weapons.

As the staff tried to enter the inner compound, the inmates with the fire extinguishers blanketed the entrance with its contents, making it impossible to enter. The Goon Squad had zero visibility because the other inmates would throw the weights into the big clouds of white dust were suspended in mid-air. When the iron weights hit the ground they would make clanging" sounds,. It would have been a suicide mission to try to run through the clouds of white sodium dust in the blind.

Next, we headed toward the chow hall. Groups of masked men ran past us with mesh bags filled with products from the commissary or the prison store. The store had been completely looted. Shelves were empty and stragglers hunted for anything of value to put into their bags. Some of the masked men walked around in brand new sweats suits and tennis shoes. I knew that when the staff took the prison back, they would be the first ones on Con Air.

Surveying my surroundings, I thought to myself, "Why aren't I angry?" I felt sad inside. How would I live in this kind of world for the next fourteen years, because that's what it is... a different world. I tried not to absorb all this hate and anger that surrounded me, but how could I not? I ate anger for breakfast, had resentment for lunch, and hate for dinner just like the other men. I wondered who was the cause of this? Just like the other men in my shoes, we blamed it on society. We blamed our co-defendants, and most of us blamed God for dealing us a shitty hand and destruction was the effect.

Hours had passed and just like the Lompoc riot, it was time to call it a day.

The helicopter that circled made the familiar announcement from a bullhorn, "If you are not involved in the disturbance, report to the soccer field."

The Native Americans were the first to head in that direction, followed closely by the Old Heads and like before, I joined them. I found a spot and fired up the last of the marijuana. I needed to get as far away as possible for the journey that lay ahead because I knew I was going to get transferred.

The yard was filled with prison staff; they flooded the compound like a big wave of black army ants and enforcing their government given authority on those who resisted. They used plastic cords to cuff everyone, when my wrist were bound by the plastic cuffs, the wound I sustained began to bleed uncontrollably, I didn't know it at the time, I thought my hand was just sweaty, as I was told to stand I became very light headed, I couldn't see clearly, felt sick. That's when I noticed that I was standing in a pool of my own blood, a vein was cut, the plastic cords that bound my wrist were too tight, I lost a lot of blood. I was taken to the physician's assistant to stop the bleeding.

Once everything was under the BOP control, the buses were brought onto the compound and quickly loaded. As we were being loaded onto the bus, Ms. Lopez spotted me and Hopper and Love, and told the lieutenant that we had saved her and that's why she got out safely.

He just looked at us for a brief moment, shook his head and told them, "Ship them too."

I looked at Ms. Lopez and gave her the same thank you smile she'd given me a few hours earlier.

We spent the next several hours on the bus. It's what the BOP calls diesel therapy.

CHAPTER 40

—

If It Don't Make Dollars

It seemed as if an eternity had passed by the time we reached our destination. I was awakened as the bus rocked and shook when we passed through a security gate. It was already the next day. By the look of the sky, I figured it was late afternoon.

The cuffs around my wrist and legs bit into my skin leaving their vicious teeth marks. In a few hours the marks wouldn't be visible. There was dried up blood on my right hand. The stitches had worked and the bleeding had stopped.

We were ordered to exit the bus and led into the institution for processing. Every time you go into an institution it's the same process. The chains are removed, you're stripped naked and searched, then put into a holding cell with one toilet for only twenty people, but they cram fifty people in there. Next you answer some bullshit questions by a mean little Pilipino doctor with poor English, and then finally you're given a bedroll and assigned a housing unit. This process takes about ten hours to complete. By that time you hate life and everyone in it.

The homie Love and I were assigned to Arkansas One holdover unit. It was a four-story cellblock tier. The two-man cells were just a touch bigger than a storage closet with steel bunk beds bolted to the floor, with a sink and toilet combination, which made the cell even smaller.

We were to be warehoused here until the bureau found a place for us to call home. Love and I were put into the same cell on the third tier together, and we would remain in holdover status for an undetermined time.

"How long do you think we're going to be here?" Love asked.

"Shit, I don't know homie," was my answer, as I began to get my bunk ready for some sleep.

The noise was constant and irritating. It was going to be hard to sleep, but I was exhausted. I heard guys singing, while others were beating on the walls with their fists to make beats while their cellmates recited rap songs. If I wanted sleep I was going to have to work for it.

I listen to Love talk about his kids. They were supposed to come visit him this weekend in Phoenix, but now that was going to be impossible. Love was serving a twenty-seven year prison sentence for selling dope in Memphis, Tennessee. Two of his Tennessee workers got popped and set him up with the feds in exchange for their freedom. Being a Los Angeles gang member and selling drugs in another state is what got him all that time, and he was as bitter as a truck full of lemons. I wondered why he didn't drink or get high. Shit, I was getting high every chance I got, but he wouldn't, and I had less time to serve than he did. I wondered why he wanted to feel it, waking up every morning sober. People thought I was crazy for pleading guilty to eighteen years, but pleading guilty to twenty-seven was crazy too, but this was the ugly side of the game.

Love had a talent for drawing. He wanted to be a cartoonist, and when he was feeling sad he would draw. While in Phoenix, he would draw portraits of the homie's kids for them. That was his hustle. That night he started drawing on the wall. By the time I woke up to take a piss, he had drawn a portrait of his kids watching their daddy sleep. I instantly became filled with emotion. As Love slept, it looked like a real picture. Love was a good dude and my heart ached for him, but I couldn't really relate because I didn't have any kids. I was happy I didn't. His kids will be adults when he went home, probably with children of their own. How could God do things like this? We slept until morning.

The CO yelled, "Arkansas One, it's chow time."

I was starving. We hadn't eaten in twenty hours and the only thing on my mind was getting some food in my belly. My hand was puffy and bruised, but it would heal up just fine. We marched in a long line to the chow hall where the smell of the food made my stomach churn with anticipation. The chow hall was big. It had six different serving lines.

Love was saying something, but I wasn't really paying attention. I was just watching to see where all the blacks sat because that's how it was, even in a transit facility.

Every available place on my tray was filled. "They feed you good here," I thought. That's when I heard a familiar voice.

"Hey. Ghost. What up, homie?" a voice called.

It was my homie, Aaron Hill. He was working the serving line. The last time I'd seen him was in St. Louis when I had to bail him out. We had gone to school together when we were kids. I remember when he got put in the hood. It was the same initiation I had gone through, he loves the banging part of life in the hood. He was wild, always beating up the customers that came through, but it didn't take much to keep him happy. All he needed was a hood rat, two forty ounces of Old English, a fifty sack of some good weed, and a motel room for the weekend and he was straight.

I made my way to him. "What up, Loco?" was my greeting.

"Oh you know, keeping it one hundred," he answered.

"I heard that you got popped and that they broke you off a gang of time," he said.

"Yeah, they did," I replied.

"And the homies let them motherfuckers come back to the hood," he said.

"Yeah, homie they didn't do a damn thang."

"So what happened in Phoenix?" he asked.

"Motherfuckers burned that bitch down, so they shipped damn near everybody out," I replied.

"Yeah, homie, there are a bunch of cats from there here. I met some niggas from Compton named Big Bear and Mondo. They came talking all kinds of shit about how they wrecked the place."

I started to laugh because those were the two that went back to the unit before it all started, and now they were talking about what they did.

"Those motherfuckers didn't do anything as soon as it kicked off they went into the unit," I told him.

Word moves fast on the prison grapevine. There was nothing that couldn't be found out. It you are a Rat it will be found out, if there is some dope on the yard, it will be found out, if one of the homies is fooling around with a punk, it will be found out. There's nothing you can hide in prison, but the downside to it is the staff always knows who's doing what, because some of the inmates try to curry favor with the staff for transfers closer to home by giving inside information.

Reputation is everything in prison. If you have a strong rep you gain a lot of respect and the people will respect your name before they even meet you. People already knew my name, but they'd never met me. They knew that Ghost was a Rider, which means that I am down for whatever, and that I am a man of my word.

My peers knew that I took eighteen years on the chin and didn't fall. What they didn't know was that I hurt on the inside and that the time was killing me softly. They would call me strong, a true gangsta, but what I really was a lost little boy who was angry and bitter, and selfish and I wish I could leave all of them behind and get on with my life. That's how I really felt, but I couldn't show it.

"You smoking?" Aaron asked.

"Nigga, you know I just got here. No I ain't smoking," I responded, laughing.

"Here, take this pack with you, and I'll have a care package for you at lunch," he said as I tucked the pack in my waistband.

"What about some chronic and zoo zoos and wham whams?" I asked.

"Don't trip homie, I got you," he responded.

Since I was in holdover status I didn't have access to the yard or the commissary. Our movement is restricted and supervised and I had to depend on the homie to provide the comfort I needed during my stay in El Reno.

It felt kind of good to have a homie from the streets here and we did hang out occasionally. The big homies didn't want me to run the streets like the homies my age; it created a conflict with the homies. I was treated differently than them because I was being groomed to lead them.

When Aaron started getting too hard to handle, his mother had sent him to St. Louis to live. When he came back to visit, he said that they were country out there and that big money was to be made.

It was the summer of '87 when Aaron pulled onto the set in a 1987 Mustang 5.0 convertible sitting on Dayton's. He said that ounces were going for eighteen hundred dollars.

"Eighteen hundred?" I asked curiously.

From that day I was done curb serving. I didn't like selling crack on street corners; it was too dangerous. We had to watch for the police, and at night there were drive-by shootings, and with all the competition, it would take long hours to make eighteen hundred dollars. The idea sounded good, and I'd get to see a different state, since I'd never left California.

I was making good money, but it was hard. Everybody and their momma were out slanging. I tried to make my quota of five hundred dollars a day. Some days I made just a little over, and other days I would make a little under, but the thought of making eighteen hundred dollars started me thinking.

There was a lot of money to be made in the projects, especially in Harbor City. The white folks from Palos Verdes, Torrance and Lomita would come down and spend thousands and go back to their safe communities to get high. There were more white people in the projects than black people in the daytime. They were the best customers.

It was time to take my hustle to the next level. I sold my '77 Cutlass Supreme for thirty-five hundred dollars, and with the money I had saved and I bought a half-kilo of cocaine, and was on the next bus headed for St. Louis. I arrived at 12:20 p.m. and sold out by 1:00 p.m. I made twenty-one thousand; six hundred dollars before I finished unpacking my suitcase, and caught the plane back to L.A. the same day feeling rich.

I sat in my first class seat on a TWA flight back to Los Angeles and wished that I had brought more with me since I didn't like catching the bus because it was too long of a ride, and taking bricks of cocaine on the airplane was risky, too many security checks.

Now Aaron, he was hard headed, didn't like to listen, just plain hard-headed. He didn't want to catch the bus, so he decided to take the plane. I told him that it was too risky to catch the plane, but he wouldn't listen. I told him to at least change clothes, and not to wear those baggy clothes because he would stand out in a crowd, but still he didn't listen. He was arrested when he landed in St. Louis. The undercover narcotics officers found only two ounces of crack cocaine in his back pocket.

Because of his criminal record, he was given a ten-year federal prison sentence, which could have been avoided.

"Damn, homie, I should have listened to you," he said.

"Can't anybody tell you shit," I answered.

"Yeah, you right. I go to the hole here all the time," he said with a smile.

Before I left the chow hall I reminded him of my care package.

"Don't trip homie, I got you."

Love had walked up and he wondered whom I was talking to.

"Oh, my bad homie. This is my homeboy from my hood," I said as I introduced Love to Aaron. They greeted each other with the Thug Hug and then we were off back to Arkansas One.

It only seemed like an hour before we heard the call for the noon meal.

"Wake up, Ghost," Love said as he shook me. "It's chow time."

I popped up and ran down three flights of stairs not wanting to miss lunch. I saw Aaron standing next to the beverage bar looking nervous.

"Damn, nigga, that's probably why you got popped, looking like you up to something," I said.

He handed me three packs of smokes, five street sized joints, which were going to be broken down to make ten descent joints, and eight candy bars, which were for Love, which I stuffed into my socks. I was happy that the homie came through for me. Shit, he owed me ten thousand for posting his bail, a few joints and candy bars was just the start.

CHAPTER 41

—

The Bigger They Come

When we were back in the cell I realized that I didn't have any matches. Love was busy enjoying his candy bars but me; I wanted to get high. I really didn't need any matches. I was very resourceful when I had to be, and the solution to my dilemma was in this unit somewhere. I just had to find it.

I walked down to the first floor and saw this dude who called himself V-Mac. He was a big motherfucker from Los Angeles. He was sitting at the domino table listening to a walk-man radio but not really listening to it because he was running his mouth about how tough he was and what he'd do to someone if they disrespected him. I really didn't care for dudes like that, it was a sign of weakness, and the ones at the table with him believed that bullshit he was talking. He was just a bully, but he had something I needed.

I approached the domino table, focused only on him. "What up, homie?" I said.

"What's up?" they all answered.

I acted like I was interested in the game, just waiting for him to ask me a question.

"Where you from?" V-Mac asked.

"From Harbor City," I responded.

"Where you from?" I asked.

"I'm from South Central."

219

"You know Man Power and Wish Bone?" I asked.

"Yeah, they the homies. Wish Bone just got two life sentences. He's up in Marion, and the homie Man Power got out of the game and is a dental assistant."

"Damn! No shit?" I asked acting surprised.

I really didn't care. I just needed the batteries in his radio.

I pulled V-Mac to the side and asked if he smoked cigarettes. "Hell yeah, I do," he said.

I told him that I would give him a few smokes if I could use his batteries to light my cigarette.

"Okay," he said.

"I'm going to need your batteries so I can light my cigarette" I said.

He looked curious as we entered his cell. I pulled out two staples and placed one staple on the negative part of the battery and the other on the positive. I used the stainless steel sink as a ground. I put the cigarette in my mouth, touched the two staples together and the tip of the staples began to glow orange as I puffed on the cigarette. V-Mac watched in amazement as puffs of smoke began to fill the closet-like cell. I jumped on the table to blow the smoke into the intake vent.

Cigarettes are a rare commodity when you're in holdover status. You have to know somebody on the yard in order to get them. While you're in holdover status, you're basically locked in a building all day. You do not have a job, and there is no recreation. You just sit and wait for the next bus or plane to take you to your next destination.

As we puffed on our smokes, the scent of tobacco escaped the tiny cell, which caught the attention of V-Mac's followers. They started to gather in front of the cell looking with hungry eyes, hoping to be offered a drag.

"What the fuck you nigga's want?" V-Mac barked.

It was clear they wanted to a nicotine fix just like everybody else. I took one more drag off my cigarette and handed it to the guy closest to the door. He looked grateful as the others waited for their drag. I always felt like a provider throughout my whole life. I provided in good ways and in bad ways, but this very moment, these men sought comfort in smoking cigarettes, so I provided for them and handed out three more cigarettes for them to smoke.

"Thank you, Ghost," the men said as I walked through the crowd, "Youse a real nigga," others said. I had to earn their respect with only a few smokes.

The holdover unit reminded me of an old warehouse with bunk beds. It was always cold. The men would walk around with their blankets on, trying to keep warm. The high warehouse-like windows were all broken allowing the Oklahoma wind to sweep through, keeping the temperature just above fifty degrees. That's where the pigeons entered, flocks of them cooing all throughout the day and night, their droppings decorated the walls of the first floor. The smell was almost unbearable.

The men huddled in groups. The religious guys continued their practice. The Christians would have their Bible studies in color-coded groups. The Muslims would perform their prayers throughout the day and the Jews would huddle and complain that they needed their kosher meals. Every one of the religious criminals would complain to the chaplain that their needs weren't being met.

When the crowd dispersed, I pulled out the good stuff. V-Mac looked on with anticipation.

"You got it going on," V-Mac said.

I stood on top of the table as he stood on the steel toilet so we could blow the smoke into the vent. I lit the joint and took a long hit, then passed it to him. Before long, we were both high as kites and our surroundings didn't seem that bad and we both smiled and laughed. Everything was okay.

We exited his cell in a good mood. The marijuana had us floating. I stood next to the wall and told V-Mac to lift me up so I could look out of the window to see if I could recognize anyone who passed by.

"Hey, homie, lift me so I could look out of the window," I said.

I didn't catch the look on his face at first. Something was wrong with him; he was deep into his head.

I asked again, "V-Mac lift me so I could look out of the window."

"Nigga, who the fuck you think you talking too?" he barked.

That's when everybody turned in our direction. I was stunned too.

"Nigga, I'm Ghost from Harbor City nigga. That's who the fuck I am!" I barked back. "Who the fuck you think you are" I continued.

"Nigga, I'm Big V-Mac," he replied, now standing over me.

221

"And what's that supposed to mean?" I asked sarcastically.

At that time I only weighed one hundred and fifty pounds and was about to square off with a guy who outweighed me by a hundred pounds, but my heart or stupidity wouldn't let me back down. My reputation was at stake.

We continued the stare down, and before I knew it, his fist came out of nowhere hitting me square on the forehead, sending me falling backwards into the brick wall. Everything seemed to be in slow motion. When my 150 pound frame crashed into the wall I was knocked back into reality, but my quick instinct allowed me to pop back up and in one fluid motion I grabbed the pencil on the table and lunged forward stabbing V-Mac in the shoulder with all my strength, which basically only made him madder.

He picked me up like I was a child and slammed me into the concrete wall. My entire body was off the ground with my feet dangling. He continued to slam my body against the wall, my head hitting the wall. I began to feel dizzy and my body began to relax. I was beginning to lose consciousness.

"You little motherfucker, you going to stab me?" V-Mac screamed.

I was at his will I was powerless I couldn't match his strength. He had me outweighed by a hundred pounds, and I was defenseless against him. I had never taken a beating like this before. I was being handled. I felt blood trickle down the back of my head from my skull slamming against the wall. The stitches in my hand opened up and I had lost the ability to get loose. I am not going to lie to you. I wished a CO were nearby to save my ass.

Out of nowhere, the homie Love came to my rescue. He was not as big as V-Mac, but he was very strong. He ran up from behind V-Mac and put him in a choke hold, yelling "Put my homie down, put him down!"

I felt V-Mac's grip loosen and I wiggled my way free. By this time a crowd had gathered. Love had V-Mac in a death grip, he was gasping for air. This was my opportunity to strike back. My head was bleeding and the stitches in my hand were ripped open but my head was starting to clear and rage filled me. All I wanted was a light and that's how I was treated?

V-Mac was flailing in Love's chokehold. That's when I hit him with three solid blows to his face with my elbow. The last blow put him to sleep. Blood squirted from his nose and mouth and his body went lifeless, but he was breathing. We dragged his big frame into the cell.

"What are we going to do with him?" Love asked.

"I'm going to tie his big ass up," I answered.

"What happened?" Love asked.

"Man, this nigga tripped out after we smoked some bud," I replied.

A group of people surrounded the front of the cell watching. Even the religious criminals wanted to see the action.

I took the sheets off his bunk and began to tear them to make rope to bind V-Mac's arms and legs. Once he was secured, I stuffed his big ass under the bottom bunk thinking about what to do next.

The word spread that Ghost had got into it with Big V-Mac. The crowd was getting bigger just to see a glimpse of V-Mac knocked out and tied up under the bottom bunk.

"Back the fuck up!" Love ordered the crowd. "This is Crip business," he barked.

V-Mac was beginning to wake up and he started making funny noises. I ripped more sheets to make sure he was tied up properly. I put the makeshift rope around his neck just in case he gained full consciousnesses and if he tried to break free I would yank on the rope, choking him.

One of the homies named C-Train came busting through the crowd ready for battle. When he saw me sitting against the wall holding the rope, he started to smile,

"Man, I thought you was fucked off," he said. "All I heard was the Ghost was getting down with V-Mac. That's when I came running," he said

C-Train was a big motherfucker too. He weighed about two hundred sixty pounds with twenty-four inch arms and a big-ass chest. He looked like a light-skinned Mike Tyson, all tatted up. He had done a lot of State time. When he found out I was from Harbor City, he told me he did time with some of my big homies, therefore I had the same love. That's how it is in the penal system.

"Yeah, homie, Love got him off me," I said and introduced them.

"What happened to his face?" C-Train asked.

"I hit him with three stiff elbows," I answered.

"What are you trying to do, hang him?" C-Train asked.

"No, just trying to keep his big ass secured," I replied.

"Don't trip. I got this mother fucker," C-Train said.

V-Mac began to stir and then he opened his eyes. As I stood over him ready to put him back to sleep, he noticed that his legs and hands were bound, and that there was a rope around his neck, with three angry motherfuckers looking at him.

"You awake?" C-Train asked.

V-Mac acknowledged him.

"Then why you fucking with these lightweights, nigga? I'm a heavy weight and your size," C-Train said.

"I tripped out homie. I fucked up," V-Mac said through bloody lips.

"So you still want to get down with somebody in your weight class?" C-Train asked.

"Ghost is my little homeboy, and you ain't got no reason fucking with him, pushing your weight around with these lightweights. Nigga you don't get no points like that," C-Train said.

"Untie him," C-Train said.

As V-Mac sat on the edge of the bed, surveying his mouth, I stood next to C-Train and Love stood on the other side of V-Mac ready to punish him if he made a foolish move.

"Something inside of me goes wrong when I smoke weed," V-Mac admitted.

"Weed?" C-Train said, looking at me. "You got some weed, Ghost?" C-Train asked.

"Yeah, I do," I said sheepishly. I was going to break you off some, but I wanted to get high, so he had batteries so I blessed him with one, then he flipped the fuck out on me. "Love saved my ass," I admitted.

That day my reputation grew. I was known as a rider, down for whatever, and would fight anybody regardless of their size. To tell you the truth, it was my homie, Love, who saved me. If it hadn't been for him, V-Mac would have inflicted greater damage on me. Love, he was the real hero. I guess it was the fact that when V-Mac hit me, I engaged with him even though the odds where in his favor. In prison, you can't ever show fear.

V-Mac's last words to me were, "Ghost, you a down ass little motherfucker. Niggas love you."

V-Mac was serving a thirty-three year prison sentence, and he hurt on the inside. I felt his pain and his punches. We would become friends later on during our sentences. I learned a valuable lesson. If you're going to get into a fight, be the one to throw the first punch.

CHAPTER 42

—

On The Road Again

It was about four o'clock in the morning when the CO tapped on the bars of my cell.

"Verrett," he said softly. "Roll it up. You got twenty minutes."

I slid down from the top bunk and began to wash my face and brush my teeth. Love was visibly sad, even in the shadows of our tiny cell. This was where we parted ways. It was going to be hard leaving him. We had gotten tight during our road trip. He didn't say a word. He just watched me.

I tucked four cigarettes into my sock, then stood on the toilet to get close to the vent and fired up a joint. Still, Love just watched. I needed to get high. It helped me get through this crazy world called prison. Still, he watched. I gave him the rest of the zoo zoos and wham whams because when you're in holdover status, you can't transfer with any property. The weed and cigarettes he could sell for stamps. I wondered why he didn't smoke or drink. The twenty-seven years he was serving should have been cause enough, but he was different from me.

Love watched for the CO as I finished smoking, I thought to myself that we had been rolling tough since Phoenix. He had come to my rescue, but I got all of the props. It was he who saved me, but he just rolled with it. We formed a tighter bond deeper than most blood brothers do.

"You got my hook up, don't you?" I asked him.

"Yeah, I do," he said checking the back of his property slip.

227

We heard the footsteps of the CO coming in our direction. It was time. Love and I gave the thug hug as the cell door slid open. I proceeded down the tier. I looked back and saw Love watching me, keeping an eye on me as long as he could. I turned and fist-tapped my chest, letting him know that he will always be with me and he returned the gesture.

"Stay strong, homeboy," Love said, as the CO ordered him back into the cell.

I watched as the cell door closed. He still stood there watching. The last image of I had of the homie Love was him standing in the doorway with both arms sticking outside the bars.

As I was led out of the unit, not knowing where my next destination would be, a wave of sadness and despair overcame me. This wasn't a good feeling to have in prison and it was happening more and more and it was fucking up my high. When you have a good cellie you could confide in each other. You share things you wouldn't say outside of the cell. Your cell was a place of safety when it came to feelings.

Cuffed and shackled, I was seated next to the window on Con Air headed probably east, no doubt. Sadness and self-pity was deeply engrained in every cell of my body. I tried to switch my thoughts to something else because if I didn't I would dwell on these feelings until we landed and I couldn't allow that to happen. I wished I had smoked two joints instead of one because I needed to numb this pain.

We were on Con Air for eleven hours, which was enough time to fly across the Atlantic Ocean to Europe. When we finally landed, one of the air marshals said that we were in Oakdale, Louisiana.

Oakdale was a small hick town. The prison was located in the middle of a swamp area called a bayou. I had never been to Louisiana before. I kind of half expected to see a burning cross or some shit like that. You know, every time they show an old racial movie, it's mostly in Louisiana where the streets are filled with 4x4 trucks with confederate flags and gun racks in the back window.

My family is originally from Louisiana. When my grandma was about twelve years old her family left Louisiana and headed for California. That was in 1935 and they wanted to get as far away from the KKK as possible.

Aunt Sissy was my Grandma's eldest sister, and her husband Prophet Jones was attacked by the KKK on his way home one evening. They caught him and beat him then tied him to some railroad tracks letting the train run over his legs leaving him to die. That's when they moved out west to California. When I was a kid I had wondered why he was so short, but I'd never asked why and or what happened to his legs.

They bought a small piece of property in San Pedro and built a nice house. Prophet Jones built that house with his own hands, proving that you can do anything. My Grandma raised ten children in that house.

I had resentment for this state and I knew that I wouldn't last here long.

CHAPTER 43

—

The Dirty South

The compound officer led a small group of us to our new housing unit, Oakdale. It wasn't any different from the other institutions I had been in in Arizona. It was hot, but the weather here was hot and sticky. I was already starting to sweat before we entered the housing unit.

The inside of the unit had two tiers. The cells lined the perimeter of the large rectangular structure. I was assigned to the first floor in a standard-sized concrete cell equipped with the steel framed bunk beds bolted to the floor, a toilet and a sink. I dropped my bedroll on the top bunk and went to walk around the unit to see if I knew anybody.

There were four TV rooms on the ground level; a room for the blacks, one for the whites, one for the Hispanics and one for the Old Heads. At first, I thought I had walked into the wrong TV room because there were three white boys in there. They were watching "Yo MTV Raps". They all looked at me as I entered. I had never seen anybody with gold teeth, especially white boys. One of them even had his hair braided.

"What up, Yo!" the one with all the tattoos said.

"What's cracking?" I responded.

"Where did you get in from?" said the one with the braids.

"From El Reno," I answered.

"Where you from?" the one with the braids asked.

"Los Angeles," I answered.

231

"You got some homeboys here. They're on the yard right now," he said. "What's your name?" he continued.

"My name is Ghost," I replied.

We all shook hands. It was weird to see these young white kids looking like this. Back in the day I had a white homeboy named Snow. He used to hang in the hood with us, but he didn't look anything like them, no braids or gold teeth. Hell, we didn't even look at him as being white.

One night Snow came to the hood to kick it with us. He had just gotten out of the hospital from being shot in the leg. He had to use a cane to walk. This particular night, some females came by from San Pedro to buy some weed.

"What's up, Ghost?" they said from their car.

"What's going on?" I answered.

"We want to buy some good chronic," they said.

I had told Snow to serve them because he needed the money. Shortly later they came back with two guys I didn't know, claiming that the weed was no good and they wanted their money back.

The two guys they brought with them stepped out of the car. "Who was the one that sold them this bullshit weed?" they demanded.

They made a big mistake coming into our hood asking questions and demanding a refund.

My homeboy, Trip, was about to get crazy. He reached for his pistol ready to pop a hot one in their asses but I stopped him, letting these two fools have their word.

"Who sold my cousin this bullshit weed?" they barked again.

"It was that white boy who sold it to us," Melissa said, pointing at Snow.

Snow looked around baffled.

"Yeah, you motherfucker!" she screamed.

We watched as Snow erupted and said. "Bitch, I don't see any white boys around here all I see is gangsters."

We all busted into laughter because Snow didn't consider himself white. He considered himself a gangster. That's when the homeboy, Trip, pulled out his pistol and pointed at them, telling them to empty their pockets.

They did what they were asked out of fear of being shot, then they received the ass whooping of their life. When the females saw what was happening, they burned rubber, leaving them behind. Those dudes were in violation and we couldn't let them leave without punishing them.

I left the TV room and headed for the pool table. A game had just finished and I asked, "Who got next?"

The old man looked at me and motioned for me to grab the available pool cue. He reminded me of the reverend Al Sharpton, hair and all, but older.

"Where you from young man?" he asked.

"California," I replied.

"You look familiar," he said, as we started the game.

As he broke, each one of the balls fell into different pockets,

"Open table," he said, caulking his stick.

"You got some kin" around here?" he asked.

"No, I don't," I answered.

He was a good talker. He was blessed with the gift of gab. I learned that he was a realtor and that he had been in that business for forty-eight years. Now he was serving time for cheating people out of their houses, and selling houses he didn't even own for high profits, and I could see why, because he was whooping my ass on the pool table. Before I knew it, he called, "eight ball in the corner pocket."

"What's your name young man?" he asked.

"My government name is De'Juan Verrett," I answered.

"Verrett, he said, making a funny face, "Are you kin to Lionel Verrett?" he questioned.

"No, I don't know anybody named Lionel Verrett," I answered.

"Are you sure, because you favor him?" he asked.

"I ain't got any family here. All my family is in California," I answered.

"That's where Lionel moved to for a short time. He went there to build some houses in - I think, Compton, because that's what he did, he built houses." he continued.

This old head was relentless with his questioning. I was too ashamed to tell him that I didn't even know my own father, let alone my grandfather. I knew no history of that side of me. I would later find out that my grandfather had another family which had produced one child, daughter, and she would grow up to be the world famous Shirley Verrett, the opera singer. It saddens me that I never had the chance to meet her in person. I also learned that we shared the same birthday, May 31st.

"Okay, youngin', I'll talk to you later," he said, heading to his cell.

I started to wonder, who was this Lionel Verrett? Furthermore, why was this Old Head so persistent in his questioning? I had been told that I looked just like my biological father, and that he looked like his father. My mind started to fill with questions. I was instantly brought back to the when I was twelve, when I found out that Mark wasn't my father. I didn't want to be filled with those thoughts. I needed to fill my mind with something to smoke and drink.

I returned to my cell to take a nap. It was hot and humid, so I opened the window to feel the breeze, which was a big mistake, because when I woke up I had mosquito bites all over my body. I should have known because the prison was in the middle of a swamp, and they must have smelled my fresh blood because they took a lot of it.

My cellmate returned. He was from Beaumont, Texas and called himself Hay Stack. He was a big ole motherfucker and soft spoken.

"Here, use some of this," he said as he handed me a can of Off mosquito repellent. I was already starting to itch, and the heat didn't make it any better.

Hay Stack just started laughing and said, "Welcome to the dirty south."

I heard mosquitos buzzing around the cell all night. I didn't get a wink of sleep.

CHAPTER 44

—

Hate the Game

The next day I met all of the homies from California. They blessed me with some prison wine and some good weed. We sat on the yard exchanging war stories about the streets. Before we knew it, it was getting close to the four o'clock count, which meant that all inmates must return to our assigned housing units to be counted, so we all agreed to meet in the chow hall for dinner.

"Hay Stack, what's for chow tonight?" I asked.

"Um, I think beef ribs," he answered.

Good, I thought, because I was starving. Our unit was released for chow. The chow hall was loud and filled with inmates seated in their color-coded sections. The men talked while enjoying their meals. I heard the sounds of pans dropping to the grounds getting everyone's attention. The food service foreman eyed every serving person, making sure everyone received the same portions.

I expected the rib bones to be cut every inch to deter inmates from turning them into weapons, like they do in west coast prisons, but they weren't. The line server put two six-inch ribs on my tray with a scoop of macaroni. Roscoe and Malo held a seat for me at their table. I sat and inspected the ribs. They weren't cut and I would take them back to the unit. They would be my weapons just in case I needed them. Living in a hostile environment you have to keep some kind of weapon. You can't take your fists to a knife fight.

"Hey, Roscoe. They gave me whole ribs. Are your ribs cut?" I asked.

"Naw, homie they're not," he answered.

"Malo, how are your ribs" are they broken?" I asked him.

Malo touched his side, rubbing his ribs, "Naw, homie my ribs not broken," he said.

"No, man, the ribs on your plate. Are they broken?" I repeated.

"They all in one piece," he finally said.

"Malo, give me your jacket," I ordered him.

"Why?" he asked.

"Because you're going to carry them out for us," I told him.

I wrapped a few pieces of bread in a napkin and placed them in my jacket pocket, knowing that the COs standing outside would spot them and stop me while Malo would calmly walk past the gauntlet of guards.

"Hey! Stop!" the CO called. "What's that in your pocket?" he asked,"

"Oh, just a few pieces of bread to make a sandwich later," I said.

Just like I had planned, they stopped me and ordered me to empty out all of my pockets, while Malo casually walked by. Malo was what we call a crash dummy. He did what he was asked in order to prove himself. He was trying hard to be a Crip and to be a part of the gang culture, and almost every other word that came out of his mouth was Cuz this, or Cuz that. Crash dummies had their uses, but their loyalty was questionable.

We made it back to the housing unit. During this time of day, the unit was scarcely populated. I told the homie Roscoe to get me some sandpaper and a Folgers coffee lid and some tape.

They returned from their scavenger hunt and met me in the inmate laundry room. The unit was practically deserted. I had to quickly make use of this opportunity. There were four washers and four dryers located on the second floor. I taped the sandpaper onto the Folgers lid, and forced the lid onto the agitator of the washer. Once it was secured, I turned the washer on spin cycle.

The speed of the spin cycle and the grade of the sandpaper were just enough to sharpen the three rib bones into perfect daggers within minutes, which would pass through any metal detectors. I gave one to Roscoe to stash in his cell. I also stashed one in my cell and told Malo to stash one on the yard just in case we needed it at a moment's notice.

Now Malo, I should have paid more attention to his behaviors, he was a loudmouth that always seemed to piss off somebody. The day before he had gotten into an argument with a Nigerian about something stupid, and the knife he was to stash on the yard, well, he used it and stabbed the Nigerian on the weight pile. This happened right before lockdown and I was already in my cell drinking with Hay Stack.

The next morning I woke up with a hangover and Hay Stack asked if I was going to breakfast. I quickly washed up and went to Roscoe's cell so we could walk together. The front door was locked. It was about 6:30 a.m. Then I went to the CO's office and there he was, locked in the office. Something was wrong.

I didn't know that someone has been stabbed on the yard the night before, and the institution was on lockdown.

"Roscoe, where is Malo?" I asked.

That's when Malo's cellie walked up and told us the news that he'd been taken from the yard last night for the stabbing. I looked at Roscoe and shook my head knowing that he was going to tell everything. I returned to my cell and began to pack all of my property because I knew that they were going to come for me. We went into Roscoe's cell and chained-smoked four joints. It was only a matter of time before the Goon Squad came for me.

Just as I predicted, they were coming, marching in formation chanting their cadence in full body armor, plastic shields and night sticks. Intimidation wasn't their strong suit; it was in their numbers.

I stood at the door of my cell smoking a cigarette watching everything unfold. I knew I would shortly be in handcuffs once again. The Goon Squad was now inside the unit. At a distance, they looked like fierce terracotta soldiers, but up close, they were nothing more than case managers, counsellors' and food service employees dressed in riot gear.

This time they brought a video camera. I guess to use as a training film for future employees.

I quickly fired up another cigarette to enhance my buzz, blowing big plumes of smoke. That's when the guy with the bullhorn called my name.

"De'Juan Verrett," slowly walk to the middle of the common area and lay face down," he barked.

I looked at Hay Stack with one of those 'here we go again' looks. "Take care, Ghost," he said.

"I will."

I continued to blow big clouds of smoke as I walked toward the mob of fake terracotta soldiers, noticing that everyone was watching from their cell windows. I stopped in front of the pool table and snubbed out my cigarette on the green material; burning a small hole just out of spite. I raised my hands while turning away, and then I lay down on the cold tiled floor as they began to handcuff me.

There was no need to say anything. I'd just wait to be given my lock up order. As I was being escorted to SHU, or Special Housing Unit, which is an 8x6 concrete cell, the CO told me that I was under investigation for a stabbing.

"A stabbing?" I thought.

And that's when it became clear. Malo, that mother- fucker, stabbed somebody last night. I knew that he must have told them that I gave him a knife. Then I thought about the knife I had stashed in my cell. No matter how much they would tear the cell apart they would never find it. Shit, Hay Stack didn't even know where it was. Then I thought about Roscoe. Would he keep his mouth shut? I was having bad luck with people telling on me.

I was placed in AD, or Administrative Detention pending investigation because I wasn't found guilty of anything. When the BOP starts an investigation, they could prolong the process. It could take one day or up to ninety days, or if they wanted to fuck with you, they could get up to three extensions, meaning you could remained locked in a 8x6 cell for nine months without ever being found guilty, and anything longer than that without a finding of guilty is considered cruel and unusual punishment by the Supreme Court.

Only twelve days had passed since I had arrived in Oakdale. This was a bad start, I thought, as I stood handcuffed in the tiny closet-like cell and the door slammed behind me. The big steel door was designed with a small opening to slide food trays through. When it opened, the CO ordered me to slide my hands through to remove the handcuffs and then that was slammed closed.

I wondered how long would I have to live in here. Not long I thought, because they don't have anything on me. It was just Malo's word against

238

mine. Then I thought about when I was arrested. I didn't get caught with anything then either. I was starting to get paranoid. Was it the marijuana making me think like this? I needed a drink to calm my nerves.

The cell was filthy it needed to be cleaned from top to bottom. The last man who'd occupied this prime piece of real estate didn't care about the next man. Before the CO left I asked for some cleaning supplies.

A few hours later the CO returned with the cleaning supplies and my bedroll, which consisted of one thin sheet, one wool blanket which looked itchy and inside my bedroll was some nasty ass tooth powder, a small tooth brush, a roll of toilet paper, and a small plastic cup, the kind your kid sister used to play with when she was three or four years old.

I began with scrubbing the walls. There were hundreds of names etched into the vomit green paint. My name would not be added to the list. It was said that if you wrote your name on any part of the prison that you would return to see it and I had no plans on every coming back to Oakdale.

The shift had changed and the OIC, or Officer in Charge, by the name of Sinclair, was making his rounds and he stopped by my cell to drop off the lockup order.

"Here's your lockup order, Verrett," he said, sliding it under the door.

As I scanned the document it really didn't say anything, just that I was being held pending investigation for an undetermined amount of time.

"You smoke, Verrett?" he asked.

"Yeah, I do," I answered.

He slid a few smokes through the food trap and lit my cigarette.

Sinclair seemed cool. He would come by every hour on the hour to ask how I was doing and light a smoke for me. It seemed like he cared. He wasn't hostile or aggressive. I knew he had been in the military from his buzz cut hairstyle. I guess if you get the same hair cut for years, it becomes the only one you like.

The first few days I was smoking like a man on death row. I was starting to go through withdrawals. My body ached. I needed to get high. I was restless and irritable. I began to lash out at anyone who stopped by my door. I wanted answers but nobody would give me any.

I couldn't even get the time. When I would ask, one of the smart mouthed COs would sarcastically say, "You got somewhere you need to be?" which would send me over the edge.

I began to flood my cell by clogging the toilet and flushing it several times until it overflowed, running under the door into the hallway and down the stairs. When they would bring the food trays, I would throw them back at the COs. I would also beat on the doors for hours. I was beginning to go crazy.

The cell began to get smaller. I could touch both walls when I extended my arms. I could walk the length of my cell in only four steps, and lights… they were never turned off. It was constantly bright in my tiny closet. I couldn't sleep, I couldn't think, I could barely breath I needed an escape. I needed to get high. I needed something. I couldn't go on like this.

There was a knock on the door and I rushed to see who it was. It was the PA. It seemed like all of the PA's were Phillipno ladies, and they were some mean little bitches.

"Hello, Mr. Berrett," she said with a thick accent.

"It's Verrett with a V, not B, I said, correcting her. She just dismissed my comment.

In my file, it states that I am an asthmatic. She had come to give me my inhaler even though I didn't need it.

"How's your breathing?" she asked.

"I'm having a hard time," I answered.

Then she gave me a bottle of Sudafed to clear my sinuses, just what I needed because they contained Ephedrine in them. I grabbed them fast before she changed her mind and I quickly swallowed four pills.

I paced around my cell waiting for them to dissolve, enjoying the anticipation of slowly getting high. Every cell in my body seemed to rejoice and thank me. My attitude instantly changed. I had gotten some relief. My pulse quickened. I felt good inside and the BOP was going to supply my need as long as I was going to remain in this closet.

The high was wearing off too quick, so I increased my dosage from four to seven. Then I doubled that to fourteen little red pills in one day. Then my heart started to beat too fast. Something was wrong. I began sweating profusely. I was losing control of myself. I started to panic.

Had I taken too many of those little red pills? I jammed my finger down my throat, trying to force myself to throw up, but nothing came out as my eyes instantly filled with tears and my breathing changed. I couldn't catch my breath. I tried to stand but lost my balance. My heart was beating too fast and chill bumps covered my body. I clinched my chest with both hands, hoping to slow my heart rate down but it didn't work. I tried to scream for help but nothing came out. I was alone. I was going to die from an overdose of Sudafed in a closet in Louisiana. A shockwave of fear engulfed my soul. I was scared. All I could do was close my eyes and hold my chest, then a name shot through my mind, GOD... GOD, please don't let me die, please don't let me die, not like this, please..."

CHAPTER 45

—

Welcome Back

I heard someone calling my name from a distance. "Verrett, Verrett." As the voice became louder, I could hear them more clearly now. I still couldn't quite make out who was calling me. Then it began to get brighter and brighter. I opened my eyes to see who it was, there was a face looking through a small three-inch window, I recognized the face, it was Sinclair.

I was back, gaining consciousness. I raised my head to smile at him and he returned one to me. I was alive. I lay in my bunk just breathing, but still clinching my chest with both hands. Then I remembered that I'd almost died from those little red pills. God had saved me once again.

The smell of urine was strong. I carefully used one hand to scan my body. My boxers and sheet were saturated with urine. I wondered how long I'd been unconscious. I didn't want Sinclair to see me with pee stains on my boxers. I slowly rose to my feet, steadying myself using the top bunk, while using my left hand to cradle my chest. I lightly tapped on the door to get Sinclair's attention.

"What's up, Verrett? Back amongst the living?" he said with a smile.

"Yeah, I am, Sinclair. Can I get some boxers and a new sheet?" I asked.

"Yeah, no problem. I'll bring some right up," he replied.

Before he left, he opened the food slot to let some air into my cell. The smell of urine saturated my tiny closet. He returned with clean sheets and a cotton blanket instead of the wool blankets and some boxers and socks.

"Verrett," Sinclair said, "you were sleep for a day and a half. You wouldn't move and you were saying something we couldn't understand and you held your chest tight with both hands. Do you want a shower?" he asked.

"Yeah, I do."

When you're in SHU you only shower two times a week. The other four days you have to take a birdbath in your cell. I was hand cuffed and led to the shower cage. Once inside, the cuffs were removed. I turned on the water letting it warm up and then stood under the showerhead letting the water drench me, hoping that it would wash away this sadness I was feeling.

Sinclair returned with a small bar of Bob Barker soap and a shaving razor. I thought there was no need to shave and declined it. I just wanted to clean my body and get the urine smell off me. I lathered my body twice before the small bar of soap was used up.

The water felt great. My mind drifted to when I was at home, getting fresh and clean to go out and have a great time somewhere, but in this case I was getting clean to go back into my cell and stare at the walls. My shower time was up. I dried off and put on some clean boxers and a t-shirt, got cuffed and was led back to my cell.

The shower water felt good, but it had a lot of chlorine in it, which made my skin very dry. I didn't have any personal hygiene items with me. Luckily, I had saved some of my fruit. Bananas make for a good skin moisturizer. I also used orange peels for deodorant, and I used butter for hair grease. When you're locked up you can become very inventive.

Now instead of smelling like urine I smelled like a supermarket. I just laughed at myself. My sense of humor was coming back as I sat on the edge of the plastic mattress thinking what do I do now. I instantly began to sweat by sitting on the plastic. I needed some extra padding to keep my body from sweating. Each week when they did laundry exchange I would give them a half a sheet, so each week I would add extra padding to my bunk.

I still had nothing to read except for the names on the wall and my lockup order. I started to wonder when somebody was going to come and tell me something. I began to grow impatient once again. I had gained my strength back and decided to get some attention by flooding my cell and raising hell. That should bring somebody to talk to me I thought.

It wasn't right that they were keeping me in here without talking to me. I felt like I'd been kidnapped. Then they cut off the water to my cell. No biggie, I thought, so I banged of the door continuously, and when they came with the food trays, I would throw them back at them. When the PA came by, I was going to ask for some more Sudafed, but thought better of it. I wanted to get high, but I wasn't willing to take that chance again.

Everyone ignored me but Sinclair. He would talk and offer me cigarettes. He took care of me and I respected him for that, but he couldn't answer my questions. Later that day, Sinclair appeared once again with a look of concern.

"Verrett," he said in a low voice. "Come to the door."

"Haven't I looked out for you since you been here?" he said.

"Yeah, man, you have, but these motherfuckers ain't telling me shit," I answered.

"Can I trust you, Verrett, because I need to tell you something? I need your word as a man that you won't say anything," he said.

"I'm solid as a rock. You got my word," I answered in a low voice.

Sinclair knew that he could trust me and I felt that I could trust him. When he worked late night, he would open the food slot and slide me some home cooked food, like crawfish. I had never eaten a crawfish before. They looked like little lobsters. He even brought me some nudie magazines. I knew we had formed a bond of trust.

I put my ear to the little hole in the door and listened. What I heard melted my inside.

"They are going to keep you in here for nine months," he whispered.

"What?" I said as if I didn't hear him correctly.

"They are going to keep you here for nine months," he said again.

"Nine months?" I said, not believing it, but what reason did he have to lie? It felt like the wind had been knocked out of me. I became light headed.

"Don't worry," he said. "I will be the number one officer next quarter. I'll take care of you."

245

I'd only been in the hole for two weeks, and to be told that I would remain in this fucking closet almost a year was unbelievable.

"It will be okay," he said. "Now remember, you gave me your word."

"Yeah man, don't trip. I got you," I replied

"And you have to stop flooding your cell and throwing trays, because if you do it again they are going to four point you in the dry cell," he said, looking straight into my eyes.

The thought of being four-pointed instantly brought some Act Right to me the dry cell was where they took inmates who were suspected of swallowing balloons of drugs in the visiting room. The dry cell is a concrete room. In the middle of the room was a concrete slab. You were stripped naked, your arms and legs were outstretched and bound to each corner, you were spread eagle, and you stayed there until you had a bowl movement. You remained like that for a mandatory seventy-two hours. Every few hours a CO would come to check of you to see if you had defecated. That was totally dehumanizing. You couldn't even clean yourself. They just ran water over you.

My cell was starting to look really nice compared to the dry cell. I wondered how I was going to spend nine months in there without going crazy. It would be May or June by the time I got out of there. What the fuck was I going to do?

I wanted to get high. I really needed a drink to calm me. I had nothing to help me with this grief I felt inside. I couldn't take any more pills. Shit, I was too scared to even take one! I would have to deal with this sober and feel every second of those nine months. I was alone with only my thoughts. How could I live in the now? How could I face reality sober? Who would help me get through this? I closed my eyes, trying to find a place of peace and comfort, searching for an answer. I couldn't find any.

CHAPTER 46

—

The 411

When you are locked up, mail is the most important form of communication with the outside world. It connects you to the streets. Any man or woman who is locked up will agree, and when you're in Special Housing mail is extra important.

After the first two weeks, I didn't receive any mail, no correspondence from anyone. I figured that my mail was being held back as a form of punishment. I was in transit for almost two months before I arrived in Oakdale, so I guessed that my mail hadn't caught up with me yet. Then one day Sinclair passed a bundle of letters through the food slot. My heart raced with excitement as I tore open the first letter. It was from Lizette.

I had met Lizette back in the day at the Long Beach mall. She had kept her promise and sent pictures of her wearing lingerie. She really didn't say much, only that she missed me and to give her a call.

The next letter was from Krystal. I had known her since we were kids. We met at a public pool one summer. We also went to the same junior high school and the same high school. In her letter, she told me that she had just found out that she was adopted.

I opened the next letter. It was from Tisha, and she told me that she was pregnant by this dude from a different hood, and that I didn't know him and this would be the last letter I would receive from her.

I really couldn't blame her or anyone else. Just because I was going to be locked up until I was almost forty didn't mean that their life must end. I knew my name would eventually fade away as every year passed, and the next generation would only hear stories about me. They wouldn't even know my face, just my name my immediate family would only remember me.

I opened the next letter it had a card in it from my mother. Her letters always started the same way, "In the name of Jesus," then she wrote a quote from the Bible. I enjoyed her letters even though they were preachy. She talked about my sisters, and how they were doing. Then she talked about work, and what was going on at the church, and that Pastor Cotton and the Prayer Warriors were praying for me. Their intentions were good, but none of that shit worked. God wasn't here, not in this closet I was in, it was just me.

The last letter I received was from my homeboy Pookie. His letters always started off with, 'what's up, Ghost?' I hope this letter finds you in the best of health and spirits."

Well, my health was good, but my spirits were low. I only received letters from him and one other homeboy. Everybody else had already forgotten about me in only four years. The Brotherhood that I thought loved me really didn't. I gave my loyalty to my hood and everybody in it, and out of hundreds of people only two wrote to me. Being Ghost from Harbor City was a pillar I stood on, and without that who was I, I had nothing else, It was my claim to fame.

Whenever Pookie wrote to me, he would give me the 411 on what was going on in the hood, keeping me updated. I was shocked when I read that the homeboy Jerome Parker was found dead. My heart started racing as I continued reading.

Jerome was the neighborhood bully; he used to chase me, and my friends around the projects when we were kids. He never hurt any of us. He just loved to punk us. After the chasing stage of our life was over, we hung out together.

The chasing started when we were playing Ping-Pong in the patio of his mother's house when we were kids. On this particular day when I was playing, he snatched the paddle out of my hand when I was in the middle of a game.

248

"Why you tripping, Jerome?" I protested.

"Shut up yellow boy," he said as he pushed me into the washer and dryer.

He began taunting me, backing me into the corner.

"What you going to do about it yellow boy?" he asked as he stood laughing over me.

Jerome was only three years older than me, but it made a big difference. I was only ten at the time and he was already a teenager. He intimidated me. I was filled with fear as I huddled next to the washer and he laughed and turned away. I felt ashamed and embarrassed as everyone laughed at me. I had to do something. I had to fight back somehow. That's when I reached for the box of laundry detergent. I didn't realize the box was open, and I threw it at him.

Jerome had just gotten his hair done with a day old greasy Jheri Curl. The box hit him on the head, covering his hair with the soap powder.

"My curl, my curl!" Jerome screamed.

Everyone started laughing while he was trying to dust the laundry detergent out of his greasy Jerry curl. Even his face was covered, which gave me time to hop the rickety old back yard fence and escape on my bike. That's how the chasing started.

Jerome chased me for three years, but never caught me. I outran him on foot and on my bike, wherever we were someone would make the call, 'Here comes Jerome' and we would take off like a flock of birds. One day I was walking back from the store for my mother, and I saw Jerome coming in my direction. My first instinct was to run, but this time I didn't. I turned to face him. To tell you the truth, I was just tired of running and that day I was going to make my stand.

Jerome grabbed me, and I grabbed him back as we wrestled in the grass just off the sidewalk. No punches were thrown, just wrestling. I thought that he would be stronger than he was, but he wasn't. I was just as strong as he was. Three years had passed since I'd made physical contact with him. I had totally forgotten about my growth spurt. I was just as tall as Jerome. Our wrestling match ended in a stalemate. There were no winners or losers as we both stood to our feet breathing hard, dusting ourselves off and staring at each other. Then we both started laughing. Our feud was officially over. I was his equal now and we have remained close friends since that day.

As I read Pookie's letter, he informed me that Jerome was dead, not by violence but due to an accident. I couldn't believe the words... Jerome dead... it couldn't be. I continued reading and learned that he had died in his mother's back yard hopping that same rickety fence I'd hopped when I hit him on the head with that box of laundry detergent. Pookie said that Jerome was getting a brick wall built to replace that old fence in the back yard to secure the property and the project was just starting.

Jerome came home drunk that night and decided to hop the back gate instead of going through the front door of the house and waking up his mother. When he climbed the fence he lost his balance and fell on top of the re-bar that impaled him, killing him instantly.

The next morning Mrs. Jenkins went to Jerome's room to check to see if he needed anything washed, but he wasn't there. It wasn't uncommon for Jerome not to have slept at home. She went to the back yard to start a few loads of laundry and that's when she saw Jerome laying on the ground in a pool of blood.

Pookie had also sent Mrs. Jenkins' phone number in case I wanted to call and send my condolences. I thought about how my Grandma must have feel when she had to bury my uncle. It must be a horrible unnatural sight for a parent to have to bury a child.

One of the toughest things for a man in prison is to lose a loved one. It makes you think about your own life and how short life is. I felt sad for Mrs. Jenkins. Her heart must be broken just as my Grandma's had been. I needed to make a phone call.

"CO!" I yelled. "I need to make a call."

No one answered.

I began banging on the door yelling, "CO, CO! I need to make a call."

Still nothing. I continued kicking the door with the heel of my bare foot; loud echoing thuds reverberated throughout the Special Housing Unit, but still nothing.

"I need to use the phone!" I yelled, but my pleas went unanswered.

There was nothing I could do. I was powerless. I wasn't in control of anything. I was locked in a closet twenty- five hundred miles away, and I couldn't do anything to comfort Mrs. Jenkins. Completely frustrated, I sat on my bunk with my back against the wall. I began rocking myself, trying to shut out everything.

Nothing seemed to work. I became tired of being tired and I curled myself into a little ball, hoping that sleep and the darkness would help me escape the grips of sadness and despair.

CHAPTER 47

—

Woe is Me

I knew the time was 11:00 p.m. because that's when the lights in my cell were dimmed, and that's how you know the shift is changing and they stay dimmed until 6:00 a.m. When you're in Special Housing Unit, you gain a keen sense of everything. I knew the CO's schedules. I knew their voices, and even how they walked.

I lay in my bunk for hours feeling hopeless and unnecessary, staring at the blank walls in my cell. I saw my entire life played out like I was at the movies. It was one of the saddest shows on earth and it was a true story.

As I looked at the wall, I saw everything I had ever done wrong. I saw nothing positive. I saw what I had become and I saw no future. I saw myself taking the place of the old men that sat in front of the liquor store in the neighborhood talking about the old days. That scared the shit out of me. I couldn't see my future. I felt lost, but what could I do different? I only knew how to survive in the streets and in prison and nothing else. I never wanted this kind of life for myself. I had never been shown a different way. Yeah, I'd been told, but not shown.

I felt that vibration from within me kick in, but this time I couldn't drown it out with prison wine or drugs. I paid close attention to it this time, and it felt good. I closed my eyes and honestly cried out to whatever was out there and said, "If you're there, please help me... please."

CHAPTER 48

—

The Traveller

The darkness brought peace and serenity to my tiny cell it delivered comfort in a weird way. I tried to sleep as much as possible so my mind could wander. I would dream and go anywhere in the world I wanted. I could be whom I wanted. I could be successful and I could be loved. I could even help the world be a better place, but the new information I needed was somewhere in the darkness of the universe. When my eyes were closed it felt like I was one with the universe. I begged the universe for answers, but when my eyes where open, I hurt on the inside. The darkness kept me safe and I didn't have to hurt more. I found peace in the darkness.

I had lost everything my money, my property, and my freedom. Now I was at the breaking point of losing my mind. Insanity penetrated my thoughts. I was now losing my will to live. I stopped caring about anything and everybody. I stopped caring about keeping myself groomed. I just wanted to keep my eyes closed as much as possible.

I felt myself being pulled into the cloudy darkness of my thoughts as I travelled deeper and deeper into the murky abyss of hopelessness. I was losing my will to continue with life. I felt broken, useless and unnecessary, so whooped by life that only death could protect me from the pain I felt inside.

I felt my soul leave my body and pace my small concrete closet. I saw myself curled into the fetus position. I looked peaceful, childlike in a way as if I was in the womb of my mother, in total darkness and safe from the world.

I stood over my own body studying the figure laying in the bed. My hair was braided and wrapped in a doo rag cap that was made from the sleeve of a t-shirt, and I had grown a thick beard. I looked old and beyond my years, like an old man in prison. As time passed, I didn't resemble De'Juan or what I thought I should look like. My soul was deteriorating and I was turning into someone I didn't recognize. The man I saw wasn't the man I saw on the inside the system was winning.

I was turning into a fixture of the system. I was becoming a part of the prison, just like the bunk I laid on, just like that toilet and sink, just like that mirror bolted to the wall, just like the bricks and bars that confined me. I had lost; I begged for freedom, the freedom to breathe fresh air, the freedom to bask in the brilliance of the sun, freedom from the torment of self; I just wanted to be free.

That night I learned that freedom is an internal concept, an inside job. It all starts on the inside with simple things. My body was telling me something. I had to pee and I rolled over and stood on the cold tiled floor and in only one step I was at the toilet and sink combination. I leaned over to pee placing my right hand on the wall to brace myself.

I felt instant relief as my bladder was relieved of discomfort and pressure I felt better. It is crazy to think that peeing could be more than just a bodily function. This might sound funny, but peeing was the beginning for me to look within myself.

As my bladder regained its freedom, my right thumb touched the cold metal of the stainless steel mirror. That simple movement caused me to focus my attention on the image in the mirror. I was slightly bent over as I looked into the mirror and I saw a pair of eyes in the reflection.

For a split second I thought someone else was in the cell with me and I turned to scan the room. I was still by myself. I wondered if I was going crazy. My heart started beating fast, not from the Sudafed, but from emotion and excitement that I had some company. I instantly became wide-awake, and someone or something was in that mirror looking at me. They gave me a caring gaze.

The eyes in the mirror looked compassionate, warm and caring. They looked deep within my very being, and they knew me. They were real; I wasn't going crazy. I flushed the toilet while continuing my focus on the eyes in the mirror. I couldn't pull away. I was scared that if I left the mirror the eyes would disappear. I didn't even blink.

I was lost for words, I couldn't even speak; I was hypnotized, enthralled in the warmth of those caring eyes. Who did they belong too? Why did they show up now in this closet I lived in? I believed that they were there to listen to me. It was a different from the looks I got from the COs or from my cellies. They were there just to listen and understand without being judgmental. They understood how I felt and what I was going through.

I grabbed the toilet paper roll and broke off a few squares and dabbed them with water just enough to make them stick to the mirror. I then covered the bottom half of the mirror. I only wanted to focus on the eyes. They eyes looked patient as I made my preparations. It was going to be up to me to make the first move. Everyone had abandoned me and I didn't want to hesitate for fear of the eyes leaving me also.

My mind raced to find the right words for my introduction. I wanted to sound intelligent and friendly. "What's up?" were the first words I blurted out. Fuck, I thought, I didn't know how to talk to anybody any-more. The eyes seemed to know what I was thinking, and they had an amused look.

I was rusty; I thought my head was going to explode as I struggled with trying to find the right words. I cleared my throat and took a deep breath.

"Who are you?" I asked the eyes in the mirror, but they didn't answer. They just seemed willing to listen, those eyes looked confident and strong. They also made me feel comfortable, giving me the courage to open up and reveal what I felt on the inside.

I kept my eye on the door, just in case one of the COs walked by making their rounds. I didn't want them to see me talking to a mirror. They wouldn't understand. They would think I'd lost my mind. Shit, if I saw somebody talking to himself I would think that they'd gone crazy.

I tried again, taking a deep breath letting my words escape as my voice trembled. I focused on the eyes in the mirror. I fired up a cigarette before I spilled my guts, letting the smoke obscure the image in the mirror.

"I am my mother's first-born child," I said. "She was seventeen years old when she had me, and I never knew my real father," I continued.

I was about to say something that I had never told anyone before. It was a shameful feeling to know that I was conceived by force instead of love, that my beginning wasn't pretty, and that's why I lived an ugly life.

The eyes in the mirror just listened; they didn't even flinch, which gave me the courage to continue.

I told the eyes in the mirror, "I was shuffled around to my eight uncles. It was cool, but it was different from having my own daddy. I had learned to live without one the substitutes weren't the same; I felt half lost, not knowing the full me."

The eyes still listened as I took a long drag from my cigarette.

"When I was a kid I used to hate myself," I confessed. The eyes seemed to have the 'Why?' look.

"One day, when I had learned that Mark wasn't my real father, I wrote on a napkin, 'I hate myself. DLV.'"

Writing that on that napkin was my way of reaching out for help. I didn't know why I did it, I just wanted to put it on paper and get it out of my head.

One of my uncles found the note and sat me down in the back yard. He had a serious look on this face. At first I thought I was in trouble, but he asked, "Why did you write this?"

Crying in his arms, I told him it was because my own real father didn't want me, and that my mother liked my sisters more than me, and that I was always being teased because I wasn't dark enough and I didn't look like my friends. My uncle just held me and told me that there was nothing I could do about it. "Dee," he said, "We have to work with what we have."

I felt a bit better talking about it to someone. I just needed someone to listen to me. The eyes in the mirror just looked at me as I continued to beat my gums. It was a great feeling to be able to reveal what lay buried deep within my soul without being judged or criticized. I wouldn't have dared to tell another person this. I began to feel bright on the inside; just a tiny flicker breaking through the darkness of my soul. I didn't know it, but I was setting myself free from the inside.

"I know who you really are," the eyes seemed to say.

The eyes in the mirror seemed to love me and I felt it. You know when someone loves you and they look deep into your eyes. Well, that's how I felt. Those eyes looked deep into very my soul making me feel protected and safe.

Telling someone your secrets without being criticized was a great relief for me. I didn't know why I had held onto them for so long. It was freeing for me, throwing away all that trash that polluted my mind and soul. I confessed to the eyes that I never wanted this kind of life for myself. I never knew that I could do something different with my life, but those eyes gave me a look that said I was worth being loved and that I could be happy. I trusted them.

I thought back to when I was so unhappy with life that I had almost taken it. When depression and despair sets in, mixed with alcohol and a pistol it's a dangerous combination. I knew that pain is powerful, and I had been in pain most of my life. Drugs and alcohol helped me mask and numb it. The strangest thought crossed my mind.

Picture this I was in a closet in Louisiana, standing in my boxers and t-shirt locked away from society, talking to a reflection in the mirror. I was beginning to feel love. Those eyes loved me and they seemed to tell me how to love myself. They told me that love is more powerful than pain and fear, and that fear doesn't have a defense against love.

When I focused on fear I gave it so much power over me that I became a different person, but because I have a fundamental belief in a power greater than myself buried deep within me, that fear fights to stay alive, causing my life to become reckless and unmanageable. But the eyes seemed to direct me to the feeling that it's all on the inside, and right then, every cell in my body began to vibrate like an old generator shooting sparks trying to get the light to shine. That was my first glimpse of feeling freedom, even in that concrete closet in Louisiana.

As I continued, I thought about the ugly side of the game, the side that wasn't glorified, and the side that I was living. They certainly don't tell you how to survive in an 8x6 cell and the hopelessness that comes with it. I saw power in those eyes, the power to make positive choices and decisions, the power to influence good in myself and in others.

I told the eyes in the mirror about a memory I had when I was a kid. I was at my mother's church when this old woman named Mother

Parsons walked up to me and said, "Son, you are special. People are going to know you before you know them. I know you can't understand what I am telling you right know, but it will happen."

Her predictions were true; people did know me before I knew them. Every time I was transferred to a new prison, the prison staff always knew my name before I knew theirs.

Mother Parson continued, "Son," she said, "You're going to walk through the valley of death. You're going to go through a lot in your young life, but you will make it through just fine. You're going to do great things. You can't understand right now and it will seem as if you're in a maze, but you will have an amazing life. Remember what I'm telling you. It will all be okay," she said.

I had no clue what this old lady was saying.

"Okay," I answered, and when I turned away my mother was standing there crying, which I never understood.

I chained smoked cigarette after cigarette as I spilled my guts. I felt good inside. I felt seen for who I really was. Those eyes gladly accepted my heavy burden without expectation or judgment. I told the eyes in the mirror, "Make sure you keep this between us," as if expecting an answer.

I was starting to get tired. Hours must have passed. I must have been standing there for hours, smoking and talking. I felt light and fresh, but physically I was exhausted. The toilet paper had dried up and began to fall from the mirror; it was time for my session to be over and I felt relieved and grateful.

"God, what do I do now?" was my last question, as I stepped to the mirror that vibration I felt on the inside told me that's just where it's at, on the inside. I looked into the mirror and saw freedom in my eyes. Then I stood back looking up with my eyes closed, and felt it. I felt freedom on the inside. As I opened my eyes, tears rolled down my cheeks and I sobbed and sobbed. I was released from bondage of self- hate. I had forgotten that tears are salty. As I enjoyed their taste, I had the ability to cry. I was human.

I had travelled many miles to get to this tiny closet in Louisiana for my moment of clarity. I lay on my bunk feeling good, and then it became cloudy as I fell in to a deep sleep. As my mind wondered in the haze of slumber, I dreamt I was reading. Why? I didn't know, but I was reading about things I'd never heard of. I was actually turning the pages, intrigued by what I read. My dreams were vivid as I journeyed to far away exotic places and everything seemed so strange but wonderful.

The banging on my cell door awakened me. "It's lunch time, Verrett," the CO said. He must have known I was too tired for breakfast and let me sleep through lunch.

"Had a long night?" the CO asked.

"Yeah, I did," I replied.

The fresh air rushed into my cell when the food trap was opened, and the stale cigarette smoke escaped into the hallway.

"What? No cussing?" the CO asked.

"Naw man, not today," I answered.

"Okay, Verrett. I'm going to leave the trap open for a while to let it air out in there," he said.

"Good looking out," I replied. I squatted, taking in the fresh air and that's when I saw the book cart.

"You want something to read?" the CO asked, as he brought the book cart closer.

"Yeah, I do, but I don't want no Jackie Collins or no bullshit like that," I answered.

Most of the books were old and beat up. I wasn't in the mood to read any westerns or mysteries, I needed something of substance, and on the bottom rack of the book cart were these thick old tattered books.

"What are those at the bottom?" I asked.

"Those are the Encyclopedia Britannica," the CO said.

A spark of excitement shot through my entire body. "Give me A," I requested.

I had never read the Encyclopedia before. I hungrily opened the book and began reading. I scanned the first couple of pages and came to the word abacus. I learned that it was a counting machine and that's when it hit me. These were the things I'd been reading in my sleep. My heart began to beat fast and my hands started sweating. I felt good on the inside. My soul was starved for this information. Was it God's will for that book cart to be taken out of the storage room and pushed in my direction? It took me nine months to read every volume of the encyclopedia from A to Z.

I went to the mirror, but only saw my reflection. Where was he? Where was God? I figured that He would always be there watching over me. I stood there looking and then I smiled and said, "Thank You."

CHAPTER 49

—

The Adventure Begins

I learned that America was named after an Italian sailor named Amerigo Vespucci, but I'd been taught in school that Christopher Columbus had discovered America. What I had learned in the Encyclopedia was that Columbus was lost at sea for several weeks, and they were running out of food and fresh water, and one early morning they saw land. They thanked God and called the land mass San Salvador, or The Savoir.

I also read about the meaning of the name Africa. Afri was the name of several people who lived in North Africa near Carthage. The Latin word aprica literary meant sunny and the Greek word aphrika meant without cold, and was later derived from the Egyptian word afru-ka, which meant to turn toward the opening of the ka. The ka refers to the birthplace or womb, and that's how that continent was named Africa.

My mind was starved for this new information. I turned the page and read about the Aztec Indians. They lived in a city called Tecukan, which is now Mexico City. One day they saw some ships on the coastline and invited the strangers to their village. The Aztecs had never seen these kinds of people and thought they were gods riding in on these strange creatures called horses. Cortez and his men were invited to their village. They were welcomed with gifts of gold and tobacco. Shortly after that the Spaniards conquered the Aztecs. Their king, Montezuma, was beheaded and the Spaniards were in control. They pro-created a new race called Mestitos, or mixed Indians, which were later, called

263

Mexicans. I was blown away by the information that I found in these books.

As I flipped to the C's, I read that China was called Chin until the first emperor united all five providences and called the new country China. I learned that people name themselves after their ancestors or continents. The name Caucasian comes from the Caucus region of Europe, which was inhabited by white people, just as the Asians who inhabited Asia were yellow skinned. My ancestors are Africans, and black people in America are now called African-Americans.

Back in my Grandmothers time, she told me that her birth certificate identified her as being colored and my mother's birth certificate says Negro and my birth certificate says black, but my nephews' and nieces' say African-American.

It seemed like every so often black people in America were given a new label. I wondered what it would be in thirty years. Would we be called Brothers and Sisters on our birth certificates? I, like many, had suffered from self-identity, who was I? This information was very important to me. I had uncovered many lies, but the most important lie was that I believed that I was no good. I learned that I was of value. I meant something, but I had to believe it first.

I finished a book every month; I fed my mind with this new information. I spent hours reading and forgetting that I was in an 8x6 cell. The books transported me around the world. With every letter I explored a new place. My mind wasn't confined anymore. I became a world traveller within my tiny cell. I went to places that many people would never see. I imagined myself seeing these places, walking where ancient kings walked, swimming in the hot springs of Pamukkale, Turkey, where Mark Anthony and Cleopatra swam, and standing in the Hagia Sophia where Constantine had stood. I made a wish that one day I would see these places.

I felt different, even the COs saw a change in me. Shit. Everything seemed all right. Even the cold and bland food tasted better. The days became shorter. I had removed the thick layers of toilet paper that covered the lights so I could read at night, and when I was too exhausted to read, I dreamt beautiful dreams.

I travelled through time; I spoke with the Puritans about unalienable rights for all men. I helped Thomas Jefferson negotiate with Napoleon for the Louisiana Purchase. I spoke with Lincoln about slavery, and helped draft the Emancipation Proclamation. I helped design the Kitty Hawk with the Wright Brothers and I was at the Counsel of Nicaea with Constantine. I performed the first open heart surgery and I marched with Martin Luther King. I even helped King Arthur search for the Holy Grail. I sat with the Pharaohs, and helped Gustavo Eiffel design and build the Eiffel Tower. I even journeyed with Harriet Tubman; I did all this while being confined to my 8x6 concrete cell.

I had made it to the last part of Z in the Encyclopedia when I heard, "Roll it up Verrett, you're leaving in the morning," the CO said.

I couldn't believe that nine months had passed so quickly. At first I thought that they were playing a joke on me. I approached the door with the book in hand; transfer?

I told the CO that I wasn't ready to leave yet. I hadn't finished the last book and I didn't want to leave my closet just yet. I found peace in here. I hadn't gotten drunk or high in months. I was safe from the world. I had created my own world, one of peace and happiness and now they wanted me to go back into a place of confusion and chaos.

"You got twenty minutes to roll your stuff up," the CO ordered.

"All right," I answered.

As I gathered my belongings and put them in a small plastic bag, I began to clean the cell for the next man who would live here.

"What are you doing, Verrett?" the CO asked.

"Oh, just leaving it clean for the next man," I answered.

"Most inmates would be excited to leave," he said.

"Yeah, I'm sure they would," I replied.

The truth was, I felt a sadness come over me. This tiny cell was what the Egyptians called ka or womb or birthplace. This was my ka. This was my birthplace. These walls that confined me had protected me, sheltered me, kept me safe, and now I was leaving them. No matter where they were going to ship me, or how they treated me I would always have what was in my head and heart. I was free on the inside.

I heard the echoes of keys dangling and the sounds of the COs boots as he walked toward my cell.

"Ready, Verrett?" he asked.

"Damn! Man, that was a fastest twenty minutes. Let me pee first," I replied.

I stood in front of the toilet and put my hand on the same place on the edge of the stainless steel mirror, looking at my reflection, remembering that night and those eyes. What I saw was me, with a thick beard and all. Those eyes had a spark in them, and then tears formed and flowed into my beard. Right then I knew I was going to be all right, I would survive. I could have sworn that the image in the mirror smiled and winked at me.

"Okay, Verrett you know the drill," the CO said.

I followed his orders and placed my hands through the food slot to be handcuffed. Once they were on the door, it was opened and a rush of air entered my cell. It looked brand new. Even the CO commented on its cleanliness. When I stood in the hallway, the door closed with a loud thud. I took one last look. This place was called SHU, or Special Housing Unit. I had given it a new name, Seeking Higher Understanding.

CHAPTER 50

—

The Test

I was leaving Oakdale, headed to some undetermined destination. I had gotten plenty of curious stares from other inmates and staff alike. I didn't care that I looked like a wild man. I was happy on the inside as I was led to the bus that waited to take us to the airport.

The bright sun shined in my face, causing me to squint, making my appearance look even more menacing. I haven't been in the sun for nine months. I was grateful for the simple things I saw. I could smell the grass that was freshly mowed and I could hear the birds chirping. I felt that they were singing to me, cheering me on. They seemed to have been waiting for me welcoming me, and seeing me off. You can do it De'Juan they seemed to sing; I flared my nostrils as I took in a deep breath of fresh air.

I arrived in Talladega, Alabama and as soon as the intake process was over I went straight to the inmate barbershop for a shave. I had met the barber and he introduced himself as "Frog".

"What's up, homie? Where you from?" he asked.

"I'm from California," I answered.

"Where you from?" I inquired.

"Cali too! I'm from Gardena," he answered.

"Yeah, I'm from Harbor City."

"Where you coming from?" he asked.

"Oakdale."

"Damn, homie! Were you in SHU, Cuz you pale as a motherfucker?" he asked.

"Yeah, they had me in there for nine months," I responded.

"All right. Let me clean you up and take that beard off," he said.

Frog began the process of removing the thick hair that covered my face. "There you go," he said, spinning me around in the barber chair so that I faced the mirror.

I rubbed my hand across my face, feeling my smooth skin that had been hidden for close to a year. I was amazed how young I looked. Well, I was young, but that beard made me look twenty years older. I looked like I should be in college or something, except for the matted braids in my hair and the orange t-shirt.

"Feels better, huh?" Frog asked.

To be honest, I had been feeling good for months now, but the shave was nice. I remembered what I had read about barbers in the Encyclopedia. The word barber was the Latin word for beard. A barber was also known to perform surgeries and dentistry, and as time passed they just stuck with cutting hair.

"What unit they got you in?" Frog asked.

"Delta B," I answered.

"We got a lot of homies there. Right now most of the homies are on the weight pile driving iron," he said.

We sat in the barbershop until the next ten-minute move was called, and then we walked to the yard. It didn't take long for the word to spread that I was here in Talladega. I had met all of the homies and I was proud of myself that I turned down the weed and wine on my first night.

Years later, after my release, I would see Frog once again. It was a Saturday afternoon. I was coming from the County Jail. I had begun doing volunteer work, working with the inmates. I pulled off the 405 freeways to get some gas. Exiting my car I noticed a homeless man pushing a shopping cart heading in my direction. He politely asked me if he could wash my windows and pump my gas for two dollars. At first I didn't recognize him and then it hit me.

"Frog?" I asked.

"Where do I know you from?" he inquired.

"It's me, Ghost from Harbor City," I answered. "We were locked up together in Talladega," I said.

"Oh, what's up homie?" he responded. "How long you have been out?"

"Almost two years," I replied.

"How about you?" I asked.

"About seven years." he said.

"What happened?" I asked.

"It's been hard out here. I couldn't find a good job to pay my bills and I lost my apartment. Homie, I've been on the streets since then," he said.

"What about school?" I asked.

"I'm too old for that," he said.

I had thought I was too old to go back to school too, but once I mustered up the courage to enroll I noticed there were people older than me who probably thought the same thing.

"Can I get twenty dollars?" he asked.

"No, but I can buy you something to eat," I answered.

I couldn't give him any money to spend on getting high. I felt sad for Frog, and here he was on Manchester and La Brea pushing a shopping cart hustling at a gas station. Back in the day, Frog was pushing sports cars, living a good life. A bolt of fear shot through me as I stood talking to him. This could be me. He suffers from deeply engrained negative thoughts and believes that he can be no more than what he is, like I once believed.

My cellie was a guy name Rudy; we'd been in Phoenix together he was telling everybody about what went down on the yard there. Rudy wasn't a gangbanger; he was smarter than that. He didn't even sell dope. Rudy was in for robbing an armoured car. It was his baby momma that turned him in when she found out he had another baby by another woman. Rudy was nickel slick. He was clean cut and spoke like white people. He could fool a lot of people with his ability to fit in anywhere, but he was scandalous, always looking for a free high.

Rudy was one of the bookies on the yard. He had the tickets for basketball, football and baseball. Rudy was so serious about betting that he even had a ticket for soccer to appease the Spanish-speaking population.

Rudy and the homies gave me a care package until my property caught up with me. It was time to call my mother and let her know where I was, and ask her to send me some money. I had allowed my mother to manage my money until I came home. She would send me what I had in my safe and I would deduct the sum every time. I needed to keep track of my money because I would need it when I went home. Sometimes I wished I had saved that money I'd paid my lawyer because I probably would have gotten the same amount of time if I'd had a Public Defender, especially with a drug case. Unless you were related to the Bushes then you could just apologize and go into a residential treatment center, but if you're not, then be prepared to do eighty-five percent of your sentence.

When I was on Con Air Charles Keating was seated only a row in front of me. Everybody knew about the savings and loan scandal and that one of his co-conspirators was a Bush, so Charles was the Crash Dummy to quiet the public. Charles Keating was given a big prison sentence, but shortly after all the dust had settled, his conviction was reversed, with the help of his Bush connection.

After two weeks of waiting for a two-day package, I called my mother to ask her about my money. I told her that I'd never received the Federal Express package. She said she had sent it, so I asked for the tracking number, calling her bluff. Then she said that she didn't have it. After years of listening to people on the phone, I could tell if someone was lying to me. It was just the little things in their voice that would alert me. Then she confessed.

"I'm your mother and I don't owe you anything. I took care of you when you were a baby," and hung up on me.

That wasn't my mother talking. She had married this guy named Martin and I didn't like him. He smoked weed and drank a lot, and now he had her doing the same thing.

My mother married Martin after I got arrested. I knew that he wasn't right for her. I loved my mother, but her picker was broken, meaning she'd always pick the wrong man. I had met him a few weeks before I got popped and I knew their relationship wouldn't last long and my money wouldn't either.

I decided to call my sister Shonie; it had been awhile since I'd called her. She was also at odds with our mother because she was pregnant. I

270

didn't know the guy she had gotten pregnant by I asked her how many other kids did he have, that pissed her off I should have been subtler with my approach, but I remember her only as my little sister, and now she was pregnant. I didn't want my sisters to have kids with anybody I knew.

"You can't tell me anything!" she screamed into the phone.

"I'm just trying to give you some brotherly advice," I shot back.

"I don't need any advice from no nigga in prison," she replied and hung up the phone up.

That was the last time we spoke to each other. It would be another fifteen years before we spoke again. I went outside to smoke a cigarette to calm down a bit.

Mark was Shonie's father and he had a brother who I called Uncle. He worked for police department. I dialled his number, and he accepted my call.

"What's up, Keith. I have a question for you," I said.

"Go ahead and ask," he said.

"I need to find my real father," I said.

"I was wondering when you were going to ask that question," he said. Can you call me back in a half hour?" he asked.

"Yeah, I can." I responded.

I quickly went to my cell to get a pen and paper, and then went outside to smoke another cigarette, trying to kill time. I was scared and excited at the same time. I wondered if would like me even though I was in prison? I wondered if we looked like each other. Would he tell me that he loved and missed me and had been looking for me all this time? All kinds of thoughts ran through my mind. I thought that there was an explanation or some kind of misunderstanding. Maybe now I could finally have a father of my very own. I would be too old when I got out to play catch with him, but maybe we could do other things together I thought.

I called Keith and he picked up on the first ring. "What's up, Dee? You ready for this?" he asked.

"Yeah, man. I've been waiting on this my whole life," I answered.

"Okay, here's the number. They are expecting your call," he said.

I nervously wrote down the phone number and address. My hands were shaking involuntarily. "Okay, I got it. Thank you Keith, for this," I said.

"No problem. Take care," he said and hung up the phone.

I stood in the phone booth staring at the piece of paper. My heart was racing. I paused and took a deep breath, then dialled the number. After a few rings someone picked up; it was a woman's voice.

"Hello, this is De'Juan. May I speak with Lawrence Verrett, please?"

"Oh, hello baby. This is Gwen, his wife. Lawrence is at work," she said. "Your uncle just called. I have been expecting your call. This is a surprise. De'Juan, can I ask what you look like?"

"Well, I'm about 5'8". I have an athletic build. I'm light skinned, my eyes are light brown, I have some freckles on my nose and my hair is wavy."

"I noticed that you live in Compton," I said.

"Yeah, we were neighbours. We started dating, and then we got married. "Oh, wait a minute. He just pulled into the driveway," she said.

My stomach instantly turned into knots making funny noises. I could hear him walking into the house. Gwen tried to cover the phone, but I heard his words. They struck me down like a bolt of lightning.

"Hello, who is this?" he demanded.

"My name is De'Juan Verrett, Catherine Pace's son," I said.

"I don't know any Catherine Pace," he shot back.

My heart was crushed. I was instantly transported back to childhood. I could barely speak; my breathing changed. I felt like I was drowning.

I got up the nerve and spoke. "I don't want nothing from you, just why? And what happened?"

"I do remember her now, but I never touched her," he said.

"Then why do I have your last name? Well, it doesn't matter now. I just wanted to know who you are," I said.

"Well, I'm not your father, and I don't know who is." His words punished me without cause. That's when his wife interrupted and asked me to send a picture and I agreed.

In one day I had lost my mother, my sister and been denied by my father. I wanted to rip my heart out of my chest. I didn't want to feel anything, and my old friend pain was back; the only consistent feeling I'd felt.

I headed up to my cell; Rudy was burning some incense and rolling up some weed as I walked in. It had been a little over a year since I'd gotten high. I couldn't fight off the obsession to escape reality. A few hits off the joint wouldn't hurt and it will calm me down. Then Rudy pulled out two gallons of wine; just one cup of wine wouldn't hurt either.

This was too much to deal with in one day. His words cut deep into my very being. The weed and wine comforted me, better than my own family did. The wine understood what I was going through. I had been sober for just over a year, and this was a good reason to give it away. I had nothing to prepare me for what life was going to throw my way.

A week had passed and I figured the picture should have made it there by now. I dialled the number. It rang a couple of times and the operator came on the line. I heard her say, "This call is from a federal prison. To accept the call, please press 5. To decline the call press 7."

Gwen's friendly voice greeted me. "Hello, De'Juan. I got your picture. You are a handsome young man," she said. "You look more like your father than your brother Lawrence junior," she said.

Time seemed to freeze for a second. Had I heard her right?

"I have a brother?" I questioned.

"Yes, you do baby. He's in the navy. Take down his address. He'd love to hear from you," she said.

"Wow! I have a brother," I said to myself.

"Hold on for a minute, De'Juan. Lawrence wants to talk to you," she said.

I instantly became rigid as if I was going into a fight.

"Hello," he said.

Our voices sounded the same, I thought.

"Listen here, De'Juan. I am not your father," he said. Those words didn't affect me like they had the first time, because I had a good buzz going.

That's when Gwen interrupted. "Lawrence, you need to look at this picture. He is the splitting image of you, and he looks more like you than Lawrence Jr.," she continued in my defense. "How are you going to tell this child you are not his father?"

"Tell him that I don't want anything from him" I said. All I wanted was to ask why? And what happened? I learned to live without a father, I don't want any money from him, and I only wanted to be acknowledged by him, that I existed."

He had placed the phone on the table but Gwen picked it up.

"Sorry baby; I have your address and I will send you a picture of us, okay?"

"Okay," I answered.

Back in my cell, I saw Rudy rolling a joint, I needed some relief and when I put one in the air it helped me get out of my feelings. It was my coping tool. As I lay in my bunk feeling the effects, I thought about how powerless and fucked my world was, but in my haze of drugs and alcohol I had control, I could choose not to feel I had failed the test.

CHAPTER 51

—

Blind Date

One of the homies named Zeus from Long Beach had moved to Macon, Georgia, and his wife and children lived there too. Zeus and I had become cool. He decided to ask his wife to hook me up with one of her friends to visit me, but first she wanted to see what I looked like.

I had sent a good close up picture to her with a nice letter, and then she agreed to come visit me. Cassandra was a nice country girl with a thick southern accent. We had corresponded with phone calls and letters for a few weeks before our first face-to-face visit.

During our first visit we talked about a lot of things. We laughed and joked throughout the visit, and then she asked could she do anything for me. That's when I asked her to bring me some weed and told her how to do it and she agreed.

I was back in the saddle once again. I felt useful doing what I did best, hustling. I had picked a couple of the homies in different units that had potential to follow orders and get that money for me.

There are two ways that drugs are brought into a prison. The first is by crooked staff members that want to supplement their income, and the second is through the visiting room. I didn't want to fool around with any COs so I chose the visiting room. When Cassandra would come for our visit, she would place twenty balloons into a popcorn bag, and I would slowly swallow them, letting them pass through my digestive

275

system, then shit into a plastic bag, clean them off and sell each one for a hundred and twenty- five dollars.

I always keep a third for myself, in case of a dry spell. I was making a slow two grand a month. I also sent Cassandra two hundred dollar checks in the mail as a surprise to keep her interested, and to let her know that she was appreciated and to keep her coming back.

Some of the homies on the yard were doing badly financially, so I let them hustle for me, and I made sure that everybody had the same things, meaning brand new sweat suits, tennis shoes and walk-man radios.

I had even formed partnerships with the hillbillies of White Mountain, Georgia in exchange for weed to learn how to make what they called white lightening by taking prison wine and distilling it and making pure alcohol, which would knock you on your ass.

My business was going great; I made twenty gallons a week. I bought a couple of cases of one hundred percent grapefruit juice from the prison store with twenty boxes of sugar, one pound of sugar for every gallon. One of the homies worked in the bakery, and he would bring me active yeast which I would add to the other ingredients in the four five-gallon milk bags and I'd let it sit for a week.

I paid this guy from Mississippi to watch the wine for me, and in exchange he never had to buy any wine. He could drink for free. I made sure that my cellie and I had something to drink every day. I was happy because the money was rolling in, Cassandra was happy, and the homies on the yard were happy walking around in their new gear.

The only one that wasn't happy was Zeus. He had just found out that his wife was pregnant by someone else and had stopped coming to visit him. He was stressed out with a fresh ten-year sentence.

I had known one of his brothers. There were nine of them, and the older brothers had started one of the biggest gangs in Long Beach. All of them were buffed out, even Zeus. One evening, as I was walking the track, he walked up to me and asked for some weed. I gave him one balloon out of respect for making this happen for me.

A few days later he came to my unit asking again.

"Hey homeboy, bless me with something I'm doing bad," he said.

I already knew what was going on, but I just waited for him to tell me. I knew he was fucked up on the inside and needed to escape the pain, but now he was interfering with my money, so I blessed him one last time.

"Make sure you sell some of this," I said to him.

"Good looking out, Ghost" he said and he shot back to his unit.

A few days later he hit me up again for another balloon, but this time I couldn't help him. I appreciated his help, but now I had to set a firm unbending boundary. He was smoking and drinking like it was going out of style. I handed him a joint.

"This is all I can do for you, now you starting to fuck with my money," I said.

"What do you mean? If I didn't hook you up with that bitch, you wouldn't have any of this shit," he said angrily.

"Nigga, if you managed your shit right, then maybe you would have something to show for it," I said.

Zeus stormed away, losing his wife and having a fresh ten-year sentence was killing him. He had lost it.

It was on a Sunday after dinner. I was walking solo back to the unit, not knowing that Zeus was plotting against me. He had waited for me in a blind spot, and as I turned the corner I saw a white light and then I hit the ground. Zeus had attacked me from behind. I was dizzy, and as he turned me over to face him, I could smell the scent of tobacco on his breath.

"Nigga, you going to break me off," he said as he shook me, and for extra measure kicking me in the stomach knocking all of the wind out of me, as I laid on the ground gasping for air. I slowly rose to my feet and marched to my unit to retrieve my knives. This motherfucker had to pay.

One of the older homies saw me storm into the unit.

"What's up, Ghost?" he asked.

"Man, that nigga Zeus was hiding behind a wall and fired on me, telling me that I'm going to break him off some weed," I grumbled.

"So what are you going to do, stab him?" he asked.

"I'm going to punish his ass," I answered.

"You know, you in Talladega. You're going to fuck around and catch another case," he said.

"Man, I don't give a fuck," I answered.

277

I wanted to strike back immediately without thinking, but Spike was right. I would have to get away with the stabbing and it was too open here in Talladega, and the chances were that I would get caught and sentenced to more time. I still had twelve more years to do and didn't want to add more. I thought about where I could catch him and jam my knife into him without any witnesses. I then gave Spike both my knives.

"So what are you going to do then?" he asked.

"I'm going to smash his head in," I answered.

"You a little wild motherfucker," Spike said.

"That nigga put his hands and feet on me. He got's to pay," I said.

"You got a big heart in that little body," he said as I left.

I waited for the ten-minute move and headed to the Recreation yard. I was going to stalk my prey. I spotted him leaving the weight pile headed toward the basketball court. I entered the weight pile and grabbed a short steel bar and slid it into my sleeve and walked to where he was standing. At first, he didn't recognize me.

"What's up now, nigga?" he asked as I slid the steel bar out and swung at him, hitting him on his collarbone. I heard his bone snap, then he took off like a jet, but I was right on his ass. Some of the homies saw me chasing him and joined in. We had trapped him on the backside of the basketball court, and he had nowhere to run; he submitted.

Zeus was trapped with nowhere to run; he held his collarbone, breathing heavily.

"Let's fuck him up," Smoke said.

"Wait, wait," Zeus pleaded. "My collar bone is broken."

"Nigga I don't give a fuck," I said, raising the bar to strike him again.

I had put the fear of God in him and he was in a no-win situation. He was at our will. I gave Turtle the steel pipe to take back to the weight pile.

Zeus looked relieved as he began to talk. "Ghost I tripped out homie, that's on Crip," he confessed.

"Nigga, I looked out for you and that's how you re-pay me by doing some dumb shit like that?" I said.

Turtle was holding a basketball and threw it at Zeus' head hitting him in the face.

278

Zeus screamed out in pain.

"Go to the weight pile and sit on the incline bench," I ordered him. "Then we all are going to say that the weight came down on you."

"All right," he answered.

We walked past two recreation staff as we entered the weight pile. Shortly after that Zeus screamed in pain and Turtle went to get the recreation staff. We explained what happened and I walked with Zeus to the prison hospital.

I had to do something to him. My reputation was at stake. If I hadn't stepped to him, then it would have opened the door for others to try me. You have to stand your ground against anyone and anything. That's how it works in here. You get more respect with violence.

Later that night I made it back to my unit and saw Spike. He just gave me the head nod as I went to my cell. I needed a drink and to put one in the air, Rudy was there writing a letter when I walked in.

"Where you been?" I asked him.

"I had some extra duty. They caught me with some chicken coming out of the kitchen," he said.

We were about to smoke when there was a knock on my door; it was the good brothers from the Nation of Islam, Brother Shabazz X and Brother Wali.

"Come on in my brothers" Rudy said jokingly.

"As-Salamu Alaykum. We come in the name of peace," Brother Shabazz said.

"And the same to you my brothers," I said.

They had joined the Nation of Islam in prison like many other black men. It was good discipline for them, the Nation's teaching of empowering the black man and woman to do for self, and to de-educate the white man's teachings that we were savages. The brothers on the yard were always clean cut, their prison clothes were always creased, their boots were spit-shined, and their shirt was always tucked in. They even wore bow ties. They looked like they were going to a job interview. I would have felt uncomfortable wearing a bow tie every day because the weather was too hot to wear a bow tie. I thought they needed some kind of summer short set, instead of being fully dressed in the southern heat.

279

I respected them, but I thought the brothers in the Nation were serious about their practice. Even their walk was different, and they would square the corners on their bunk like military men do, and salute each other. Too serious, I thought. At least cut a line every now and then, or say a cuss word.

Brother Shabazz ordered Brother Wali to stand post in front of our cell.

"Why is Brother Wali standing outside our cell Brother Shabazz?" I asked.

"He's on his post, Brother," Shabazz answered.

"Can't he post up in here? That shit ain't cool, brother, because we smoke weed and drink up in here," I said.

"He must stay on his post and practice his discipline, and you brother should too! The white man gives you this poison to keep you deaf, dumb and blind," Shabazz preached.

"With this right here," Rudy said, holding a fat joint, "I see no evil, hear no evil and speak no evil."

I tried my best not to start laughing and to keep a straight face.

I respected Shabazz for staying on his square and wanting to be a better man. I silently envied him for that. Shabazz was the Supreme Captain for the Nation of Islam in Talladega. He was diligent with his studies and from a correspondence course he received his X in the mail.

"Would you like a honey bun, my Brother?" I offered.

"Brother, do you know what is inside of that honey bun?" he asked.

"Yeah, some frosting, cinnamon, sugar and a whole bunch of calories," I said.

Rudy started laughing, but Shabazz found nothing funny.

"Shabazz, when are you going to order some bean pies? I'm tired of eating this unhealthy stuff," I said.

"This week," he said. "Then I'm going to sign you up."

"For some bean pies?" I asked.

"No, for some FOI training," he said.

"FOI training?" I questioned.

"Yes, black man. The Fruit of Islam training," he responded.

"If they have a smoking section, sign me up too," Rudy said.

Shabazz just gave Rudy a serious look and dismissed his question.

"Brother Ghost, you need the teachings of the honorable Elijah Muhammad," he said.

"I don't know my brother. That means I would have to get haircuts every week," I said.

"Don't worry. Brother Melik X will take care of you."

"I'll think about it," I said.

The reason Shabazz came to my cell was to talk about the incident that happened with Zeus and me. He wanted to do his part to stop the black-on-black violence.

"Brothers, we got to wake up. Our beloved prophet taught us to be upright, to stand up straight, that the white man loves to see us act savagely against each other. I ask you, brother Ghost, to come to the chapel and meet with Brother Zeus. We can work out our differences."

I respected what the brothers from the Nation of Islam were doing. They were trying to better themselves. I understood the teachings just by hearing them. Their founder, Elijah Muhammad, empowered them to believe that they are more than what they are told they are. The brothers on the yard were a tight group. They worked out together, they ate together, and they were always studying together.

"Okay, Shabazz. I'll be there," I answered.

"All praises are due to Allah, who came to the wilderness of North America in the form of Master Fard Muhammad to bring salvation to the lost black man," he said. Then he gave me a hug and left.

Rudy re-lit the joint and said, "I ain't going," as he passed the joint to me.

CHAPTER 52

—

Finding Religion

In prison most inmates turn to religion as a crutch. Many became practicing Christians, Muslims, Jews and Buddhists. I, like many, chose to keep it gangster. The Nation of Islam taught not only from the religious point of view, but also from a historical view, which fascinated many young angry black men. I was even impressed by what they taught.

The Nation of Islam's goal is to raise men out of boys and to teach them that they are more than what they were told they are. The teaching boosted self-worth and self-esteem, and taught that the black man in America suffered from the conditions of self-identity and history.

"The white man is the devil," I would hear some of the brothers say, but I was taught when I was a kid that no one is superior over anyone because of the color of their skin, it's in their actions. The Nation of Islam's goal was to educate these men and to turn them into mental giants so they could become productive citizens.

I respected their teachings, but it wasn't for me. I knew deep down that being a good person made me feel good on the inside. I really liked helping people no matter if they were white, black, Asian or Hispanic, and I based all of my decisions on character, not color. I respected the brothers who joined the Nation of Islam. It just wasn't for me. I needed to find my own way to peace.

I studied the concept of Islam. Islam is the Arabic word for peace, and just like me, the brothers in the Nation were looking for peace internally.

I remember reading about Islam in the Encyclopedia, and about its founder. I read some Islamic literature. The Nation of Islam's teachings were slightly different from the ancient teaching of Muhammad, who founded Islam in 635 A.D. Muhammad promoted and taught the concept of only one God, just as Abraham had taught, and that we all have a personal relationship with God even without a mediator. They taught that we all have that direct connection with God, we just have to water that spiritual seed that we all have on the inside.

I had been watering my spiritual seed with wine and drugs, which kept me from growing spiritually, and I was becoming tired of the bitterness and anger that came with it. I knew that it wasn't really me, but I felt that I had to do that in order to survive. Alcohol and drugs were my coping tools. They helped me forget about the remaining eleven years I had to do. I had been living in a violent environment for five years now, and before that I lived in fear and anger as long as I could remember. It seemed that there was no end, no light at the end of the tunnel. I began to study all of the major religions, hoping that one of them would nurture the seed that was within me to grow.

At mail call, my name was called and I received a few letters. It was from Gwen, my father's wife. I quickly ran to my cell and sat at the desk and opened the envelope. The pictures were of a man I would have called Daddy under different circumstances. I looked just like him! My hands shook involuntarily. This was the first time I had laid eyes on the man that denied me and our resemblance was unquestionable.

Rudy came into the cell complaining that his girl hadn't sent the pictures of her wearing some lingerie.

"What's up?" he asked as I lay in my bunk.

"I just got the pictures of my father," I replied.

"Let me see them," he asked.

I gave him the pictures.

"Damn, homie. You look just like him," he commented.

"Yeah, I know, huh?"

I propped up the pictures so I could look at them while I read Gwen's letter and smoked a cigarette. She said that I looked more like my father than my brother, Larry, Jr. She told me that my brother was in the Navy and stationed in Hawaii, and gave me his address. I remembered praying when I was a small boy asking God to give me a brother, and now I had one. I guess God did answer prayers sometimes quick and sometimes slow.

CHAPTER 53

—

Meeting Time

I had sent word to the rest of the homies on the yard that we would be meeting in the chapel with the brothers from the Nation of Islam at 6:00 pm. The prison chapel consisted of a big sanctuary and several small rooms for each faith.

Brother Shabazz, and the rest of the brothers set up the meeting from the Nation of Islam. Rudy decided to go, but complained all the way there that he was missing the Lakers and Houston game. I told him that he could catch the highlights on ESPN. I never really went to the chapel and when I did, I went just to watch old movies. When we entered, I saw the brothers on their post, standing on either side of the doors. They stood like those guards that stand in front of Buckingham Palace. They didn't even blink as we walked past them. It was amazing how they transformed former drug dealers and bank robbers into clean-shaven, well-disciplined soldiers in their creased up khaki prison uniforms with not a wrinkle on them, while wearing bow ties. Even their boots were amazingly shiny.

"As-salamu Alaykum," Brother Andrew X greeted us.

"Thank you my brother and the same to you," I answered.

They even had ushers to tell us where to sit. At the far end of the room was a podium with three big pictures, one was of Master Fard Muhammad, the other was of Elijah Muhammad, and the other was of Minister Louis Farrakhan. On either side of the podium were the

American flag, and the Turkish flag, which was used by the Nation because of the Star and Crescent.

Shabazz was making small talk when he saw me and motioned me to him.

"All praises are due to Allah," he said giving me the customary Muslim hug.

The room quickly filled up as the men took to their seats. The last man to enter was Zeus. All eyes were on him as he sat across the room with his shoulder in a sling. There were about twenty-five homies, Crips and Bloods. There was no set tripping here in Talladega because we were all from California. Our clique was called the Cali Car. The southern people would wonder why Crips and Bloods fought and killed each other in California, but not in Talladega. We had strength in our numbers and reputation. Without that, the southerners would have had control of what we did on the yard. The homies watched Zeus, giving him dirty looks. Shabazz walked behind the podium to start the meeting as his two bow-tied guards stood on both sides.

Shabazz asked everyone to close their eyes and to lay our hands in our laps with our palms up as if receiving a gift, and then he opened with a very long prayer.

"Brothers," he said, "Black is beautiful."

"That's right" one of the brothers shouted. "I called this gathering in hopes of stopping this senseless black-on-black violence here in Talladega. The white European-American men love to see us killing each other. It's less work for him. If we stay divided, then we'll stay conquered."

"Speak on it black man," one of the other brothers said.

Shabazz continued, "This evening, my family, I have asked our Brother Ghost and our Brother Zeus here to work out their differences because that's what families do. We talk. Would everyone please welcome Brother Ghost and Brother Zeus to the podium?"

Everyone began clapping.

As we both stood at the podium, brother Shabazz instructed us to look at each other and to be totally honest about what had happened.

Well, I was going to be honest as I could. "The violence started when Zeus fired on me when I was walking back from the chow hall. I didn't see him, and then he kicked me in the stomach, and told me that I better give him some contraband, that's how it started. He threw the first blow."

"Brother, is that correct?" Shabazz asked Zeus.

"Yes, it is," Zeus, answered.

"Why did you ambush Brother Ghost?" Shabazz asked.

"I was stressed out and tripping," Zeus responded.

"Brother, we all have to be honest here," Shabazz, said.

"Ok, it was about some weed," Zeus said.

"You mean to tell us that you have a broken shoulder because of some reefer?" Shabazz inquired.

"The white European American male puts that poison in our hands, which make us deaf, dumb and blind, and we will harm not only ourselves, but our family, and our communities. The white European American male is a genius and diabolical. He puts that poison in our communities to keep us deaf, dumb and blind. When a brother is all of those, he doesn't know any better, brothers. I was just like that. I had beastly ways, savage behaviors. I was a Negro. Do you know the definition of the word Negro?"

I had read in the Encyclopedia that the word negro is derived from the Latin word necro, which means mentally dead, and that the word negro in Spanish means black, so to be deaf, dumb and blind is to be mentally dead, not knowing my history or identity.

Shabazz continued, "Master Fard Muhammad came to the wilderness of North American to find the chosen one to teach him the seven books, then use them to wake up the black man to show him his history. Some of us woke up, but many are still sleep and will remain mentally dead."

One of the brothers shouted from the back of the room, "Not me!"

The meeting was coming to a close. Shabazz asked Zeus and I to shake hands, and we did. Then the room erupted in applause. Shabazz grabbed both of our hands and raised them up in unifying our brotherhood. I still didn't trust Zeus.

We went back to our unit and as I lay in my bunk I thought about what I had when I was in SHU. I had freedom from all of this bullshit. I was happy. I wanted to regain that feeling of joy that I felt on the inside.

The following Saturday Cassandra was coming to visit and to bring my weed to me. I enjoyed the time I spent with her. We spent the entire day just talking, and then we took pictures and kissed. As we were talking, Zeus came into the visiting room. He had a look in his eyes that revealed treachery. I was about to take all the balloons, but decided not too.

"Go flush all of those balloons," I told Cassandra.

"Why?" she asked.

"Just do it now," I ordered her.

Cassandra got up and went into the ladies bathroom and flushed them. I had a weird feeling inside. Zeus was not to be trusted and I didn't want to get popped with bringing in drugs into the prison, let alone getting Cassandra caught. Donald Ray and his wife sat next to Zeus. As Donald began swallowing the weed-filled balloons, Zeus motioned to the CO that he had to use the bathroom. Right after he left, three lieutenants came into the visiting room and went straight to Donald Ray and his wife. I figured that they were there for me, but I was clean.

The lieutenants grabbed the bag of popcorn and found the remaining weed-filled balloons and arrested Donald Ray's wife on the spot and marched him to SHU to be placed in the dry cell until the balloons came out of his body.

The entire visiting room watched what was happening in shock. I had to get back to the yard and let the homies know what happened.

I said to Cassandra, "Baby, I got to go. That nigga can't stay on this yard, and I have to let the homies know what happened."

"It's none of your business," she protested.

"He's from California and it makes us look bad," I answered.

Once I made it back to the yard, I called a meeting with my homies and the Mississippi car and told them what had happened in the visiting room.

The shot caller for the M-Car was called Sticks. I guess Jheri curls were still big in Mississippi, because they all had one. He was an older guy and real laid back.

"What's up, Ghost? What happened with Donald up in there?" Sticks asked.

"That nigga, Zeus, set him up. I couldn't get to Donald in time. He was sitting right next to Zeus. I figured the lieutenants were there for me because it happened so fast. It was like they were waiting, but when I saw Zeus come into the visiting room I told my girl to flush all of it."

"So he set Donald up instead?" Sticks asked.

"Exactly," I replied.

"What's the next move?" Sticks asked. "He's a California boy and we can't put hands on him unless you give the green light."

"I wanted to give your car the option, because if you don't want to take action, the California car will," I responded.

"We want it," Sticks answered.

"Okay. I'll let the homies know that you got the green light," I said.

Most of the riders in the Mississippi car lived in the same unit as Zeus. It went down after the 4:00 pm count. They put pool balls into their socks and wrapped their faces with bandanas and surrounded Zeus and beat the crap out of him. I was told later that he was close to death. The COs found him unconscious, lying in a pool of his own blood with his front teeth knocked out and a broken nose. He'd been viciously beaten.

I thought about what Shabazz had said about black-on-black violence and being divided. We were definitely lost.

CHAPTER 54

—

Good Behavior

Three years passed while I was in Talladega. I was now twenty-five years old. I couldn't believe that I didn't go to SHU. Not one time during my stay. I guess I was perfecting my prison skills of staying out of the way. The youngsters that hit the yard considered me an OG, and my name rang like a high school bell.

When we congregated on the yard the new arrivals would come to introduce themselves. Most of them were just babies. They were trying their best to look and act tough. Their pants would hang off their waist and their shirts were three sizes too big. I saw myself in each of them, as an angry teenager in a savage world not knowing what to expect and wanting to make a name for them.

Not long ago I was in their shoes. Sadness crept into me as I watched those young men posturing, playing the game we all played. I began my own version of the introduction to prison and the rules that my clique had to live by which were given to me by my uncle.

Next, the new arrivals had to produce their court documents. This was important to insure that they did not cooperate with the government in their case. Rats were not allowed in our clique or on the yard. If their paperwork checked out, then they were inducted into the clique.

It was a big responsibility to manage, discipline and take care of everyone's needs. I was respected because I stood behind and kept my word. See, in prison that's all you have is your word, and your actions must match. If I gave those men my word you could count on it being the Gospel.

Anger and sadness mixed with despair is what my eyes revealed. That's why I constantly wore my black shades. I had to be a different person when I was on the yard, uncaring and unbending, stone faced and stone hearted, but when I was in my cell I was just De'Juan. The mask of bitterness was removed and I could relax a bit.

I received a letter from my case manager instructing me to report to his office. When I knocked on the door I was told to enter.

"Hello, Mr. Verrett," he said.

"What's up?" I answered.

"You have been here for three years now without a write-up, and I took the liberty of putting in a transfer for you," he said.

"Is that right?" I responded,

"Yes, that is correct," he said with a grin.

"So where are you sending me too?" I asked curiously.

"Where does your mother live?" he asked with a smile. "That's for running a good program," he said.

Well, I managed not to go to the Special Housing Unit while I was here so I guessed that was a good thing.

"Thank you for doing this for me," I said.

"You did all the work. Congratulations, Mr. Verrett," he said as I exited his office.

I called a meeting with the homies on the yard and told them my news and I let everybody know that Smokey would be taking my place. We then had a big pow wow, or a smoke out.

It was going to be hard to tell Cassandra that I was going to California, but I would offer her the option to move there if she wanted too, knowing that she would decline.

CHAPTER 55

—

Back 2 Cali

We were taken to the Birmingham airport where the all too familiar Con Air plane waited to take its bound passengers to their next destinations. As I boarded the plane, I was reminded of a slave ship except its cargo wasn't Africans, the BOP didn't discriminate.

It had taken five weeks to finally reach California, and as the plane began its descent through the cloud of smog, LAX airport came into view. I was happy as hell to be back home. Everything looked different as the plane taxied to where the armed U.S. Marshals and BOP staff waited to receive the not-so-precious cargo.

We were ushered into one of the buses that were headed to FCI Terminal Island. I had taken a window seat, and I wanted to see everything. My heart pounded with excitement as we pulled onto the new 105 freeways toward the always-congested 405 south. I was home, well not really home, but in my hometown and I felt well.

The driver of the bus then merged onto the 110 south freeways. We were going to drive past my house, where I was arrested and it even passed through Harbor City. Five years had passed since I had seen these familiar streets. Not too much had changed.

The big green Vincent Thomas Bridge came into view. My entire body involuntarily shook with anticipation and excitement. I thought about how many times I'd travelled across this very bridge. I never thought that I would cross it in handcuffs and leg irons in a bus filled with inmates.

I saw gigantic cruise ships preparing to take their smiling and laughing passengers to a fun-filled vacation while we were headed to a place of incarceration. I saw the prison's gun tower" at a distance. We were getting close. I caught myself smiling on the inside. I hadn't been this close to home since I was arrested.

I saw a glimpse of myself in the reflection of the bus window. I was looking more like a grown man. There was a hint of maturity in my reflection. I had learned and been through a lot in the last five years. I was beginning to get the hang of this thing called adulthood. I was becoming and basically growing into adulthood in prison, while most of my friends grew into men and fathers on the streets.

It was August of 1995 when I arrived in FCI Terminal Island and I didn't waste any time getting settled. I made my way to the recreation yard, which was located on the south yard to see some of my homeboys to get my hook-up. Back then; Terminal Island was just like the streets. Corruption ran wild with the staff. Drugs and real alcohol was abundant and the female COs sold sex at a high price. For five hundred dollars and a referral, you could have some real sex, instead of using a Fe-Fe bag, which was a latex glove into which you poured baby oil or lotion, and then you wrapped it in a towel, Get the picture!

I was given a care package from my homies, which consisted of a street ounce of weed, a knife, a real pint of Jack Daniels whiskey and some tennis shoes until my property arrived from Talladega. My first day on the yard was great. I was received by the homies with much love and respect. Everyone donated something. I was comfortable. I had to be careful of not going overboard with drinking and using because the staff performed random drug tests, so I cut down on smoking weed, but I drank a lot.

A dirty urine test was a fast ticket for a transfer and I planned on finishing my remaining eleven years at Terminal Island. I would use the marijuana only as currency.

The south yard is where the baseball field and the weight pile are located and inside recreation, they also had two inmate housing units. As I walked the track, I could see the ocean and people riding the same ferryboats I used to ride, and they laughed and waved to us. I could also see San Pedro and the street where my family lived, where I used to ride my bike as a kid. It hurt to be so close, but yet so far. The loud horn of the cruise liner got my attention as it sailed right next to the prison headed to some far off exotic destination.

The O.J. Simpson trial captured the world's attention, even in the prison world. It was on in every TV room, and everyone had their opinion. The trial was better than any written show on television at the time. It was probably the birth of reality TV.

Even in the visiting rooms most of the conversations were about the O.J. Simpson trial and what they thought about it. In the black TV rooms most thought that he shouldn't have been fucking with a white girl in the first place, and I am sure that in the white TV rooms it was the opposite.

I didn't think that O.J. had committed the murders with his own hands; but he'd hired some people to do it for him. He wasn't stupid enough to be caught holding the knife.

Back in my day, when I played pop warner football, my coach called me O.J. because I ran like him on the field. The only reason I ran so fast was because I was small and didn't like to get tackled, so my fear turned into speed which turned into touch downs. I always outran the defenders.

A few weeks later the verdict was in. O.J. was found not guilty and the entire black population erupted in cheers. O.J. had beaten the system. It was a win for all of us. He had the best lawyer, Johnnie Corcoran. He gave the LAPD a black eye. The white population was angry. The white correctional officers were pissed off, openly calling him a woman killer. The COs got madder by the second, as the inmates laughed and chanting over and over, "If it doesn't fit, you must acquit."

You could feel the tension on the yard even between the black and white staff. Everyone chose a side, which brought out the ugly in everyone.

It seemed like the staff wanted to re-try the case, and the inmates would be the defense. The trial would continue to be discussed everywhere, in the chow hall, in the inmate laundry rooms, and in the law library. To tell you the truth, I really didn't care because I was still in prison with eleven years left.

CHAPTER 56

—

Smile Now, Cry Later

The same thing that makes you laugh will make you cry. Shortly after the O.J. verdict, the ruling striking down the proposal that challenged the Crack Law that would reduce the lengthy sentences was once again denied. This shocked everyone who'd been convicted of a drug case. I had been in three prisons that erupted in striking back at the system. The only thing a riot brings is more and more security to the prison and long bus or plane rides to the other side of the country.

I had gotten a clerk job working in the inmate paint shop, where my responsibility was to type up passes for the painters to walk across the compound when the yard was closed. My job was sweet. I sat in an office listening to the radio. The job was stress free and I enjoyed it. I could spend the rest of my time doing that. The staff paint foreman was cool. He didn't bother me even when he caught me typing personal letters, just as long as I did my job. That's all he wanted from me.

"Recall, recall!" was shouted over the PA system. "The institution is on lockdown," the voice said. "There is no movement on the yard."

The paint foreman had only been working with the bureau for under a year, and was clueless about what was going on. He was contacted by radio. "Paint foreman, Riley," the voice said, "Return your inmates to their housing units."

"Copy that," he replied.

I knew exactly what it meant. There was drama on the yard. There was no warning that there was going to be a riot. We were ordered to return to our assigned housing units. I had managed to stay under the radar and out of trouble since I'd been there, but trouble seemed to find a way into my life.

As we were being escorted to the north yard a shockwave of panic engulfed me. The disturbance was in my housing unit only. The windows were broken and chards of glass covered the pavement.

The Lieutenant ordered the compound officers to open the door and force us to enter the unit.

I spoke up. "Why are you going to put us in harm's way like this?" I said.

Mr. Riley also spoke up. "Sir, this group was with me. It would be unsafe to put these inmates into the housing unit."

The Lieutenant just shot him a dirty look and ordered the compound officer to open the door.

As we were forced to enter the building, I instantly changed my personality. I maneuvered my way to my cell. As I walked through the unit, havoc and destruction surrounded me. I knew that when it was over I was going to be transferred back to the east coast. I felt like those old men when I was at Lompoc - these motherfuckers messed up a good thing.

I began to pack all of my personal belongings. I knew I would be leaving soon. I found my stash of marijuana and began to roll cigar-like joints. I didn't care about getting a dirty UA test now. I needed to get my mind away from here. The men ran around the unit screaming and yelling as I just blew big clouds of smoke. I just waited. It wouldn't be long before the disturbance was quashed.

All of my good intentions went up in flames. I tried to do right. Yeah, I wasn't perfect, but I'd tried! I was tired of all the transfers and layovers, the long bus and plane rides and being chained up. That shit was old.

Tear gas canisters were propelled into the unit. The time had come. It wouldn't be long before I would be chained and sitting on a bus headed to God knows where.

The institution was now under the control of the prison staff. As they entered the housing unit, I sat on my bunk waiting for my name to be called, and it was. I was taken to R&D with about a hundred other inmates. Once there, the chains were put on, and we were escorted to the bus that awaited us.

I became quiet. I tried to summon that old veil that covered my emotions, and then I felt it. I was wrapped in its protection.

"State your name and number," the CO ordered.

"Verrett, 92857-012," I responded, as I found a seat next to the window. Looking out at the hill where my family lived, I thought that at this time they were probably having dinner. I was only at FCI Terminal Island for thirty-eight days.

CHAPTER 57

Back to the Hole

I remained quiet as the prison bus began its two-hour trek heading to San Diego. I couldn't believe that I was only on the yard for thirty-eight days. I had tried my best to change some of my behaviors, but what good did it do, and what would my mother think? She was expected to visit me the next day. Now she would have to wait for a phone call or letter from me explaining why I was transferred once again. She wouldn't believe me. In five years I had been transferred six times. My track record was bad.

The bus was filled with loud young men who had never travelled outside of California. I hated every last one of them. They had fucked up a good thing for me. For most of them Terminal Island was their first prison and it was my fifth. I was considered a seasoned convict.

"Yo, Ghost, you been down awhile. What do you think they're going to do with us?" one of the youngsters asked.

"We are all going to the East coast," I answered.

The bus became deathly silent. I knew that would get them to thinking and to put some fear into them.

"No shit!" one of them said.

"Yeah, I just spent almost three years out there," I continued.

When we arrived at the Metropolitan Correctional Center or MCC in San Diego, we were quickly placed in the SHU. I didn't even bother to look into the mirror. I knew that if I did those eyes would be disappointed in me.

The next day I learned that the Bureau of Prisons had issued a nationwide lockdown, and when I was interviewed by the DHO (Disciplinary Housing Officer) I was told that FCI Talladega was the first institution to lash out against the government's rejection of the Crack Law, sending a shockwave of violence throughout the BOP.

Incident reports were issued to the men that were involved in the riot. An older Mexican guy and I were the only ones who didn't receive a write-up.

"I see that you were only at Terminal Island for five weeks," the DHO officer said.

"Yeah, I was only five minutes from home," I answered.

He began shuffling through his stack of paperwork, and then got on the phone. "I'm sending two back," he said.

I was happy as a motherfucker to hear that.

"And why not?" he asked. "Inmate Verrett has been cleared of any wrong doing. He was only there for thirty-eight days, and his family lives in San Pedro," he said.

"They do not want you back there," he said.

I was heartbroken by the news, but there was nothing I could do about it. My past had caught up with me.

"Well, there's no use of keeping you in SHU," the DHO officer said, and I was immediately moved to the ninth floor. And that's where I saw my former cellmate from MDC, Freeway Rick.

"Damn homie, it's good to see you," he said as he and I shook hands and gave the homie hug.

"Are you back here on a violation?" I asked.

"No, Ghost, I caught a new case," he replied.

"What happened?" I asked.

After he told me the whole story, I said, "That's fucked up. So, how much time are they talking about?" I asked.

"If I lose the trial, life," he said.

"Then what's the deal?" I asked.

"Eleven years."

"How long have you been in here?" I asked.

"Eighteen months."

His case was widely publicized he was being interviewed by major news anchors, even Maxine Watters came to interview him. There had been a lot of corruption leading to his arrest.

"So what are you going to do?" I asked him.

"I'm putting twelve in the box," he said.

"So you're going to leave it up to twelve strangers to decide your fate?" I asked.

"If it's my fate to receive a life sentence, then so be it," he answered.

As the weeks progressed, Freeway Rick was found guilty and given a life sentence, which was later reduced to a twenty-year sentence. Then four more years were taken off, leaving him with a new release date in sometime in 2009.

Two months had passed and I was called to 'roll it up'. Rick gave me his mother's address so we could keep in touch. I met up with some of the youngsters who remained in SHU during our stay in San Diego. They all looked pale and starved. The spunk they had on our way to MCC wasn't in their eyes anymore. They looked like I once looked, defeated. I wondered if they had had an awakening while they were in that small 8x6 closet.

As we were being chained up, I asked one of the COs where I was going.

He flipped through his paperwork and said, "You're going to USP Florence."

USP Florence was the new maximum-security prison in Colorado. I remembered reading about it in USA Today. They nicknamed it the New Alcatraz because of the new design. No one would ever be able to breach the walls. I couldn't believe that my security level had been bumped up three levels without receiving a write-up.

I was the only one going to the super max. This was fucked up!

When you are going to a USP or United States Penitentiary, the protocol is to be black-boxed. That contraption was the most uncomfortable devise known to an inmate. You cannot move your hands, only your fingers.

The black box was designated for only high-risk inmates. It's an evil device, tortuous. The black box completely restricts any movement; you can't even scratch your nose, and if you had to pee, well that was almost impossible. Your hands remain at waist level until the box is removed. You have to be mentally strong while the box is on. It's like having your hand stuck to your waist with no possible movement whatsoever.

Once the black box was secured on my wrist, it forced me to learn how to meditate to get my mind off the torturous devise that bound me. For the weak at heart, the box consumed you. I had heard stories of men breaking their wrist trying to free themselves of the box. I had to travel deep within myself not to go crazy. The box was designed to break you. I needed to find a place of comfort in order to survive the long hours I would spend with the box.

I completely zoned out as I boarded Con Air once again. The black box had all of my attention. The leg irons didn't hurt as much as they cut into my ankles. I sat in the chair and closed my eyes and drifted to my childhood. I was at the golf course collecting golf balls, riding my bike and swimming. I loved to swim. When I opened my eyes ten hours had passed. We were now in Pueblo, Colorado.

CHAPTER 58

—

Thunder Dome

The prison bus labored its way through the twisting mountainous two lane roads of Pueblo, Colorado. The view was actually beautiful and I pretended that I was on a field trip with my classmates.

A sign came into view: 'You are now entering the land of the Pueblo Indians'. I had read about them in the Encyclopedia. They had built their homes on the sides of the mountains. The pictures in the book came to life. I actually saw holes in the side of the mountains where the Pueblo Indians had lived. I imagined myself walking inside them. I could really see how they lived and how they protected their homes. I had re-created colourful scenes from what I had read in the Encyclopedia. For a brief moment in time I lived with the Pueblo Indians. I hunted and I danced with them. I even sat around the fire while the elders told stories to the kids. Then I heard the call. The enemy was advancing and we prepared to defend our homes. Once everyone was secured, the ladders were pulled up and we began to defend our land.

Arrows blotted out the sun, filling the sky as they found their targets, but it wasn't enough, for this new enemy we faced was different from the other tribes we fought against. Our brave warriors began to fall, the sound of crackling thunder echoed throughout the valley. We couldn't win. We were defeated. We surrendered and we were chained up and put on a wagon headed to a reservation, never to see home again for many years to come.

I was brought back to reality as someone asked, "CO, how much longer before we get there?"

"Not much," the CO answered.

I kept those beautiful images of the endless miles of the pueblo Indian land burned into my memory. My eyes became the camera lens, and I would zoom in and blink, capturing what I saw. I made sure that what I saw would stay burned into my memory forever.

We had finally reached our destination. As the bus pulled into the parking lot, the bus seemed to be elated that we were here as it sat idling trying to catch its breath.

My eyes were glued to the window as I surveyed what seem to be air-conditioned units that were on ground level. I had learned that Florence had four facilities, and what I was looking at was the ADX or the Ultra Max. It was partially underground, and that's where we were headed.

I saw a large group of armed prison staff getting into their combat positions as the large triple razor wire entrance gate opened. We were surrounded. I thought, "Fuck, what did I do to deserve this?" Everybody on the bus remained quiet. I began to say a useless prayer, for I knew everyone else was doing the same thing. Next, a large steel door opened as the bus began its descent into what seemed like a cave, except there were no trees and rocks, only steel and concrete. Then the heavy steel door closed, cutting off all natural light.

We were now in a holding port. On the wall I saw a sign that read 'Welcome to the underworld' as the "Goon Squad surrounded the bus. The ADX is the most secured prison in the United States. Located partially under the earth's crust, there is no chance of escaping, and it felt like we were entering the bowels of hell to meet Satan. There was no natural sunlight or air, only fluorescent lighting and re-cycled air. This was a place where a man could be forgotten about.

The lieutenant boarded the bus. He was a big burly man, one of Satan's soldiers here in partial Hell. His voice was piercing as he made his announcement.

"Everyone shut the fuck up and follow my orders!" he barked. "And if you do not, I will physically correct you in an aggressive manner. This is your only warning. I am going to call your name, and when you hear your name, do not say anything until I command you to acknowledge."

I hated life, wishing I had chosen another way to live. If I could have looked into the future and seen this, I truly would have stayed in school, maybe even gone to college. I knew my big homies had never experienced this kind of treatment.

The first name was called. It was this white dude who was going to spend the rest of his life here. He had killed a CO in USP Lompoc with a hammer, beating him on the head. I noticed he had a black box on too. My stomach was in knots.

"Acknowledge," he barked. The guy did what he was told.

"When I say step to the right, only take one step. Remain in total compliance and you will not be corrected, got it?" "Now step!" And as the inmate became closer, the lieutenant pulled out a bullhorn and continued shouting even though he didn't need one.

"Good job convict!" he yelled into the bullhorn.

Once he reached the outside of the bus, he was promptly surrounded and four pointed by the Goon Squad. I knew they hated him for killing one of their own, and I'm sure that they were going to make him pay for it for the rest of his natural life. As he followed the commands, the Squad had their riot sticks cocked at the ready. I hoped that the guy wouldn't make any false moves, like sneezing or trip.

My survival mode kicked in and my body went into protect mode. An invisible shield surrounded me. My emotional state flat lined. I couldn't feel; I was now safe. Step by step, the inmate and the gauntlet of COs finally faded away, as I was preparing myself to be called.

The engine started and the door closed. He was the only inmate to be called. A sigh of relief was felt amongst the remaining passengers. I couldn't wait to get back on ground level and feel the sunshine pierce the barred tinted windows of the bus. I was grateful.

The ADX housed some of America's most notorious criminals. The most popular resident was the Italian Mafia boss, John Gotti. ADX is where he died. I remembered reading about ADX in the USA Today newspaper. It was designed for no other human contact other than a CO. You couldn't even physically read your letters, couldn't touch them, they had to be read on a screen, even the showers were in the cell, absolutely no other human contact.

The bus was headed to the USP, which was only across the street. That's where I was going. At least I could see the sky and clouds and breathe fresh air. I was grateful for that.

CHAPTER 59

—

Main Line

Once in R&D (Receiving and Discharge), the intake process began, and the black box and the chains were finally removed.

"Verrett," the lieutenant said as he read from his clipboard. "All black box arrivals go to SHU for the captain's review for seven days, and then you go to the mainline."

I didn't even protest. I was exhausted. I needed some sleep and I felt like I could sleep for a week. USP Florence was a new prison. The old steel bar doors were replaced with thick heavy metal doors. Inside the cells, the toilet and sink weren't connected. The rooms were almost modern and clean, but there was a funny smell coming out of the vents like something had died in there. Once inside the cell the smell grew stronger over the next couple days.

When you're in SHU, you're allowed to shower twice a week. There was also a cell rotation every month, which meant you changed cells. I looked forward to shower day; otherwise it was birdbaths in the sink.

The guys in the cell next door declined to take showers and recreation. I didn't understand why. The smell was almost unbearable. It stuck to your skin, and when it came time to eat chow, that foul smell disrupted my appetite. Everyone thought that a big rat had gotten trapped in the vents and died and everyone started to complain about the smell. The COs said that they would put in a work order to have the vents checked, but that process would take up to a month, and truth be told, they really didn't give a damn while they sat in their air condition command room.

On the day of the cell rotation, which meant that you had to change cells every thirty days; everyone learned what the bad smell was in the cell next to mine. The occupants were ordered to roll it up, to move to another cell. What I heard next made the hairs on the back of my neck stand straight up. The sound of a devilish laugh echoed throughout the Special Housing Unit. The inmate laughed uncontrollably, like a mad man in a horror movie kind of laugh. I knew that he had totally lost his mind.

"Oh, shit!" I heard of the COs say, as another CO ordered the mad man to cuff up.

What we all learned was that the mad man had killed his cellmate. He had cut his throat with a Bic razor that was given to him by a CO. I had learned that they had gotten into an argument, and as the victim slept the crazed man held him down and slit his throat.

"He's been dead four days, you stupid muthafuckas. What? You can't do anything to me. I already have two life sentences," he said, as he began laughing and sounding like Vincent Price.

The Lieutenant tried to get him to cuff up, but to no avail.

"Come in and get me," he taunted them.

It appeared that the COs was unprepared for this kind of behaviors and they were clueless as to what to do.

The lieutenant ordered a cell extraction that means that the staff brings in their tactical team who are armed with pistols that shoot salt rocks. The salt rocks don't penetrate the skin, but it causes enough pain to make you think you've been shot.

I stood at my cell door looking out of the small window as all the other inmates watched with curiosity. It was like watching a real life horror movie, but with no pushy director.

The lieutenant fired into the cell, *bang, bang, hitting* the crazed man as he screamed in pain. His shrieks reverberated in his tiny cell, which only seemed to fuel his rage. Lethal rounds were not authorized when extracting an inmate from a cell. The next course of action was to use pepper spray.

The prison staff stood in combat formation in full riot gear waiting to pounce on the prisoner. They all started to put on their gas mask, and I knew it wouldn't be long before the crazed man gave up. I quickly grabbed my towel and soaked it in water and wrapped it around my nose and mouth.

They fired a canister into the cell and within seconds the gas filled his tiny cell. I could hear him gasping for air and laughing at the same time. He had given up as they rushed into the cell, four pointed and hog-tied him. The pepper spray began to seep out of his cell into the hallway and into everyone's cell. My cellie and I began to cough. The wet towels didn't work as good as a gas mask. Our eyes instantly teared up and it was hard to breathe. We quickly lined the door with wet toilet paper in hopes of stopping the pepper stray from entering our cell.

As the prison staff dragged him away, all we could hear was, "Fuck you! You can't do anything to me! I got three life sentences!" he shouted between his coughing and laughing.

His voice penetrated the entire building and my ears. He was right. They couldn't do anything to him but keep him locked in a room for the rest of his life, where they had to let him use the phone, take a shower twice a week and feed him three times a day.

I had never in my life witnessed such a disregard for life. Yeah, I lived the street life, but this was different. I felt bad for the man that had been killed. His family would only get a quick phone call informing them that their son or husband or brother had been killed as he slept. To die in prison was almost unthinkable; yeah in a hail of gunfire, but not in prison.

The body was taken out of the cell on a gurney. Rigormortis had set in. I watched the stiff and lifeless body bounce as they guided it down the tier. I had only been in USP Florence for a few days. Back in the hood, I could bet that my big homies had never witnessed this kind of stuff before. It will forever be engrained in my memory.

I learned that after he killed his cellie, he used the razor to open his chest and remove all of his internal organs, and then he flushing them down the toilet as his body began to rot. My cellie opened his Bible and said a prayer for him and his family.

A few days later, the stench of the decomposing corpse began to lift, but the thoughts of what happened next door to me stayed with me. Only a twelve-inch concrete wall had separated me from that murderous act.

My time was up and the Captain's review was complete. I was released from Special Housing Unit and assigned to Delta A. As I was being led down the walkway with my bedroll, a shot of adrenaline shot throughout my body. It was V-Mac coming in my direction, but he looked different. He was wearing a Fez, which was only worn by the Moorish Muslims. V-Mac had converted and joined the Moorish Science Temple of America.

I instantly became defensive as I greeted V-Mac.

"What up, Loc?" I said.

"Hello my brother" he responded.

"You a Muslim now?" I asked.

"I have always been a Muslim," he answered. "What unit do they have you in?" he continued.

"Delta A."

"There are some good brothers in there," he replied.

"All right then, V-Mac," I said as we shook hands.

"I go by Brother Vincent now," he said.

"Okay, Brother Vincent. How long have you been here?" I asked.

"Two years." he responded.

It was amazing to see the change in him in only a few years. I wondered what drove him to want to change. Being religious in prison wasn't for me. I enjoyed getting high and drinking. It helped me not to deal with reality and I liked it that way, but joining a religious group just wasn't for me.

"As-salaam aleichem, brother," he said

"And the same to you," I answered.

"Oh yeah, I want to invite you to the temple real soon. Okay?" he added.

"I'll think about it," I answered.

As he walked away, I watched the tassel on his Fez flop from side to side. He was now under the teachings of Noble Drew Ali, the founder of The Moorish Science Temple.

I made my way to Delta Unit and I checked out my surroundings. The yard was small, the softball diamond was deserted, and the grassed looked like it needed to be watered and on the far side of the yard I saw the weight pile. It was crowded with men pumping iron. I could hear grunts and groans from the distance and the sounds of weights being dropped onto the thick rubber mats.

I was now at the entrance of the unit. Above the door there was a security camera mounted to the wall. I was being watched.

"State your name and number," the voice coming out of the speaker said.

"Verrett, 92857-012," I answered.

Next, the big heavy metal door opened and I was ordered to step inside. Once inside, the door closed with a loud thud. I was now standing in what seemed to be a holding area. It was only about ten feet wide and ten feet long. That's when the Unit Officer appeared behind the other security door.

"Drop your bedroll and shake everything out," he ordered me. "Now strip. Remove all of your clothing."

By this time, I was used to stripping and going through the motions. It didn't bother me any longer. I remember the first time I was told to remove my clothing. It was the most incomprehensible demoralizing act I'd ever experienced. Now it was almost second nature.

I entered the unit and followed the Unit Officer to his office. It was still new and the design reminded me of MDC, only bigger. It was the same scalene triangle shape. The cells on the upper and lower tiers lined three of the scalene walls. The showers were located at each end of the unit, four showers on the second tier and four on the bottom, and one shower for the handicapped.

There were four different TV rooms. The first room I was occupied by the Spanish-speaking inmates. They were watching some kind of game show. They watched me as I passed. Next was the black TV room. It was partially empty, except for a few guys watching BET. It was filled up with empty chairs. I knew that everyone had their designated spot, and I would find mine later. In the white TV room, they were watching an old movie, and one was for the old men. Now the funny thing about the old men they were all of different races. I guess that they were too old to play the race card. It reminded me of the Old Heads at Lompoc.

I was assigned to cell number 103, but before I went to the cell, I went to the black TV room to ask who lived there. As I entered there was a guy standing in front of the television.

"Say homie, who lives in 103?" I asked.

"That's me," a guy spoke up, looking at me as if sizing me up.

"Yeah, homie, they put me in there with you," I said.

"Where you from?" he asked.

"I'm Ghost from Harbor City," I answered.

"Where you from?" I asked.

"I'm Bones from South Central," he said.

We then shook hands our neighbourhoods' were allies. I was then introduced to the rest of the homies, Bloods and Crips. There was no set tripping in Florence. Basically, it was State against State. Bones continued to talk as he gave me the tour of Florence. We stopped at the bleachers of the baseball diamond to talk to some homeboys who were just about to fire up a joint and Bones introduced me to them.

"Where you from, homie?" asked the one who called himself Cycho.

"I'm from Harbor City," I answered as he passed the joint to me. I was nervous to be smoking outdoors in the open like this. Massive gun towers surrounded the small coliseum-like prison yard.

Two COs escorted a guy across the baseball field. He was handcuffed and heading to SHU. All of a sudden two Mexican guys bolted from the stands headed toward the handcuffed inmate. As if in slow motion, they pulled out what seemed to be an ice pick. The two COs and the guy handcuffed didn't even see them coming until it was too late. They leaped on him like a cheetah does and impala. It was like watching the Discovery channel, only with humans. The two COs were taken by surprise as the predators began their attack, leaving the bound inmate helpless. The inmate laid face down in the dried grass, as his attacker stabbed him several times. His screams crackled like thunder. I felt his pain. The man was helpless. Something inside of me wanted to help.

My body involuntarily began to rise, but Bones grabbed my arm. "It ain't our business Ghost."

The deuces were activated, which means no movement on the yard. All of the guards in the gun towers took their aim. With no warning shots, the crackle of gunfire reverberated throughout the prison yard, and throughout my body. I didn't know if anybody else felt it, but I did. One of the attackers screamed in pain as he bowled over and clutched his hand. The sharp shooter had shot the ice pick out of his hand that's when they were both rushed by a half dozen guards.

"Everybody down" was the announcement over the PA systems. We all lay in the dirt, waiting for our next instructions.

I had only been in USP Florence for seven days and already two men had died violent deaths. I had learned that the Texas Family was beefing with the Kansas City car. The Texas Family or TF was thick in numbers. That's the reason the Crips and Bloods had to unite. It was said that the shot caller for the TF ordered the hit and used what is called a Crash dummy to carry it out. Crash dummies were expendable. They either did the hit, or they got hit. A lose, lose situation.

USP Florence was like being in Gladiator school where only the smart and strong survived. The atmosphere was like an ancient Roman arena, where you ate, exercised and waited for your time to defend yourself. Alcohol was prevalent. It kept me numb to my surroundings. Every night in my drunken state, I would offer my inebriated prayers not to be in a position to use the knives I'd been given to kill anyone.

CHAPTER 60

—

In The Name of Islam

I had signed up in the chaplain's office to attend the Jumah Muslim services that were held on Fridays. I learned that the word Jumah means Friday in Arabic. I attended the services, not because I was interested in their messages. It was only to get out of work early.

The two-lane corridor was congested with men as we stood waiting to pass through the metal detector to get into the chapel. We passed the security checkpoint and entered the sanctuary, which was filled with different groups of Muslims. I instantly recognized the Muslims that represented the Nation of Islam. They always looked intense. The next group was the five percenters. They were founded by the radical Clarence 13 X who was found shot to death in New York. The Moorish Science Temple of America was congregated in the second largest room. I saw Brother Vincent performing his prayers. As the tassel on his fez dangled, I couldn't help but think of that Flintstones cartoon when Fred and Barney wore their fez hats as they went to the lodge to pay homage to the Grand Pubbah.

I walked into the Sunni Muslim service. The room was filled with different races, even whites. I had never seen a white Muslim before, especially an ex-biker with tattoos who had turned Muslim. He looked like he was at peace with himself as he sat on the ground reading his Qur'an. I wondered what the Arian Brotherhood thought about him. The transformation must have been hard, from being a White Supremacist to a Muslim. The Muslims were larger numbers than the Arians. No one messed with the Muslims, not even the Crips and Bloods.

The others, they all had on their Kuffie hats, and some were doing their prayers as I found a place to sit. The Sunni service was different from the other Muslim services. Everyone sat on mats whispering words in Arabic. An Asian Muslim who called himself Hamza stood to his feet and began to recite the call to prayer. The sounds and words were beautiful. It penetrated my soul even though I couldn't understand a word. The room was completely quiet, and as he finished, Ahmed the inmate Imam approached the podium and began his sermon.

I recognized Ahmed from his trial. He was charged with the failed attempt to blow up the World Trade Center in New York back in 1993. The explosive packs he had didn't go off as the others had. He was quickly arrested, charged and convicted, then sentenced to six hundred years, and now here he was preaching about Oneness and peace, but his eyes revealed that there was no peace within him, only hate, which seemed to be deep rooted. He wanted the United States to fall. Ahmed was one of those dudes that would blow up a bus with my mother on it thinking it would take down the United States. Muslims like Ahmed made Muslims look bad, especially any Arab-looking people. He should have gotten the death penalty. What made him dangerous was that he was a great speaker. He could recite the Qur'an beautifully, and he was in command of the entire prison Muslim community.

Over the next several months I studied the Qur'an and the Islamic Constitution. I came across this word Jihad, which meant Holy War. I had read that during the time of war a Muslim is forbidden to harm the man in the field. They are even forbidden to even cut down a tree. They are only supposed to fight those who fight against them, so that cancels out blowing up innocent people on busses.

Rahsool was the younger of the two that was convicted of attempting to blow up the World Trade Center. He seemed very different from Ahmed.

When the Jum'ah service ended, and as I was leaving the chapel, Ahmed tapped me on the shoulder and introduced himself. "Salaam aleichem, Brother. I am Ahmed the Imam."

"What's up?" I said.

"Brother, are you thinking about converting to Islam and joining the brotherhood?" he asked.

"No, I'm not. I'm a Crip," I told Ahmed.

He gave me a long stare as if sizing me up, and from then on I was invisible to him. Rahsool was cool with it. We became friends, I guess. We would meet in the leisure library and watch videos, or drink coffee on the football field bleachers and talk. I was curious about how he got hooked up with Ahmed.

The penitentiary is filled with good men that lacked the proper guidance and the support they need to make positive choices and decisions. On the other hand, there are men who are just plain evil like Ahmed, who manipulate inexperienced minds like Rahsool into doing acts of terrorism, who probably thought that he was doing something that was just. Because of that bad information, Rahsool would send the rest of his life in prison.

Rahsool told me that he has been selected for the mission to attack the United States and that his family had been given fifty thousand dollars for his part.

"Ghost, I was treated like royalty after I agreed. They gave me everything. They told me that Allah would give me seventy-two virgins when I got to Paradise, and that I was doing Allah's work."

"Did you ever have second thoughts?" I asked him.

"Yeah, I did, but once you're selected, you can't refuse. If you do, then your family can't buy, sell or trade," he said.

"That's fucked up," I answered.

"Yeah, it's fucked up if your family can't eat," he responded.

"But what about the people you harmed and their families?" I asked.

"You don't think about that, only your family and that you're doing it for Allah," he said.

"Wow, that's a trip," I said.

I thought back to how I had been groomed by my big homies to get that money. I never thought about blowing up a building or harming people, but what I was doing had the same affect. I harmed people and their families by selling drugs. Rahsool and I were like many other men and women who thought they were doing the right thing. Deep down we would have picked another way of life. I never wanted to grow up and be a drug dealer, and I'm sure that Rahsool hadn't wanted to grow up and be a suicide bomber either. Just like the thousands of men I'd came in contact with, we all would have chosen education and employment. What it boiled down to was the information, guidance and the choices and decisions we'd made.

CHAPTER 61

—

Snowflakes

Restless, I woke up in the middle of the night to use the toilet and thousands of thoughts shot through my mind. The entire unit was quiet, and I enjoyed the silence except for the heavy breathing of my cellie. I needed to talk to someone, so I stood in front of the mirror, hoping those eyes would appear, but they didn't. It was just my reflection.

Looking out of the tiny window of my cell, my heart began to race with excitement. IT WAS SNOWING. I had never seen snow before and it was beautiful. The entire prison yard was blanketed with it. For a brief moment, I was transported to some far away winter wonderland where prison didn't exist. All the bad things that had happened on the yard were covered. The snowflakes drifted and accumulated on the window ledge and I noticed that every snowflake had a different design. I remembered when I was in elementary school our teacher would have us cut snowflakes out of paper to decorate our classroom for Christmas. I hadn't believed her when she said that all snowflakes had different designs until now. Thousands of random thoughts that raced through my mind didn't seem so important as I counted snowflakes and drifted off into a peaceful sleep.

The next morning, as I prepared to leave the unit and walk in the snow, there was an old man in a wheel chair with a stack of books on his lap. I figured he was headed to the law library. It was obvious that he was having a hard time keeping the books from slipping off his lap, so I asked if I could help him since I was headed to the leisure library to watch old movies.

"Can I help you?" I asked him.

He gave me a look of gratitude and answered, "Thank you young man."

The ten-minute move was called and we headed out. The snow covered everything and it was thick. I couldn't tell where the grass and the sidewalk met. Mr. Gossett was a big man, and I struggled to keep him on the sidewalk. We lost traction on a patch of ice and I lost control of the wheelchair. We slid off the path and tumbled into the snow bank.

I hopped up and said, "Mr. Gossett, are you all right?"

He looked at me and started laughing uncontrollably He started making half a snow angel, then I joined him.

Mr. Gossett was nearly three hundred pounds of dead weight and he was tall. I was going to need some help to pick his big ass up and put him in his chair. We both continued to laugh.

"Laughter's good for the soul," he said. "It's been years since I laid in snow."

"I never been in the snow," I said.

"Thank you for asking to help me," he finally said, as a group of guys came running over and surrounded us.

"Mr. Gossett, you okay?" they asked, while giving me dirty looks. I held my slippery ground and returned their gaze.

"Who's this? one of them asked.

"He's okay. Tell 'em your name son," Mr. Gossett said.

"I'm Ghost from Harbor City," I announced.

I didn't like the looks I was getting from those dudes. They probably thought I had caused the accident or pushed Mr. Gossett over. I just wanted to help out the old handicapped man get to the law library and now I was being confronted for my kindness. I learned that Mr. Gossett was the founder of the notorious Chicago Gangster Disciples, the largest organized gang in Chicago. They were bigger that the Crips and Bloods.

"I have a lot of respect for this young man," Mr. Gossett told the crowd of his soldiers. Once he said that their faces and demeanour relaxed. I instantly felt at ease as they began to guide us to the law library. The entire Chicago Disciples treated me with respect.

"I've been watching you up in the unit," Mr. Gossett said. "You act wild, but you're not. You're not supposed to be here. There's something about that's different."

Mr. Gossett and I talked a lot about different things. He gave me a lot of game about life.

"You're just missing pieces of information," he said. "Everybody has a gift or a talent. We just need to take the time to understand that vibration we all have inside of us."

I was blown away by his words. Chills ran through my body because I knew what he was talking about. I had always masked that vibration. I thought I was the only one who felt it.

"Be thankful that you have another chance at life because I don't have a date to go home," Mr. Gossett said. He was fighting the courts to get a release date. He was serving a natural life sentence and was going to die fighting.

We would play chess and drink coffee. Usually I would beat him, or maybe he would let me win, but I was so enthralled by what he told me that I didn't pay attention as he said, "Checkmate," with a laugh.

"You're smart, young Ghost," he would say. "You talk like everybody here, but you're not like everybody here, you really don't fit in here. What's the last book you read?" he asked.

"The Encyclopedia Britannica," I said. "From A to Z."

As he continued talking, something happened on the yard with the California car. One of the homies named Sito had gotten into it with a DC Boy over a pair of tennis shoes. Sito was known for being a fuck-up and was on thin ice with the homies. The next thing I knew, all the homies were summoned to the yard because it was about to go down. All the Crips were armed with what we called bone crushers.

I started to walk away.

"Where you going?" Mr. Gossett asked.

I respected Mr. Gossett, but I was a Crip, not a Gangster Disciple and when the call was made I had to show up.

"I gotta go," I told him. I went to my cell and padded my jacket with books, which was my prison armor in case I was stabbed. The books would stop the knife from puncturing my skin. I walked to the gym at a fast pace with Jack-Nasty, Jay-Bone and Self-Made.

Once we entered the gym area I was approached by the homie, Psychotic. He grabbed me by the arm like a big brother would do and asked, "What the fuck are you doing here?" he asked.

Psychotic was serving a life and thirty-year prison sentence for killing an undercover DEA agent.

"The same thang you doing," I answered.

"Niggas gonna die in here today, and the ones who don't are going to catch murder beefs." "Ghost, homie, you only got ten years left, most niggas in here is washed up."

I didn't want to be viewed as a coward, but Psychotic made a lot of sense. He got so close to my face I could smell the tobacco on his breath and he looked directly into my eyes.

"Homie, you got work to do when you get out. Most motherfuckers aren't ever going home. This is our world, not yours. Take your ass back to the unit," he said.

Before I could protest, he grabbed my arm and said, "I know you're a rider. I'll let the homies know that."

Everything he said started to sink in as I headed toward the exit with the homie, Self-Made.

Back in the housing unit, I saw Mr. Gossett waiting by his cell. As I approached him, I saw the look of disappointment on his face. I leaned against the wall, lost for words, not knowing what to say.

"You need to listen to that vibration, Ghost, and let people see you for who you really are," he said, as he wheeled himself into his cell, leaving me with those words.

I went into my cell and fired up a joint, waiting for the sirens to blare and I watched the snowfall. It seemed like an eternity before Psychotic and the rest of the homies returned. Everything had been squashed.

"Ghost homie, you haven't got to prove nothing we know you're a rider," Psychotic said and he exited my cell.

It was now 1997. Two years had passed so quickly. I was headed to the chow hall when the Unit Manager called my name. At first I thought I was going to be given a piss test.

The Unit Manager said, "You were never supposed to be here. Your security level was never high enough. Someone messed up your paperwork. You haven't had a write up in over two years and we have to get you out of here ASAP.

That news was unexpected and I was excited and sad to leave. For some strange reason I went to see Mr. Gossett to tell him that he'd been right. I was never supposed to be here. That night we played chess and drank coffee until lockdown.

In the early morning hours I was awakened and told to report to R&D. As I walked the compound with all of my personal property, I was grateful for the lessons I'd learned and for the men that understood me.

CHAPTER 62

Reunited

Con-Air landed at the Portland, Oregon International Airport and we were quickly loaded into the prison buses and taken to FCI Sheridan. After the arrival process was complete, I was assigned to Unit 3-B. That was to be my new home.

I was dog tired and needed to get some rest after spending ten hours handcuffed on an airplane. I entered the cell and saw my new cellie lying on his bunk. He rolled over to see who was coming in, and a big ole Kool Aid smile replaced his frown. It was C-Style. I hadn't seen him since 1991, when I was at FCI Lompoc.

He jumped up and gave me the homie hug.

"Damn, Ghost, what's happening? Where you coming from"? he asked excitedly.

He had a lot of questions and wouldn't give me the time to answer any of them. I knew he was as happy to see me as I was to see him, but I was burned out from the long flight. I threw my bedroll on the top bunk and flopped down on the plastic chair and collected my thoughts.

"Well, when I left you, I went to Phoenix. From there I went to El Reno, then Oakdale. I was on the yard for only twelve days before they put me in SHU for nine months. Once I left there I went to Talladega, Alabama. I stayed there for a while, then went to Terminal Island. I was there for thirty-eight days before they had a riot and they shot me to USP Florence, and now I'm here."

"Damn, homie, you been fucking up," C-Style commented.

"Man, I ain't had a write-up since Phoenix."

"Then how in the fuck did you end up in USP Florence?" C-Style questioned.

"Shit, it was a conspiracy," I said jokingly.

Being transferred constantly was stressful, but it helped break up my time. I never really got used to being in one place for a long period of time. I became used to being transferred. If Con Air had frequent flyer miles I would have the platinum card. There was an endless rotation of men and women being shuffled from prison to prison. I wondered if it would ever stop I was always prepared to be shipped out at a moment's notice. Sometimes I felt like a slave going from one plantation to another.

Sheridan was built in 1987, and was the home of nearly eighteen hundred inmates, mostly from the Northwest part of the United States. Back when I was on the streets, crack cocaine was the cheapest and highly addictive street drug you could purchase which was sold mostly by black and Hispanic dealers. Crystal Meth, which was homemade and extremely addictive and the new cash cow now rivalled it for drug dealers. It also cut out the overseas drug trade because the manufacturers or cooks could buy all of the ingredients at the local supermarkets.

I didn't like the weather in Sheridan because it rained constantly, and the skies were always grey. It made me feel depressed. I understood why the suicide rate was high in the northwest. What I did enjoy was the inside gym with a second story track where I could walk my laps and smoke, that's where everybody went to get high and drink, the perfect blind spot.

I went down to sit on the bleachers and feel sorry for myself while listening to the oldies on my walk-man. I noticed this young white dude leaning over the safety rail on the second story level, and then all of a sudden he jumped and fell almost fifty feet, landing head first on the basketball court, snapping his neck, killing himself instantly.

"Man down! Man down!" I yelled.

"Go get the Rec CO!" I screamed. "Get the Rec CO!"

Everyone stared in shock at the young man's twisted body. I felt for him and how his family would feel once they received the news that their son killed himself in prison. He had given up and couldn't handle the ugly side of the game. My feelings were mixed. I became angry with him. He could have made it; he could have walked out of prison a different person. He hadn't given it a chance. He lost the fight. He could have found it within himself.

"Hey, that's Jason!" someone in the crowd yelled. "That's Jason!"

"He's a coward!" another yelled.

I began to shake involuntarily with anger as the comments continued. Like a volcano, I exploded, spooling obscenities that flowed like hot lava.

"Shut the fuck up! He's not a coward. He wasn't as strong as us!" I barked.

The crowd of inmates looked confused as I stood over his lifeless body and that's when all of my crew made their way through the ever-growing crowd.

"Back this motherfucker up!" I ordered my homies.

Just as the crowd began to back up, the Recreation Officers arrived with a stretcher and placed Jason's lifeless body on it. Jason was a nineteen-year-old kid serving a ten-year sentence for selling Meth. He was in pain and didn't want to feel anymore. I felt a strange connection with him. What made me different? If he would have weathered the time he would have been out before me by eight years and moved on with his life. Jason was like me and many other people who made bad decisions and listened to the wrong people.

The crazy thing was he hadn't even screamed when he jumped.

CHAPTER 63

—

Shot Calling

My reputation as a Rider placed me in the position to lead or call the shots a responsibility I did not want, but was necessary to keep our fraternity of gang members organized. Just like in the military, I had risen through the ranks and earned my stripes. I counseled the homies on the prison politics of diplomatic relations with other gang leaders to discourage potential race or gang riots. I also chaired our disciplinary board, which meant if one of our soldiers got out of line or disrespected another race, that race could not take the matter into their own hands. They would contact me and the other OGs and I would hold our own form of justice.

Our numbers were growing rapidly. There were too many dudes coming off the bus claiming to be Crips and Bloods. I was positive that it was for protection. I was becoming paranoid, so I called a meeting on the yard, requesting that everyone bring their PSI (Pre-Sentence Investigation) reports.

This court record exposed the truth about your case and most importantly, if you testified against anyone. I didn't want any rats in our clique. There were only two sections that needed to be reviewed in the PSI Report. The first was the government's recommendation for a 5K1.1 downward departure, which meant that you had cooperated with the government. That section should state NONE. The second section indicated if there had been a plea in the case.

333

Only half of the men returned with their paperwork. The other half knew that they could not stay on the yard and immediately turned them over to SHU (Special Housing Unit), which instantly became over populated. Later that day, I was called into the lieutenant's office for questioning. I was known for being the leader or shot caller.

After the four o'clock count C-Style and I remained in the cell.

"Man, you changed," he said.

"What do you mean?" I responded.

"Man, you running around here telling motherfuckers what to do, like who can stay on the yard and who can't," C-Style replied.

"I have a lot more experience than most homies here."

"One thing for sure and two things for certain, you aren't never going to tell me what to do," C-Style said.

I sat listening to him, and then reached for my pack of Camel cigarettes. "Give me a light," I told him.

C-Style struck a match and lit my cigarette, then noticed the smile on my face, and realized what he was doing. We instantly busted out into laughter. C-Style and I were tight, but seven years and seven prisons had passed. While Sheridan had only been his second prison, a lot had happened for me during those years.

Shortly after the Bureau of Prisons changed the security point system, which affected me, I was going to be transferred again. In the early morning hours, I heard those familiar words, "Verrett, roll it up."

Sitting once again on Con Air, I drifted to a place of peace within myself. Ten hours later, I woke up in Safford, Arizona.

CHAPTER 64

—

Y2K

A decade had passed. As the new millennium began, I was now twenty-nine years old. A full ten years of my life had been spent locked away from society, but internally I didn't feel it. I was basically growing into manhood in prison, being reared by the justice system.

Deep inside of me I was free, for my spirit could not be handcuffed or locked away by the Bureau of Prisons. Only I held those keys to my freedom, but occasionally I would misplace them when I didn't want to deal with reality, and alcohol was my vehicle that would transport me to another dimension. That's when the ugly side of me would surface. When I got loaded I wasn't De'Juan. I was Ghost, bitter and unbending. I didn't know how to control that part of me. When I would drink I instantly became a different person and ultimately end up being placed in SHU and transferred.

Safford, Arizona was about thirty miles from the Mexico border. The inmate population was sixty percent Mexican Nationals that were waiting for deportation. The announcements over the PA system were even in Spanish.

My homie, Big Dollar, knew I was coming to Safford, and waited for me to exit R&D (Receiving and Discharge). I saw him before he saw me. He didn't recognize me at first. I had gained forty pounds and most of it was muscle. I could understand why he didn't recognize me.

The last time he'd seen me I was seventeen years old and now I was a twenty-nine year old grown man.

"What's up, Ghost?" Big Dollar shouted with a big smile.

I returned his smile with one just as big. The last time I'd seen him was at a nightclub in Hollywood, and he still looked the same, tall and slim.

"What's up, homeboy?" I responded. "What's it like here?"

"It's laid back, but the black population is short. There are only eighteen of us here. You make nineteen," he said.

"Damn."

Big Dollar walked me to the inmate laundry where he had the hook up on new clothes. After that, I met all the homies. I was disappointed that half of the black population was old men and the other half was OTCs (Out of Town Crips) and OTBs (Out of Town Bloods). I wondered if we could count on them if anything ever went down.

The AW (Assistant Warden) named Hawkins remembered me from Lompoc. He had risen through the ranks fast in only ten years. When he saw me standing in the chow line he motioned me to go to him and I obeyed.

"Mr. Verrett, are you back on a violation?" he questioned.

"I ain't ever got out yet," I answered.

"How much time do you have remaining?" he asked.

"Six and a half left," I replied.

He stood there surrounded by his subordinates, trying to look important as they almost stared a hole in me.

"I need to talk with you, Mr. Verrett," he said. "So when you're finished eating wait for me outside of the dining hall."

"Okay," I simply answered.

"And by the way, how old are you now? You were a kid when you first came in."

"Yeah, I was nineteen. I'm twenty nine now," I answered.

His colleagues winced at my answer.

I felt bad for a moment. I had instantly lost my appetite and I just picked at the food on my tray. Big Dolla knew something was wrong with me. A wave of self-pity overcame me and I felt the strong urge to get loaded.

After hearing what Hawkins had to say, I went on the hunt. I needed a drink-a big drink. I still didn't know how to deal with reality. I hurt on the inside and I hated it when someone told me about how much time I'd been in prison. I already knew that. I didn't need anybody reminding me.

"Damn Ghost, you drink everyday like an alcoholic homie" Big Dolla said.

"Alcoholics push shopping carts and live under bridges," I said. "I only have three small cups a day." I defended my actions while finishing my third cup.

What I enjoyed about Safford were the sunsets. It reminded me of how I felt inside. During the day, the sun would shine bright, proving its power and strength, just as I would put on my mask and posture on the yard, basically saying, 'Don't fuck with me,' but when the sun began to set, it would reveal its softer side. The gentle light would pierce the scattered clouds revealing different colors and the beauty of the heavens. When I was in the safety of my cell I would reveal the real me. I remember reading in the Encyclopedia that all stars had different surface temperatures and different colors, which are seen in rainbows and sunsets.

The months passed by quickly. My eleventh birthday in prison was just a few weeks away. My mother had planned on driving ten hours from San Pedro, California to Safford, but she was going to bring my sister and her kids. It had been three years since I'd seen my mother, and nine years since I'd seen my sister. During those years she had two more children. I was getting used to not seeing my family. It kept me safe from showing my feelings that I was human. Yeah, I would talk to them on the phone and send pictures, but physically seeing them was different.

I woke up on May 31st, 2000 and it was official. I was a thirty-year-old convict who had spent all of his twenties in prison. A deep sadness engulfed me. Big Dollar dropped by my cell to give me a card and a bag of M&Ms. I just smiled and thanked him.

As I was dressing for my visit, I heard my name called over the PA system. "Verrett, report to the visiting room, you have a visit."

I was excited and nervous at the same time. I grabbed my photo tickets and prison ID and headed toward the visiting room.

Once I entered the visiting room I heard a little girl's voice yell out, "Uncle!" To my right was my family. My niece, Tiara, sprinted across the visiting room and jumped into my arms, squeezing me tight while my mother, sister and nephews watched. This was the first time I'd seen my four-year-old niece in person, and she knew me and loved me. The boys had gotten big. Terry was now eleven and Lynell was eight. I had watched those kids grow up only in pictures, now here they were with their arms wrapped around my neck. Being loved was the greatest feeling I had ever felt. Nothing could compare to it. Those kids showed that I was capable of being loved.

I was stricken by a wave of sadness as I sat in the plastic chair. I just realized that the choice and decisions I'd made affected my family, even the ones not even born yet, and these kids had no business coming into a prison. My sister revealed to me that she hated me for leaving because she didn't have a big brother around, and that my mother had had a nervous breakdown because of my incarceration. I had never realized that being locked up could destroy a family even though they were free.

All I could do was hold on tight to those two little boys and that precious little girl and squeeze them, letting them know that Uncle is real and that I love them. At that very moment I understood the meaning of unconditional love. When I looked into their sparkling eyes, they loved me.

When the hugging was over, my oldest nephew asked, "Uncle, why are you in here?"

His question took me by surprise.

Then my sister interrupted with "He's in school," she said.

I gave my sister a confused look. Everyone instantly became quiet and I broke the silence.

"Where do you think I am?" I asked.

"In school," they all chimed in.

I looked at my sister and mother. "I'm going to tell them the truth," I said.

Turning my attention to the kids, I said, "This is not a school. I made a bad decision when I was young, and that's why I'm in prison."

Tiara leaned in real close, looked me directly in the eyes and asked, "Uncle, did you steal some candy from the store?" she innocently asked.

My heart almost melted right there. "No sweetie, I sold something that is illegal and I got in trouble and they put me in here. It's like being on punishment," I said.

"Well, I'm never going to do anything like that," she said with conviction. "I was on punishment for one hour, and mommy sent me to my room and I missed my favorite cartoon, Dora the Explorer."

My mother and sister just started laughing, while the boys remained quiet.

"I don't care," Tiara said, breaking the silence. "You are still my Uncle."

I ain't going to lie, I was choked with the emotion, of the unconditional love this child gave me. I tried my best to hold back my tears. My mother and sister failed at the task, as tears filled their eyes. I was stuck and had to find something to divert my feelings, so I adjusted my ponytail.

"Uncle, can I comb your hair?" she asked.

"Yes, you can, baby," I answered.

She was gentle at first, and then really got into what she was doing.

"Uncle, your hair is long like a lady's hair. It's longer than my Mommy and Grandma's hair," she said with a small laugh.

Long hair was part of my identity now. I was known as the light-skinned one with the long hair.

When you're in prison you forget how gentle a child's touch can be. I noticed the children of the other inmates. Their children would hold onto their faces, constantly keeping contact with their fathers. I had only seen it on television. I'd never experienced this before. Holding my nephews and nieces filled my empty void with love.

I noticed that something was wrong with Terry. He wouldn't make much eye contact with me, while Lynell was busy trying to wrap his hands around my bicep and comparing his eight-year-old arm to mine. Tiara was oblivious to my situation as she focused her energy on combing my hair.

After we had eaten from the visiting room vending machines, it was time to take our visiting room family pictures. This was unnatural to take family photos in prison. Grief and despair, coupled with sadness began to creep into me. I realized that this is what it's all about family and love. When it came down to it, it was family that travelled ten hours to come visit me. Not one of my homies even attempted the long trek. I swore to myself that things would be different when I was released.

Visiting time was coming to a close and the COs made their announcements. "Visiting is over in five minutes."

I stood to give my mother a hug and her eyes were filled with tears as I held her tight. "I love you mom, it's going to be all right," I said, trying to comfort her as she wept in my arms.

"I love you too, son," she said between sobs.

My mother and I had had problems, but they all seemed unimportant at this moment. I hugged my sister and thanked her for introducing me to the kids. With my nephews, I gave them both hugs and gave them the hammer handshake. Last was Tiara. This was a different story. Saying goodbye to her was the hardest. She did not want to leave and she let everybody in the visiting room know it.

Tears ran down her little face even before she began to cry. As her sobs began to grow, her little chest started heaving, and then she exploded, letting everyone in the visiting room feel the level of her pain. The walls around my heart began crumbling. I was defenseless.

"I want to stay with you!" she shouted at the top of her lungs.

I had to choke back my tears. This feeling I was experiencing had been locked away for years, and it took a four year old to teach me about love. What had I done to receive this love? These kids loved me even while I was in prison. These feeling were tearing me up on the inside. Tears began to form and everyone was watching Ghost.

"I'm staying here!" she protested.

"Come on Tiara, we have to go," my sister said.

"No, I'm staying!" she yelled at my sister.

My sister went to take her by the hand. That's when she bolted across the room and grabbed onto my leg, pleading with me.

"Uncle, tell my mommy I can stay with you, please," she begged.

My sister came to unpry Tiara from my leg; she seemed to be holding on for dear life. I was fighting that wave of emotions that were killing me. The entire visiting room was in shock and in silence as they watched. The pain I felt inside was almost unbearable to handle. I was feeling dizzy, it was hard to breathe, and I began to sweat. I was power-less to a four year old. She had won.

I looked at my mother and sister for help, while my nephews watched from behind teary eyes, the other inmates with their families seemed as if they been through this before. Tiara wasn't responding to anyone, so I had to take the matter into my own hands. I knelt down and held her little face and looked into her eyes.

"Sweetheart, you have to go now. You can't stay here with me," I said

"But why?" she questioned.

"Because there is no room for you here," I answered.

"But why?" she repeated.

I said in my best parental voice while attempting to pry her little arms from my leg, "You have to go. Listen to your mother," I said.

Tiara loosened her grip and I gently picked her up and gave her a big hug while walking to my sister and handing her over.

As my sister carried her out of the door, I heard Tiara yell out, "He's my Uncle!"

That tore me apart. I couldn't hold my tears back any longer. This little girl's love penetrated the depths where I kept my emotions locked away. It shook me to my very core and embarrassment showed on my face because the other inmates saw big bad Ghost cry.

The CO was kind enough to process me first. I entered the changing room to get strip-searched. I stood in the changing booth and the CO told me to take a minute to compose myself. I sat on the plastic chair and honestly cried. I let it all out. During the last ten years, I'd acted as if nothing bothered me, and here I was, an emotional wreck, torn apart by a child.

"I've never seen anything like that," the CO said. "How do you feel, Verrett?" he honestly asked.

"Drained," I answered.

"Go ahead to your unit. I'm not going to strip search you," he said.

I grabbed my black shades and headed out of the door toward my unit. I acted if nothing bothered me, while my black shades hid my red and swollen tear-drenched eyes. As I lay in my bunk, I felt soft and vul-nerable. Family visits made me feel things I didn't want to feel.

341

Later that day, I called my mother on her cell phone.

"You see what you have done to us?" she said. "We love you, but it's hard to leave you there!"

"Please don't yell at me right now. I didn't call to hear that. I already know… I'm just calling to say thank you, that's all."

From then on, I swore no more family visits, only females.

I avoided the homies on the yard, even Big Dollar. I sat on the bleachers watching the sunset with half a gallon of wine and two joints. I didn't want to feel. I needed an escape because I was an emotional wreck. I reviewed my day. I had spent all of my twenties in prison and today was my thirtieth birthday. I had been torn apart by a four year old. What a life, what a day! I raised my cup for a toast and silently said, 'HAPPY BIRTHDAY DE'JUAN.'

CHAPTER 65

—

Shift Change

The first time I admitted responsibility for my actions was in the chow hall in Safford, Arizona. Mr. Wesley was the head of food service. He was an older black man that had a good vibe about him. He always seemed very peaceful, even when the chow hall was full of chaos, especially on chicken night. I wondered how he did it. For some reason, we made some kind of connection. I don't know how, but, he took a liking to me and would allow me to help in the kitchen on the weekends and by my service to him, I was able to make any kind of dish I wanted.

"I know you have a lot of influence on the yard," he said out of the blue.

His comment caught me off guard. "What do you mean?" I asked.

"You know what I mean. You're powerful and don't even know it," he said, while reviewing his clipboard.

A shot of adrenaline coursed through my body as my heart began to beat faster.

"The influence you have could be used in a different way," he said, without looking at me.

What do people see in me that I don't see in myself I wondered. I've been told this my entire life. I was shaken by Mr. Wesley's words. I remained quiet and listened to him.

"I wasn't always on the right side of the law, you know," he confessed.

"I could tell that you had shit with you back in the day," I replied and he smiled.

"Yeah, I did, but I woke up one day and I knew I couldn't continue life the way I was going. Everyone I knew was going to prison or to the graveyard, so I went to the navy," he said. "I needed structure. I wanted to help people in some way. I wanted to be of service to others and preparing food was my way, and that's why I work in this prison. To be of service to you," he said with a smile.

"To be honest with you, sometimes this food is garbage," I admitted.

"I make the best of what I have to work with," he answered.

"Do you believe in God?" he asked.

I paused. "Sometimes I do. What about you? Do you believe in God?" I asked.

"Yes I do. I choose to call Him Yahweh. I have a strong connection with Him," he said.

Mr. Wesley noticed that I was preparing to make an exit because I didn't want to hear him preach.

"I don't want to preach to you. I just wanted to answer your question," he admitted.

"May I ask you a question?" he added.

"Go ahead and ask," I said.

"Why are you in prison?" he asked.

"Because my co-defendants set me up," I said.

"What were you doing for them to set you up?" he questioned.

"I gave them some cocaine to transport for me and they got arrested by the feds, and that's why I'm in here." "Oh," he said, rubbing his chin. "So what you're saying is that you had no choice but to sell drugs?" he asked.

I was about to defend myself, and then it hit me. I realized that I did have the choice. It had been mine all this time and I had chosen to sell drugs. Mr. Wesley saw the light come on in me and smiled.

"It was never my co-defendants fault that I'm in prison. It's my fault," I said out loud.

For some strange reason I felt different at that very moment. All the pent up hate I had for my co-defendants instantly vanished. I didn't need it anymore. I was briefly lost in my thoughts and when I looked up I saw that Mr. Wesley had tears in his eyes.

"This is the beginning, this is the beginning," he said as he pulled out a handkerchief to wipe his eyes.

"Thanks, Mr. Dubb. I appreciate your advice." I said, as I left the chow hall.

"Use that power for good!" he shouted as he stood in the doorway. "Use it for good."

I felt light as I walked across the yard to my unit. The day seemed brighter. At that very moment everything was okay. Life was good, even though I was in prison. I knew I had a lot of things to work on, especially my drinking. For some reason, I didn't want it anymore.

The weekend had arrived, as Big Dollar and I headed to the movie house he noticed that I didn't have my water jug filled with a gallon of prison wine; instead it was filled with Tang.

"What's up, homie? No wine tonight?" he asked.

"No, not tonight. I choose not to drink, that's all," I answered.

The next morning, on September 11, 2001, after breakfast, everybody was standing under the outside gazebo smoking cigarettes and drinking coffee while watching the news. I was more interested in the NFL highlights than what was going on in the world. It was around 6:45 a.m. The images that flashed on the screen caught everyone's attention. We all stood there in disbelief as a plane crashed into the World Trade Center in New York.

At first we didn't think it was real, that a plane would fly directly into the World Trade Center. We all thought it was a preview for a new movie until we actually saw people jumping out of the windows. We all stood there speechless and in horror, not believing that this was actually happening.

Every television on the yard was showing the same thing. The compound was silent as we watched. I became sick to my stomach and I was sure the other inmates felt the same. This was crazy!

Then the announcement came over the PA system in English and Spanish. "All inmates return to your assigned housing units."

A few days later the news announced that the planes had been taken over by Muslim terrorists. I thought back to when I was in USP Florence with Ahmed and Rahsool when they had tried to do the same thing in the early nineties and failed. It was all driven by hate, and those men chose to hate. They had received misguided information and acted on it.

CHAPTER 66

—

Déjà vu

Once again, I was taken to the Special Housing Unit where I would spend the next four months locked in a concrete closet. I automatically shut down all feelings and this time there were no Encyclopedias to read. I was too ashamed to even look into the mirror that was bolted to the wall. I had let those eyes that cared about me down again. I summoned the courage to look into the mirror and what I saw sent a shockwave of fear throughout my body. I looked tired and worn out. I was defeated.

I had been in prison for over fourteen years and I had not accomplished a damn thing, well, except for building muscle. I was a muscular two hundred pound scared little boy with no future. The first few days in the hole were the hardest. My body was going through withdrawals and the pain was almost unbearable. I had nothing to take the edge off. I was craving, irritable and restless. I wished I had just one drink to calm my nerves or just one hit to relax me. I felt like screaming, and banging on the walls would help me get rid of the anxiety I felt. Then anger and bitterness set in and I started to punch the walls. Each cinder block had the face of everyone who had betrayed me and I started hitting the wall harder until my fists started bleeding. With the last punch I had broken my left hand.

Breathing hard, I stopped and noticed that the CO was watching me in the window.

"That wall ain't going to give in, Verrett," he said.

347

I remained quiet, breathing heavily, looking at my hand. For some strange reason, my hand didn't hurt compared to the pain I felt on the inside.

"Put your jumpsuit on Verrett. I'm taking you to the hospital," he said.

The prison hospital could fix my hand, but they couldn't fix the pain I was feeling on the inside, so I refused all pain medication. As the months passed, my hand healed, but my spirit was still broken. I was then transferred back to Safford, Arizona.

I had left Safford only fourteen months ago, and everyone wanted to know what had happened. Then I saw Big Dollar and he gave me a look of disappointment. I was ashamed to look him in the eye. I tried to avoid him for the first couple of days, but he finally caught up with me and asked me what happened.

"You went crazy off that alcohol," he said.

"It wasn't that," I said. "Hawk started hating on me and set me up," I said defensively.

Big Dollar didn't buy anything I was saying. "Just look at all the times you got in those situations homie, and look at what you did before it happened. You might find the answers," he said.

I thought about what he was telling me as I walked to the leisure library. The leisure library was a small room with books that lined all four walls with two eight-foot bookshelves in the center of the room. There were a handful of older inmates reading quietly. I began my search, scanning for something different. I noticed an old book at the bottom of the bookshelf. It was old and tattered, but unique in a way. I made out the name on the spine of the book. Norman Vincent Peale was the author's name.

I opened the book, looking for the title. "Stay Alive All Your Life." The title jumped out at me. The book was old and dusty and forgotten about. I was intrigued by what I read. I left the leisure library feeling lighter and stopped to watch an intense volleyball game.

A Samoan guy who called himself UT was arguing about a call with the referee. The debate got heated and the Paisa's or Mexican nationals began to crowd around UT, yelling in Spanish. Then it happened. "UT" hit the referee with a haymaker, instantly knocking him out cold before he hit the ground.

"Shit!" I said, as I ran over to try to calm the situation. The crowd grew triple its size in a matter of seconds. I had some respect from the older Mexicans, and worked with them trying to isolate the incident, but it didn't work. The word already was in the wind. I took "UT" by the arm and headed for the black and Islander TV room. I told everyone to be on guard because something was going to go down.

A few days had passed without incident. It was now a Saturday. That's when the blacks and Islanders played basketball and after the game we all had a prison picnic. This ritual took place every weekend to show unity for the new arrivals. As we were eating, a large crowd of Paisas stood at the entrance of the walkway. At first glance I didn't think anything of it until another fifty joined them. My heart started beating fast. Something was going to happen. I motioned to Big Dollar to look. Without saying a word, I went to my stash and grabbed both of my knives. I said a silent prayer and waited for them to advance.

The new guy I was schooling named Eric had just arrived to Safford with a fresh ten-year sentence and was clueless to what was going on. Then it started. The large group of Mexican nationals began to shower us with rocks. We were outnumbered ten to one. We needed to stay together, but some of the guys who were from Arizona took refuge in the library. Our small number dwindled even more.

"Cowards!" I yelled.

"What are we going to do?" Eric asked in a panicked voice.

I surveyed the advancing wall of people, hoping to find a weak point, because if they came in too far we were done. I saw an opening.

"What are you going to do?" Eric asked again.

"I'm going to run straight into the crowd and poke everyone in arm's reach," I said as I studied the crowd.

"What do you mean?" he said in disbelief.

"Dollar," I said, "I'm going to be the spear."

"Okay, we got your back," he answered.

Eric was a big youngster, about two hundred and sixty pounds. I told him to hold on to my belt loop and push me through the crowd and not to stop until we were through.

"Are you crazy?" he questioned me.

"I've done this before. I've been in prison for fifteen years now," I told him.

After the next wave of rocks, I turned into a lion and led the charge, screaming like a madman as I entered the wall of people, poking anyone close to me as Eric pushed me deeper into the crowd. The Paisas had brought rocks to a knife fight. This was a matter of life and death for me. I really didn't want to hurt anyone, but I didn't want to get hurt either. I had to defend myself at all costs.

We made it through unharmed except for a few scratches. Eric was still pushing me until I told him to stop. We re-grouped and stood our ground. I gave one of the pokers to Big Dollar and advanced on the crowd. During this time I heard the sirens and I knew the institution would soon be on high alert.

The staff quickly gained control of the institution and the buses rolled in. Half of the Paisa population was transferred that day. We remained on lockdown for a week, and then the peace talks began. Big Dollar and I were called to delegate with the Paisas, and a treaty was reached and enforced.

Four months passed without further incident. I was given a transfer to Terminal Island for keeping the peace. Ten years had passed since I was transferred from Terminal Island and I wondered if this would be the last prison I would be in before I got to go home. I only had fourteen months left. I prayed that things would be different this time. Something had to change.

In the early morning hours on March 14, 2005 I heard those ever familiar words, "Verrett, roll it up."

CHAPTER 67

—

Treasure Island

The white 747 Con Air plane touched down safely at LAX airport. The plane taxied to the Bureau of Prisons hanger where U.S. Marshals waited with their assault rifles and handguns drawn. None of that mattered to me. It was all routine now I was just relieved to be on the ground once again.

A lot has changed in ten years, except for the bumper- to-bumper traffic on the 405 freeway. That would probably never change. The prison bus laboured its way toward Terminal Island. I remained quiet with my eyes glued to the window, taking in the landscape. I thought to myself, "I'm not going to mess this up this time."

I was sure that the word had spread through the prison grapevine that Big Ghost was on his way back to Terminal Island. I had to find a way to let the homies know that it was going to be different this time. I had the reputation with the homies as a Go Getter or a Play Maker, but I seemed to always get sacked, and with the staff I was known as a fuckup or shit-starter. Something had to change. Fifteen and a half years had passed and I had accomplished absolutely nothing. Now was the time. I knew I had to be open to new things and ideas.

We arrived at Terminal Island on March 8, 2005 at about 1:00 p.m. As we exited the bus we did the prison shuffle to R&D (Receiving and Discharge) where the chains were removed and we were placed in holding cells waiting to be processed.

I was the last inmate to be seen. The CO heading the intake process looked familiar to me. I noticed that she kept her distance from me while watching me without looking directly at me. At first I thought maybe I had gone to school with her, but she was about ten years older than me. Then I remembered. She was my aunt by marriage. I hadn't seen Shelia since the early 80s in Harbor City.

The last time I had actually seen her was at her brother, Herald's, house, which was my cousin's father. Herald would pay my cousin and me to walk and clean up after his Dobermans, and once the yard was clean Shelia would make us lunch. And now, almost twenty-five years later, here we were, I was being finger printed by my aunt in a prison.

"Don't tell anyone that we're family," she whispered to me.

"Shit, you don't tell anyone," I replied.

The truth was, if the administration found out that we were family I would be on the next bus out of here.

"So you have been here before?" she asked.

"Yeah, about ten years ago," I answered. "They shipped me out because of a riot," I added.

The intake process was complete and I was assigned to K-Unit. This would be my home, hopefully until I was released. I was then assigned a job as an orderly in the psychology department. It was a sweet job and where most of the pretty female staff worked. I lucked out. The job consisted of emptying trashcans and sweeping the hallways, and for the rest of the day I could write letters or read.

The psychology department offered classes from meditation to drug prevention, or if you just wanted to talk to someone, the psychologist's offices were always filled with inmates wanting to talk.

I found myself standing just outside the doorway listening to one of the drug counselor's talk about addiction, prevention and recovery, and how her own drug use affected her family. I felt everything she was saying. I understood her. The crazy thing about it was she was a staff member with over twenty years of sobriety. This woman was from the streets, she'd lived in the streets, and now here she was working in a prison wanting to help inmates who suffered from drug addiction.

We called her Mrs. T. She was one of the realist staff members I had ever known. When she would facilitate a class it was standing room only. She spoke from the heart. I took my position by the door with my broom in hand and listened to her.

"No matter what you go through or what you've been through, you can always recreate your life," she would say to the class. I was mesmerized by those words, just as the people in the room were.

The word recreate echoed throughout my soul. Was it really possible for me to recreate my life as Mrs. T claimed to have done? I knew that she was from the streets because she spoke the language of the hood and I believed her.

"You have to be open to new things," she continued.

Mrs. T was different. She really cared! She was a powerful woman even though she was only five feet tall and there was a real sense of peace in her. My job as an orderly allowed me to go into each office and clean up. I made my way to Mrs. T's office and I noticed all the books on the shelves and posters that hung on the walls. As I cleaned her office I would Eye Hustle, which means I read all the titles of the books. She had books on meditation, another was called the "Art of Power," and one called "Chakras" Another was called "The Mindfulness". She had some shit I'd never even heard of before.

"Pretty interesting stuff, huh?" she said as she watched me reading the titles.

"Yeah, it is," I answered.

"Go ahead and see if there is anything that interests you," she said.

I took a few minutes scanning the bookshelves. I wondered if they would help me in any way.

"Mr. Verrett, have you ever listened to a mantra?" she asked.

"I don't think so," I answered. "What is it?"

"It's a chant you recite while meditating," she replied.

Mrs. T handed me some headphones and I listened. The sounds were strange, but very relaxing, and I felt it in my heart. The soft low vibrations reminded me of what I had felt inside for so long. I closed my eyes and started humming with the voice in the headphones. I was caught in the moment. When I opened my eyes Mrs. T looked shocked.

"What's wrong?" I asked.

"You were in the flow with the mantra," she said.

"It seems like I've heard it before, but I don't know where," I answered.

"You've heard it on the inside" she replied. "It's been there all your life," she added.

The first time I heard it, I memorized it. My entire body tingled with a warm sensation. I still remember that mantra to this day. Mrs. T was my catalysis for my spiritual change. She made it easy for me to learn new things.

"We have to live what we are taught," she always said.

Mrs. T carried a lot of weight in her ninety-pound frame. I didn't even look at her as prison staff. All I saw was a human being who cared.

I began to uncover clues of who I really was. My heart began to open to new ideas. "Recreate", "Be Willing." For a change, those books seemed to shout at me. I learned that I am a spiritual being having a human experience, but how can one be spiritual in a violent environment I wondered. My inward journey began. There was a lot of healing that was needed and I was open to it.

Later that day I sat at a table in the leisure library reading.

"That's a good book," the guy across from me commented.

I instantly went into my hard prison gaze. 'Open for change' quickly filled my mind.

"Yeah, it is," I answered.

"What's your name?" he asked.

"Ghhh. My name is De'Juan," I answered.

"Nice to meet you, De'Juan. I am Ishmael. Do you know what your name means in Arabic?" he asked.

"No, I don't," I replied.

"It means spiritual change."

CHAPTER 68

—

Powerlessness

The word spread on the streets that I was back in Terminal Island and at mail call I received a boatload of letters with pictures from females I had known from back in the day. I broke weak and sent out as many visiting forms to all of them as possible. I was powerless.

A part of me didn't want to get back into hustling. It was becoming too stressful and I was close to going home. Uneasiness crept over me and in the blink of an eye I reverted to my old ways, which justified my actions by manipulating them to bring me what I needed to get high. I struggled with the obsession as it tormented me. I was powerless to it.

I lay in my bunk and wondered what Mrs. T heard or read that made the cravings go away. What did she do? What happened? I couldn't continue life this way. My eyes followed the path of my dimly lit cell and rested on a book Mrs. T had given me to read, "The Art of Power." I was having a power struggle. It felt like a war was waging within me. I was experienced in the art of negative power, the power of getting loaded, and the art of self-will. I had mastered the art of manipulation, but I had failed in the art of life.

I reported to my work assignment on Monday morning empting trash cans and setting up the classroom as Mr. Reed and Mrs. T walked down the hallway. I tried to avoid eye contact with them, not wanting them to see how I felt, which was just as empty as the trashcans I emptied.

Mr. Reed was a tall man, about 6'5". His hair was almost completely white. He wore a uniform similar to the US Surgeon general. He was a good man, and respected by the inmate population. He kept it real, just like Mrs. T.

Mr. Reed was a predictable man. Every morning he would go to his office and turn on his CD player, which was always tuned into smooth jazz. He whistled as he started his coffee maker. As I walked past his office, he motioned me to enter.

"How was your weekend, Mr. Verrett?" he asked.

"It was all right, I guess," I said, not wanting to look him in the eyes, as Mrs. T walked in.

"You know, Mr. Verrett, people are attracted to you," Mrs. T said. "You have the power of attraction, but you use it in the wrong way," she said, as if staring into my soul.

Mr. Reed went to his coffee pot and poured himself a cup and without looking at me said, "I can feel your energy when you walk into the room."

Mrs. T nodded in agreement, "And now your level is low," he added.

I had been told the same thing my entire life by different people, even strangers, but something was blocking me from fully accepting it. I heard their words as I focused on the image on the wall.

"What does that mean?" I asked, pointing to the picture?

The picture on the wall was of a Hindu figure with a bright a light bursting out of his chest. It was the heart chakra and the image was powerful.

"I would like to invite you to our meditation group on Friday night in the chapel," Mrs. T suggested.

"I'll think about it," I replied.

"If you don't like it, you don't have to go anymore," she said. "I think you would enjoy it, just like you enjoyed that mantra you listen to the other day," she added.

I truly respected Mr. Reed and Mrs. T for giving a damn! They helped the men confined within the prison walls find the path that leads to a different life. I heard what they were saying, but I didn't fully accept it. I still made my prison wine and I still got high, but it wasn't the same. The thrill was gone. I got high just to get high.

July 2, 2005. That was the day that everything changed. I started drinking right before the four o'clock count. I had my spot in the TV room, and everything I needed. I needed something stronger than a joint and decided to snort some heroin. I only used it occasionally and in moderation, and I was too afraid of shooting it. I made my way back to the TV room, sat down and enjoyed my high. Heroin made me feel peaceful inside.

The room became cloudy but serine. I was already into my nod. I was conscience of my surroundings but unresponsive.

"Hey, Ghost, hey Ghost" one of the homies said as he tapped me on my shoulder.

"He ain't going to answer you. He's fucked up," another voice said.

"Yeah, that nigga turned into a drug addict," I heard another say.

"Shit, Ghost been like that ever since I've known him."

I recognized the voice. It was my close homeboy, Trey, as everyone agreed and began laughing.

They repeated the words, "He's been like that ever since we've known him."

Those words echoed throughout the room and my soul and cut me deep, and they were right. I had been like this for almost sixteen years and I hadn't accomplished anything. I was now a thirty-five year old man with the life skills of a nineteen year old. Those words bounced around in my mind while tormenting every cell in my body, then everything became completely dark.

CHAPTER 69

—

Just For Today

I found myself lying in my bunk. It was absolutely silent in the unit. I checked the time. It was just after 3:00 in the morning. I had been out for nine hours. My bladder begged to be relieved of the discomfort and pressure. I made my way to the urinals and found immediate liberation.

The sink area was just across the hall. As I turned on the water to wash my hands, I looked up and saw my reflection in the mirror. I looked away because the eyes were back, and they were the same ones that kept me company when I was in SHU. I stood there and just stared, for I hadn't seen them in twelve years. It seemed as though I was standing there for a while, but it was only less than a minute. I lost myself in the warmth of those caring eyes.

"It's count time, Verrett," the CO said.

I didn't even hear the CO walk up. I was that entranced with those eyes. I pulled myself from the mirror and shuffled back to my bunk. I had a hard time getting back to sleep. Memories of all my experiences flashed through my mind as I stared into the darkness. I was lost within it. I remembered all the times when I'd been transferred, I remembered the riots, and I remembered the cold steel chains that bound me like I was a savage animal, corralled into small over crowded cages. I remembered the feeling of being empty.

I remembered the peopled that I'd hurt, I remembered my mother and sisters, I remembered the first time I'd seen my niece and nephews, I remembered the unconditional love they gave me and I remembered holding onto those feeling for as long as I could until the darkness crept in. I remembered what Mother Parsons told me when I was a kid, that I was going to go through something and that I would make it out okay. I remembered that she told me that I had a lot of good work to do in the world. A part of me told me that she was wrong. I remembered the faraway places that the Encyclopedia took me and I remembered the peace I'd felt.

I also remember what Mrs. T and Mr. Reed told me, be open to new ideas, you can recreate your life. I remember Mr. Reed telling me that I could change the things I could, but could I? Was I strong enough? I was terrified of tomorrow, and what did new ideas really mean? Accept the past, Mrs. T would tell me, accept your past.

I cried out into the darkness in a low whisper, "God I can't go home like this. Please help me, please! I don't know what to do."

I woke up sober that morning. It was July 3, 2005, the day before the United States celebrated its independence, and little did I know that it would also be mine. The unit buzzed with the morning sounds of inmate traffic. I felt the need to remain silent as I maneuvered my way through the hallway to the sink area.

I stood in front of the mirror with my eyes closed and took a deep breath. When I opened them, the man in the mirror was sober. His eyes were clear. I smiled and he smiled back as if he knew something I didn't know. I completed my morning ritual and went back to my bunk and felt the strong sense to remain quiet and still. The room was no longer spinning. It was still. I was still. Blame and excuse no longer invaded my thoughts. I was now willing to listen. I was open; I needed the courage to make it through the day. There would be no more excuses. I was ready to meet the challenge.

As I sat on my bunk, Trey came by to check on me.

"What up, Ghost!" he said, "You were fucked up last night," he added.

"Yeah, I was, huh." I answered.

"Are we going to drive some iron today?" he asked.

"No, not today homie. I ain't feeling it."

"I feel ya," he said, then gave the homie handshake and went about his business.

The truth was, I didn't have the strength to lift weights, and I needed to reserve my strength to make it through the morning. I grabbed my Walkman and put on my headphones and pretended that I was listening to some music so I could be left alone. I needed to remain quiet and listen. It was my way of getting closer to myself and I needed to withdraw from the world for a bit.

Shortly thereafter Trey came by. "Hey, Ghost, they just released the unit for chow. You going to eat?"

"Naw, homie, I ain't hungry." The truth was, I was still waiting for something to happen, or some kind of revelation to hit me.

"Last call for the dining hall," came over the PA system.

I felt the urge to go outside and stand in front of the unit and survey the people on the yard. I fired up a cigarette, blowing a big cloud of smoke, and that's when I saw a group of people in street clothes walking across the yard with the counselor. There were two women and an older man. I noticed that one of the women was carrying a pink box, which got me curious. I figured that it contained donuts, and I hadn't had a donut in almost sixteen years, so I followed them.

I had no clue that the volunteers were. I assumed that they were some Christians or some Jehovah's Witnesses wanting to preach to the lost souls wandering the prison yard. What would it hurt if I went and said a couple of amens and a few hallelujahs to get a donut?

I followed them to a small room on the second floor of the psychology building. I peeked through the window on the door, and that's when the lady with the donuts motioned me to enter.

"What's this?" I asked.

"This is a support group for recovery," she answered.

"A support group? Oh, no," I replied. "I thought this was something else."

"Would you like a donut?" she asked.

For the life of me I couldn't turn them down so I entered the room and grabbed a donut. I noticed that there were six other inmates in there. I had seen them congregating on the yard and I figured that they'd turned religious or something.

"What's your name?" she asked.

"I'm Ghost," I answered.

"Welcome, Mr. Ghost. I'm Beth. It's nice to meet you," she said with a gentle smile.

"It's nice to meet you too," I responded.

Beth was an older woman, about sixty years old. She had a smile that made me feel that everything was going to be all right. I felt relaxed.

The other people in street clothes also introduced themselves.

"Welcome, I am Norman," he said as he extended his hand to me. I balled my fist at first, preparing to give him the homie hand shake, but decided not to. It felt funny shaking hands this way.

Norman was an older white guy who had good energy about him. I respected the fact that he and Beth had been coming into the prison system for years just to carry a message of change and recovery.

Samantha was the youngest of the three; she was Chicana with a long ponytail. I wondered how all three of them knew each other. They all came from different backgrounds and now they were all friends doing the same thing, carrying a message.

As the meeting started, Beth asked everyone to bow their head as she recited the most profound words I had ever heard, which struck me to my core.

"Relieve me of the bondage of self. Take away my difficulties that victory over them."

I knew that those words hadn't come from the Bible because I'd read it over a dozen times, so who wrote them? Where did they come from?

The room was quiet as Beth began her story. I was mesmerized by what I had heard. She was telling my story of what I had gone through and experienced. I listened. She spoke of the feelings of hopelessness and despair. She also spoke of how she had lost her way. She told stories of how she had wanted to make the ultimate sacrifice of taking her own life because the pain was too great, but decided not to.

I felt her pain as she spoke and remembered the time when I sat in the bathtub with a bottle of gin and a gun. I just wanted the pain to stop, but I couldn't kill my mother's only son.

I hung onto every word she said. I related and I felt a strong sense of safety in that small room. I was choked with emotion as she spoke. This was powerful! Everyone in that room related in some way, even though we all came from different backgrounds.

Norman was next. His story was just as compelling, and he told his story from behind tear filled eyes and no one laughed at him. The room was quiet as he spoke.

Last was Samantha, she was a home girl who had been through it, and now she was living a different life because she was willing to follow a dozen simple suggestions.

As the meeting came to a close, Beth asked everyone to hold hands as she recited a prayer. I closed my eyes and listened to the words. When the prayer was over I opened my eyes. Traces of tears appeared as I quickly put of my black shades. Something had happened and I felt different; I felt free I knew I was home, just for today.

CHAPTER 70

—

The Miracle

Something magical happened in that room. I left feeling light and serine. As I walked back to my unit, I heard someone calling my name. It was Justin and Caesar.

"Hey, Ghost, thanks for coming to the support group," they both said.

That's when Cesar handed me a card and asked me to read it every day. "Okay, thank you. I will," I said and headed into my unit.

On the morning of the fourth of July, the prison was on holiday schedule. Damn near everyone was making preparations to celebrate with the rest of the country. Me, I had to get out of the unit and decided to burn off some frustration and go lift some weights. I had been lifting for ten years now and my muscular build showed it.

The weight pile was partially empty which I liked because I didn't have to wait for anything. On the other side of the fence there was a guy playing the guitar, and he played it beautifully. His fingers danced on the strings as he made the guitar actually sing. It was amazing to hear. For some strange reason, the music drowned out the voices in my head. I guess they were right when they said that music could sooth the savage beast, and that beast was between my ears.

I completed my workout and exited the weight area as he continued to play. His appearance didn't fool me. He pretended to look like he was crazy his hair was matted and unkempt, but I knew that he wasn't insane. He wore wrinkled but clean prison clothes and his beard was matted up, but his eyes were clear, even though he wore thick prison-issued glasses.

I approached him and he stopped playing. "Am I playing too loud?" he asked.

"No," I answered. "You're playing great."

I guess I looked intimidating walking up to him; because of my muscular build. "What's your name?" I asked.

He seemed to blank out for a second, probably wondering why I was talking to him.

"My name is Marvin," he finally answered. "Marvin is my name."

"It's nice to meet you, Marvin. I'm Ghost," I said as I extended my hand in friendship.

Marvin looked confused as to why I was showing him kindness. He walked around the yard totally invisible to damn near everyone, and I saw him, I acknowledged him and I spoke to him.

"You play really good," I said, as I pulled out a pack of smokes, and lit one. "You smoke?" I asked.

"Yes, I do, but I really can't afford them at this time," he said.

"Take a few of them"

I handed the pack to him and as he lit one, he said, "Thank you."

"Don't trip," I answered and we sat for a moment, looking at the ocean.

"You know what, Marvin? You ain't fooling me," I told him.

Marvin looked confused. "What do you mean?"

"You know exactly what I mean. You run around here looking crazy and always by yourself. You do that just to keep people away from you, and it's worked, but when I saw you playing that guitar, I knew you had all of your senses. The jig is up."

Marvin remained silent. He knew I was telling the truth.

"Look at everybody on the weight pile" I said pointing, "We all go there to posture and to get big. Most of us are just scared little boys. The bigger our muscle, the more protected that little boy is. It's like our armor. The appearance says 'Say away. Don't fuck with me,' just as your appearance says, 'I'm crazy.' The concept is the same."

For the next few months, Marvin and I sat in the yard watching the boats sail by while he played his guitar. I was his only friend.

Marvin revealed to me why he was in prison. He told me that he had lost his job, then his house and he became homeless, that he had been living on the streets for eight years, and that he got tired of living that way and decided to rob a bank, claiming he had a gun. Then he waited in front of the bank for the police to come, knowing that when he went to prison he would have a place to sleep and three meals a day. It was sad to hear that he had given up so easily on life.

I continued going to the support groups. I listened to every story that was shared. It helped me and I was getting something out of it. I assessed what my life could be like if I remained sober. I had thought that if I had plenty of money that I could be happy, but I wasn't. I related to the story of being on top of the world but being unhappy and almost blowing my brains out. I looked for happiness in all the wrong places money, women, drugs and alcohol none of that made me happy *none of it!*

I learned that prison is a state of being. Yeah, I was in a physical prison, but the prison of the mind and spirit is far worse than being confined to a concrete cell. I had imprisoned myself long before the U.S. Government imprisoned me.

I finally accepted my responsibility for the way my life had turned out. I accepted that fact that it wasn't my co-defendants' fault that I was in prison. It was because of the decisions I'd made to sell drugs. That's what put me in prison. That's when I was struck with the sense of internal freedom.

I changed some things about me and the homies on the yard started to notice. One day I went to my counselor's office and asked him to remove all of the females on my visiting list. He thought I'd gone crazy, but I didn't want to be tempted to do anything stupid.

One afternoon I was in my cell when Trey stopped by to talk.

"What up, Ghost?" he said.

"Just chilling," I said, putting down the book I was reading. I knew that he wanted to tell me something because he was hesitating.

"What's on your mind, young homie?" I asked him.

"You know the homies are starting to talk about you?" he finally said.

"About what?" I inquired.

"They say that the sixteen years you been locked up has finally gotten to you. They're saying you finally lost it," he said, as if unloading a heavy burden.

"Is that right?" I asked. "Well, you go tell them that I finally found it," I said with a smile. "Tell all the homies that I found it," I said.

I guess it would have seemed as if I'd finally gone crazy because I had stopped making my prison wine. I had stopped hanging on the yard getting high. I had stopped all of the politics that go on in prison. I had started walking the track with a mixed group of inmates and we talked about life after addiction and how are we were going to live life after prison. I related to those six men. We were all scared of the unknown and we let each other know how we felt. I guess it would look like I'd lost it from my past behaviors.

On the advice of Mrs. T and Mr. Reed and with the encouragement of Justin and Cesar, I started to attend the weekly meditation and yoga classes in the chapel. At first, I felt weird and uncomfortable. I was moving at a rapid pace but it all seemed so natural. I would be the first person to exit the unit so none of the homies would see me heading toward the chapel. I enjoyed the practice, but I was not ready to fully share what I was doing with the homies just yet.

The yoga instructor was escorted into the prison chapel. He was an Indian man with long black hair, which complimented his dark brown skin and a graying beard, and he looked like he was always at peace with himself as he sat with his legs folded.

There were fifteen of us inmates in the group. We all sat on the mats with our legs crossed when the instructor started the class. He told everyone to focus on the sound of the bell and to breathe.

The chanting began slowly at first, which brought out the vibration that was deep within us. The feeling was unexpected. I felt bright on the inside. I believed that I caught a glimpse of what other people saw in me and I felt good. I actually looked deep within myself and I saw it. It had always been there waiting for me to claim it.

I left the chapel feeling light on the inside, just like that poster of the blue figure that had the light shining from his chest. That's how I felt, powerful. I returned to the unit where Trey was waiting for me.

"What's up Ghost? Where you been, homie?" he asked.

"I was in the chapel practicing yoga and meditating," I answered, as Trey gave me a funny look.

"Meditating? Yoga?" he said. "Well, how was it?" he finally asked.

"It was some cool shit," I answered. "I think you should try it," I said with a smile.

"I might," he replied. "Maybe soon."

"I think you would like it," I said.

He smiled and said, "I better not find you at LAX chanting and shit with a tambourine." That's when we both started laughing.

CHAPTER 71

—

Still Learning

I began attending different classes and workshops. I was opening up to the new idea theory. I was invited by Justin to participate in a workshop that was hosted by a group of volunteers from this place called Agape, which means unconditional love in the Greek language. It was a non-denominational spiritual center. It was amazing to see people from different religious backgrounds coming together to spread the message of love. When I first heard what they had to say, I thought, 'Don't drink the water.'

Love was their message. "You are love," they would say. I instantly became defensive because love was something I didn't understand. I got to thinking, "How are these motherfuckers going to come up in here and say I love you," when they didn't even know me.

I had an issue with what they were trying to sell. I had never loved another person in my life. I liked a lot of people, but never loved anyone. Shit, I don't even know if I loved myself. I was just starting to *like* myself.

The Agape group leader named Marvell spoke up and started the meeting. He was an older black man with a slim build, baldhead and a goatee. He had a powerful way about himself and very peaceful. I watched him with a cautious eye. The others were on the same page as Marvell. The woman name Jennie sat in a plastic chair with her eyes closed with a smile on her face. She was a white woman with long sandy brown hair and a strong aura that was highly visible.

Shortly after Marvell opened the meeting for questions, I was compelled to raise my hand and voice my opinion on this thing called love, and he picked me.

"Excuse me, I don't want to sound disrespectful, but how can you love everybody?" I asked.

"That's all there is, is love," he explained. "The spirit that resides in all of us is the power of love," he said.

"Okay, but you come up in here saying that you love us. I don't know if I even like you. You seem like an all right dude, but I can't say that I love you," I responded.

"I'm not saying that you have to like everybody, but you should love everybody," he said as he stepped toward me. "What's your name, young man?" he asked.

I became uneasy in my chair and shifted my weight, and answered. "My name is Ghost," I answered him, looking straight into his eyes.

"Well, Ghost, I love you brother and there's nothing you can do about it," he said without breaking eye contact.

"I ain't ever loved anyone!" I blurted out defensively, as my heart pounded. I wondered if this complete stranger looked within me, did he really know that I wanted to be able to love? I'd always felt it, but was I even capable of loving another person?

"Man, I was taught to only love with my eyes and hands," I said.

"Interesting," he said, as he scratched his chin. "Well, who taught you that?" he asked.

"My big homies," I answered, which I knew sounded stupid.

"Well, that's what they were taught and they needed to think like that in order to survive. I too once lived in that life, until something happened."

"I could tell that you had some shit with you back in the day," I said, as the group laughed.

"I did, but that was an eternity ago," he admitted.

"Well, I can say that I've been in like and in lust a lot, but never in love," I added, and more laughs came from the other guys.

372

I began attending the Agape workshops once a month, and on my last session with them, just a week before I was to be released, they came in and had a going home ceremony for me. They brought in some unfamiliar faces. There was a guy with some long dreadlocks who sat and watched me and there was a woman with dreadlocks who sat next to him, as they watched me walk in.

Marvell asked everyone to place the chairs in a circle and asked me to sit in the middle, and I agreed, Marvell asked everyone to point a finger at me to send me white light. The Agape members and the inmates and I felt it. Something was happening and it was powerful.

Next, Marvell asked everyone to whisper some words of encouragement in my ear. I started with Marvell and slowly moved around the circle. Each person had a unique message. I expected at least the first ten people to say the same thing, but no one did. Not one word was repeated.

After I completed the circle, I was filled with so much emotion that I felt tears of joy form as I looked to the ceiling, not wanting them to fall. I couldn't cry in front of the other inmates. I had a reputation and I couldn't be seen crying, not in prison. The tears felt heavy and I couldn't hold them back any longer. As I wept, the circle closed in on me and embraced me. Not one person laughed at me.

"You are strong, brother," Marvell said. "You're strong."

"Thank all of you," I said between sobs. "Thank you for loving me until I could love myself. Thank you for putting up with me during these last few months. Thank you for understanding me and being patient with me."

"That's what we do," Jennie added.

The man with the dreadlocks finally spoke up. "Brother, I have heard so much about you that I had to come and see who they were talking about. I am Reverend Michael Beckwith, the founder of Agape. When you come home I would like to have you come to attend our service," he said.

"I will," I answered.

Marvell gave me a few minutes to talk.

"When I first came to this service I was curious and skeptical, especially when you told me that you loved me and didn't even know me."

"We know who you are," Marvell said from his seat.

"Something happened, something on the inside. It's like I tuned into a new channel or a new frequency, and now I send out positive wave signals which attracts people on the same wave length."

"It's the law of attraction," the reverend added.

"Yeah, that." I said. "I feel different. I like this feeling, and I love this feeling for I am love."

The room erupted in applause. The woman with the dreadlocks stood up and began to sing as the other Agape members joined her. At that moment it didn't seem as if this was a prison. I was free.

CHAPTER 72

—

Coming To America

I woke up shortly after the 4:00 a.m. count on Monday, May 8, 2006. That was the day that I was going back to America. I had waited sixteen and a half years for this day, and it was finally here. A lot had changed. I had changed and I wondered how much America had changed! the strange thing was, I wasn't nervous, I felt peace I was surprisingly calm and ready.

The unit was still quiet except for faint distant snoring of the slumbering inmates. I made my way to the mirror to have one last conversation with the man in the mirror. As I stood in front of the mirror, I remained still for a moment, taking a deep breath and holding it. I closed my eyes, clearing my mind. As I exhaled and opened my eyes looking into the mirror, I saw those familiar eyes. My heart raced. I was instantly wrapped in the warmth of their gaze, and I saw freedom in those eyes - freedom from the bondage of self- hate, the freedom from deeply engrained negative thoughts. I looked deep into his eyes and he was truly free. It had been *an inside job* all this time, and that's all I had to do was take a look on the inside. He had seen freedom in me long before the prison system was to set me free. He gave me strength, self-assurance and confidence for my new life in America.

'Change the things I can,' I remembered Mrs. T telling me. I believed it now. Every cell in my body believed it now. I thought about every prison I'd been in and I had never changed anything, but I expected different results, and nothing ever changed. I now had a program to follow with guidelines to live by in order to have a new way of life. I was told that if I followed those simple suggestions my life would change. I was given the courage to take the steps and I truly bared witness that my life could be different and I was determined to make it work once I was back in America.

I told the man in the mirror about the strong support system I had in place, and all I had to do was show up and they would be there for me just as he was always there watching me from the mirror. I thanked him for listening. We both knew that this would be our last session together. He smiled and I smiled back.

I quietly walked back to my bunk. I realized that this was going to be the last time I would ever sleep in a bed like this. This would be the last time I would wake up in prison and this would be the last time I would view the outside world from behind steel bars and razor wire looking out of a window only to see the sun set behind gun towers. This was going to be the last time I showered with flip-flops on.

I remembered telling Mrs. T and Mr. Reed, "The next time I come into a jail or prison, I will be wearing a visitor's badge. I'll never be an inmate again," and they believed me.

I sat on my bunk and took a couple of deep breaths and began to meditate silently, chanting a peaceful mantra I'd memorized. "Om nah mo, guru de nah mor."

It seemed as if only minutes had passed when Trey shook my bunk.

"What's up homeboy? You don't want to go home?" he said with a big smile.

"What time is it?" I asked.

"Its 6:15."

I quickly washed up and gathered my personal belongings. The extra sweats and tennis shoes, radios - I had passed them out to the guys who didn't have family members sending them money. I knew that they would appreciate them. I had learned the art of giving.

As I was exiting the unit with Trey, a few of the guys I had befriended stopped me to shake my hand. I had become friends with this big ole bald white guy with a handle bar mustache who called himself Polar Bear, which fit him perfect because he was about 6'8 and weighed about three-hundred, twenty pounds and was covered in tattoos. He was a very intimidating figure, but he was actually a gentle giant.

"Ghost, you take care of yourself, brother," he said as he picked me up, squeezing me in a bear hug.

"I will, Bear," I said. "You can put me down now." We both laughed.

Bear handed me a slip of paper, which had his mother's home address on it. "Let's keep in contact," he said, looking down at me.

"Most def," I said, putting it in my phone book.

I felt sadness as the guys in the unit waved goodbye. Prison had been my home since I was nineteen years old. I was now thirty-five years old and about to leave this dysfunctional family and enter a new world. I didn't know what to expect, but I was ready for the challenge.

February 6, 1990. It seemed like a million years ago when the judge had given me that nineteen-year prison sentence. I couldn't imagine this day. Gratitude filled me. I had made it. I'd survived. I was going home.

I stepped onto the yard with a sense of accomplishment and confidence. I wasn't in fear or worry. The only thing I was, I was maybe outdated like Rip Van Winkle, but I could change that. For some strange reason, it didn't seem as if I had actually served all that time and had been transferred to all those different prisons. It didn't seem as if I was getting out of prison. It felt like I had just woken up. Yeah, prison had been my home for half of my life, but I felt at ease and peaceful. I had had an accelerated spiritual experience, which prepared me for this. My life would be very different. I could feel it.

As Trey and I walked across the yard and turned the corner, at first we thought that J-Unit was having a fire drill because there was about a hundred people standing in front. As we got closer, I started to recognize the faces and they were all smiling.

"Here he comes," I heard someone in the crowd say.

The men gathered at the gate to greet me and to send me off. I looked at Trey and he had a big ole Kool Aid smile of his face.

"Did you plan this?" I asked him.

"Naw, Dog, these are the people you touched and they have love and respect for you, homie," he said.

Tears began to run down my cheeks and I wasn't ashamed. There were men of all nationalities waiting for me. I was speechless. I was choked with emotion and joy that I couldn't explain. I was one of them.

For that very moment, everything was perfect. Our differences didn't matter, no set tripping at all. It was only respect and love. I remember standing in this same crowd over the years seeing the homies go home, but this was different - it was my turn. I remembered what Mr. Reed told me, that I have the power of attraction and that I could use that power to influence people in a positive way, and it was true. Men who wouldn't normally mix were right here waiting and talking to each other, it was amazing.

I stood in the crowd shaking hands with the men when someone came busting through the crowd. It was old man Lawrence Livingston with his usual bundle of law books tucked under his arm. This was the same old dude from FCI Lompoc who had told me that he was going to cut me.

He handed his law books to Trey without looking at him. We locked our gaze and as if on cue we both smiled. Lawrence still had a bright smile and bright eyes.

He gave me a hug and said to the crowd, "I have known this jitterbug since the first day he came in and he was wild and foolish."

The crowd laughed.

He continued, "I have watched him turn into a man in here, and now he is going home different."

Without looking at me, Lawrence grabbed his books and made his way out of the crowd without looking back.

I fought back my tears by continuing to shake everyone's hand and exchanging addresses. I promised to write everyone and send pictures.

The last guy that I saw was Marvin. He stood by himself with his guitar case and a manila envelope. I excused myself and went to talk with him.

"What's up, Marvin?" I said with a smile.

"Um, hello Ghost," he said, looking at the ground.

"I'm going home today," I told him.

"Yeah, I know. I have something for you," he said, handing me the manila envelope.

"What's this?" I asked curiously.

"Open it," he responded. "This is what I see you doing," he said, still looking at the ground.

Marvin had painted a picture of me on the back of a Krispy Kreme donut box he'd found in the trash. The picture was of me leaving prison and standing on the Hollywood walk of fame in front of Grumman's Chinese Theatre.

"What does this mean?" I asked him.

"I had a dream that people are going to know you before you know them," he said.

"Well, thank you, but I'm going to work at the oil refinery," I answered.

"Nope," he replied. "God has a different plan for you. People need to hear your story. You're going to help a lot of people like you helped me," he continued.

I stood there momentarily speechless, lost for words. I extended my hand, which he took, then I gave him a hug and thanked him for the painting and carefully put it with the rest of my paperwork.

The R&D officer opened the door. "Come on Verrett, you want to go home?" she said in a joking way.

I gave one last look to the crowd of men, then I gave Trey the homie handshake and told him to write me.

"And you know it, man," he replied.

Everything had already been prepared. My books had been closed. I had twenty five hundred dollars in my inmate account, but the bureau could only give me five hundred in cash. The remaining two thousand dollars was already in a U.S. treasury check.

As I sat in the bullpen for the last time, I could almost hear the chatter of men and the clanging of chains being dragged across the concrete floor. Thousands of men had sat in this very room and thousands more would have their chance. I felt sorry for them. I remembered all the times I had sat in this kind of room chained like a wild animal waiting to get on Con Air to take me to some unknown prison.

"It's all over now," I thought. I quietly said a prayer for them.

"Here are your clothes, Verrett," the CO said.

Taking me out of my semi-trance, I took a deep breath and began to undress in private this time. I put on my street clothes and felt good;

I wondered why I wasn't nervous. I was only twenty-five feet from America.

"Okay, you ready, Verrett?" the lieutenant asked.

"Yes, I am," I answered.

As we walked the last mile, I pulled out my phone book, and thought about whom I should call. The gigantic steel gate began to groan in protest as it was being opened, my breathing changed as my pulse quickened. I paused and took a deep breath and steadied myself, exhaling slowly while taking the first step. I was now in America. I was officially an American again. I looked back at the lieutenant as he watched me with a smile.

"Take care, Mr. Verrett," he said.

"I will LT. I will."

Across the street was the pay phone. I fumbled in my pockets for some change. I looked at the piece of paper with the phone number on it, and then dialled the number. The phone rang a few times before someone picked up.

"Hello, who is this?" the voice asked.

"It's De'Juan I'm out."

THE END! WELL NOT REALLY!!

PART TWO COMING SOON!

"DREAMING OUT LOUD"